M000304623

The Ways of the Lord
Volume II

Earline Kline

Vivian,
God bless you
as you read
these pages.

Earline

endurance press
2019

The Ways of the Lord Vol. II

by

Earline Kline

ENDURANCE PRESS
577 N Cardigan Ave.
Star, ID 83669

ISBN 9781733550369

Permission to reprint these devotionals given by Haven Ministries and Anchor.

All Scripture quotations are King James Version public domain in the United States.

Interior Design: Endurance Press
Cover Design: Teal Rose Design Studio's

Foreward

Around 1985 Haven of Rest began to publish a daily devotional called Anchor. It was always on a theme. Dan and I read it at breakfast each morning. The I began to take a correspondence course in writing. I began looking for things to write about. One evening we attended a special meeting where the speaker spoke on the "Ways of the Lord." It struck me as a good theme for an Anchor. So I began a search of scripture for all the ways of the Lord I could find. When my notebook was full, I began to write an Anchor on "The Ways of the Lord." When the manuscript was done I wrote Haven and told them what I had done. They wrote back and said, "We don't accept free lance work. All Anchors are written on assignment. But if you will send it to us we will look at it." Such a tiny crack in the door. Why should I send it. But Dan insisted I send it. My writers group insisted I send it. So I scraped together the postage and sent it off to Haven. A couple weeks later the phone rang at 4 pm on a Tuesday afternoon. It was Joyce Gibson the editor of Anchor. She said to me, "We want to publish your "Ways of the Lord" as an Anchor." I protested that I was only a housewife and did not have the education of many of their writers." She said, "That did not matter." So "The Ways of the Lord" was published that summer. I went on to write for Anchor for 25 years. I wrote 25 Anchors and the first 12 are in the first Volume of *The Ways of the Lord*. This is the second volume of devotionals.

To my husband Dan who stood beside me and encouraged me when the writing became a challenge.

January

Why Pray?

"The eyes of the Lord are on the righteous and His ears are attentive to their cry" (Psalm 34:15).

Have you ever asked, "Why pray?" I have. At one time when I was going through deep depression, I wondered if it was worth praying at all. My devotion time was a mere routine and it meant little to me. The only cry I could utter was, "Restore my joy." Did God hear me? So far as I could see, nothing was happening very fast.

Three-year-old Lexie made a nest out of her quilt on our lawn. Stopping her constant chatter for a moment, she looked up to the sky and called loudly, "Jesus, are You awake?" Then a little louder, "Jesus, are You awake?"

I could have assured her, "Yes, Jesus is awake, and He heard you just now."

Jesus never left me in those dark days of depression. He stayed close beside me, and He heard the cry of my heart. In time He healed me, and my zest for life returned.

Why pray? Because God is listening for your voice, and He is more than willing to help you. He has a generous, compassionate heart. You may not feel Him there, but He has never left your side.

Yes, Lexie, Jesus is awake. He has heard you, because He never sleeps.

Insight

God is always listening for the faintest cry from one of His children. Remember, you are precious to Him.

DAY 2
Matthew 7:7-11

Invitation to Pray

"Ask, and it shall be given you; seek, and ye shall find; knock, and it shall be opened unto you" (Matthew 7:7, KJV).

Prayer is our means of communicating with God, and His invitation is an open one. We can come to Him. We can ask Him to meet a need, or we can talk over a problem, or we can lift up someone else's need before the throne of God.

Why does He tell us to ask when He already knows our need? Most of us have raised the question. Through my work with children in my day care, I have found an answer that satisfies me. I know the needs of the young children, and I am committed to their care. However, I don't want them going to the refrigerator and pouring their own juice or climbing into the cracker cupboard and helping themselves. They may have those things, of course, but they need to come to me and ask. When they do, I gladly take care of their needs.

Similarly, our Heavenly Father wants us to come and ask, believing in His loving-kindness. He wants us to know from experience that He delights to give good gifts to His children. He hears our requests, and He answers in the way that is best for us.

His invitation is open. Come, make your needs known to Him. Your Heavenly Father's cupboard is full to overflowing, and He never has to go to the grocery store to replenish it.

Insight

God is committed to you. Prayer is asking and receiving. It is your Heavenly Father giving to meet your need.

DAY 3
1 John 5:13-21

Prayer With Confidence

"This is the confidence we have in approaching God: that if we ask anything according to His will, He hears us. And if we know that He hears us-whatever we ask-we know that we have what we asked of Him" (1 John 5:14-15).

If prayer is asking, then how do I ask? How can I be confident that God will answer my prayer? God says I need to ask according to His will. Then I ask, how can I know I'm asking according to His will? God's will is revealed in His Word. If I'm filled with His Word and pray His Word back to Him, then I'm sure of His answer.

My husband Dan and I were praying for another car. Our LeBaron had 190,000 miles on it, and four months before, the engine burned up in it. We replaced the engine and kept on praying. At that time Dan was driving 20 miles to another town to work, and the prison where he volunteered as a chaplain was 17 miles away. We needed a dependable car. So we prayed the promise of Philippians 4:19, confident God would meet our need in His time and in His way. What we needed was patience to wait until God answered. By one miracle after another, God provided our car fund goal and we purchased a car. Two weeks later, Dan would be let go from his job and be officially retired.

Hold God to His promises in your life. You can be confident that He will answer. He will meet your needs, whatever they are.

Insight

You can come boldly to the throne and pray with confidence, relying on the promises of your Heavenly Father.

DAY 4
Hebrews 4:14-16

Come Boldly

"Let us therefore come boldly unto the throne of grace, that we may obtain mercy, and find grace to help in time of need" (Hebrews 4:16, KJV).

When Jesus died on the cross, He did a marvelous thing. He opened the way into the very presence of God for us.

In Old Testament times, the only one allowed into God's presence was the high priest and then only once a year. All others must stay in the outer court.

Today, Jesus, our High priest, is entered into the very heavenlies for us. He knows how weak, poor, and needy we are, and how much we need His strength and grace. He invites us to come boldly, without fear, into the very presence of God, there to have our needs met.

Do you need strength just to face another day? Come! Do you need wisdom to make a decision? Come!

Do you need joy to lift your heavy spirit? Come!

Do you need an awareness of how close and how loving the Lord is to you? Come!

Do you need love for someone who is hard to love? Come!

Do you need patience with young children, or with an elderly person who is dependent on you? Come!

Do you need grace to live with continued physical weakness? Come!

Whatever your need, the door is open. God's invitation is out. Come boldly! Your need will be met.

Insight

Jesus has opened the way so that you may come boldly to the throne of God in your time of need.

DAY 5
Philippians 4: 1-8

Pray With Thanksgiving

"Do not be anxious about anything, but in everything, by prayer and petition, with thanksgiving, present your requests to God" (Philippians 4:6).

We have learned come to God asking Him to meet our needs, to pray with confidence according to His will, and to come boldly into God's presence. Now we need to learn to pray with thanksgiving.

I have always struggled with worry when faced with a problem. My custom has been to worry over an issue much like a dog worries over a bone-gnawing and gnawing, unable to let go of it. However, over the years I have tried to do exactly what Paul admonishes in our verse for today.

First, to stop worrying and begin to pray about the matter, laying it out before the Lord. Then to begin to give thanks for everything I can think of that surrounds the problem .Then, most of all, to thank God that He is still in control and that He is going to work things out in His own time and way.

I have learned that there is something about thanks giving that begins to release the power of God in even the most difficult situation.

Are you troubled about something today? Use these steps in prayer and experience the peace of God that passes understanding (v. 7). Begin today to learn to pray with thanksgiving and praise.

Insight

End your worry by praying with thanksgiving. You'll begin to experience God's wonderful peace.

DAY 6
Luke 18:9-14

Pray for Mercy

"Hear my voice when I call, O Lord; be merciful to me and answer me" (Psalm 27:7).

We all struggle with pride, either thinking we are better than someone else or thinking that no one could possibly love us. Too high or too low an estimate of ourselves is still pride because we are still centering on ourselves.

That pride must be broken if we are ever to come to Jesus as our Saviour. We must realize how much we need Jesus and we must acknowledge what He has done for us by dying for our sins. We need, like the tax collector in Jesus' story, to utter a sincere cry for mercy (Luke 18:9-14). When we do, Jesus saves us and makes us a part of God's forever family.

Mercy is God placing the punishment for our sins on His Son, so He can freely forgive us, not treating us as we deserve. Mercy is God welcoming us, though we have rejected Him in times past.

Have you ever come to that point of realizing how poor, sinful, and needy you are? Has your stubborn pride been broken? With a truly humble heart, have you come to Jesus and uttered a prayer for mercy? Then you belong to Him forever. He promises never to leave you nor forsake you. You will never be alone again. What a wonderful promise! Once you come to Him, He will begin to bring forth His glorious plan for your life.

Insight

God is at work in your life to humble you, breaking your stubborn pride, that He may show you His mercy.

DAY 7
Ephesians 6:10-19

Pray for Boldness

"Pray also for me, that whenever I open my mouth, words may be given me so that I will fearlessly make known the mystery of the Gospel" (Ephesians 6:19).

Paul was in prison and would probably have been advised to keep silent. Instead, Paul asked the Ephesian believers to pray that he would have boldness to proclaim the Gospel. Now how many people can a prisoner contact? Every time the guard changed, Paul told the new guard about Jesus. Soon there were many who had become true believers.

I am a Gideon Auxiliary member. Each member is asked to give out two New testaments a month. At one time I had probably given out two in the last two years. I needed this prayer for boldness. Being rather shy, I find it very hard to speak up and share the Gospel.

One December, as we traveled to California for Christmas, I determined to give out at least two New Testaments. As we checked out of our hotel room, I mustered up my courage and offered a New Testament to the hotel clerk. She was delighted to accept it.

Then, as we finished breakfast in the restaurant, I thought of our young waitress. She was so busy. Dare I ask her? I did, but she had to leave in a hurry to get an order out to another customer. To my delight, she came back, received the New Testament, and gave me a big hug! My heart was filled with joy. I had trusted the Lord for boldness, and He had helped me.

Insight

Pray for boldness to share the Gospel. God will give you courage to make the contact, and He will give you the words you need.

DAY 8
Acts 16:16-34

Pray and Sing

"About midnight Paul and Silas were praying and singing hymns to God, and the other prisoners were listening to them" (Acts 16:25).

Paul and Silas were in prison, their feet in stocks, their backs lacerated, bleeding, and painful. There could be no sleep for them that night, so at midnight they began to pray and sing hymns of praise to the Lord, in whose name they were suffering. God intervened miraculously with an earthquake, and delivered them from prison.

It was not midnight for us, but it was a summer of mild recession. Both our college sons were home, but there were no jobs available for them. Dan's construction business was dead. The only family income was my day care. In our need, we decided to set aside an evening for prayer and fasting. I prepared no dinner. Instead, we gathered around the dining room table with an outline for an evening of prayer and sharing. We trusted God to feed our hungry hearts.

We shared memory after memory of God's faithfulness in the past. Then we simply gave thanks and praise to God for who He is and all He had done for us. Two hours later, our evening ended in spontaneous singing of "How Great Thou Art."

It was an evening we would long remember as a family. Still no one found jobs, yet God provided so that our needs were met, and the boys were able to return to college.

Insight

In the midnights of your life, when the problems press, remember to pray and sing to the Lord.

DAY 9
Matthew 8:1-4

Prayer Out of Pain

"A man with leprosy came and knelt before Him and said,
'Lord, if You are willing, You can make me clean.' Jesus
reached out His hand and touched the man. 'I am willing,'
He said. 'Be clean!'" (Matthew 8:2-3).

He was dressed in rags, covered with sores. He had been
cut off from his family for perhaps years, banished to live outside the city in a cave. Whenever he approached other people,
he was required to cry out, "Unclean, unclean!"

The man was an outcast, but he had heard of Jesus, and
he sought Him out. Falling down before Jesus, he cried out
of his deep pain, "Lord, if You are willing, You can make me
clean." And Jesus was willing. The man went away cleansed
and whole.

Who of us has not cried to God out of our pain? I remember the days when my husband was very ill, and I was carrying the entire load of the family. I would fall on my knees by
my bed and cry my way through a psalm, beseeching God to
heal Dan and to carry me through my days.

In later years, I would beg God for relief from my physical
pain, certain I could not endure it another day. As I wept before Him, I would be given the strength to go on.

Are you crying out to God in your pain today? He hears,
and He will help you. He is the God of compassion, and He is
touched by your pain.

Insight

*Prayer out of pain touches the very heart of God, and He
reaches out to comfort you.*

2 Corinthians 1:3-11

Helping Others in Prayer

"On Him we have set our hope that He will continue to deliver us, as you help us by your prayers" (2 Corinthians 1:10-11).

How important is it that others pray for us? Why does God choose to work through the prayers of His people? He certainly doesn't need my feeble prayers for others, but He chooses to work through them anyhow.

Years ago as we moved from California to Idaho, God chose to have me pray for Dan, who had taken a ranch truck with our stuff to our new home. Still in California, the boys and I were spending the night in our boss's home, while they were out of town. At 4 o'clock in the morning the fire alarm went off just outside the bedroom. By the time I got up and shut it off, I was wide awake while the boys slept on. I must need to pray for Dan, I thought. Later, I learned that at just the time I was awakened, Dan was about to fall asleep at the wheel as he drove back to pick us up. I do not doubt that God alerted me to pray for him.

One of my greatest comforts is to know people are faithful in praying for me when I have a need. When ever special needs arise, we contact our circle of friends and family members and ask them for special prayer in our behalf.

What a joy it has been to add to my mailing list new people who are willing to pray for us, then to share with them God's answers to their prayers.

Insight

God works through the prayers of His people, so set your heart to pray for the needs of others.

2 Corinthians 12:7-10

Unanswered Prayer?

"Three times I pleaded with the Lord to take it away from me. But He said to me, "My grace is sufficient for you, for My power is made perfect in weakness' " (2 Corinthians 12:8-9).

Is there such a thing as unanswered prayer? Or is it rather that God does not answer our prayers in the way we would like Him to? We think we know what is best for us. But do we?

The apostle Paul was troubled with some kind of ongoing affliction. He pleaded with God to remove it, but God did not deliver him from it. Instead, He gave something better. He told Paul, 'I'm going to leave this thorn in the flesh because I will manifest My power through your weakness."

Four years ago I injured my sacrum while moving some playground equipment. I could not walk, stand, or sit without intense pain. Nothing I tried could bring me relief. Week after week I begged God for healing, but I continued to suffer.

After eight months of physical therapy, the medical personnel sent me home to live with the pain the best I could. God's word to Paul became God's word to me. "My grace is sufficient for you." And these are His words to you as well. God will give you a ministry through your weakness or your pain.

My physical pain will always be a reminder of the grace of God, a grace that will carry me through whatever a day may bring.

Insight

Your weakness is a reminder to depend on the all-sufficient grace of God. Lean on Him today.

DAY 12
Nehemiah 2: 1-5

Arrow Prayers

"The king said to me, "What is it you want?' Then I prayed
to the God of heaven, and I answered the king . . . " (Nehemiah 2:4-5).

Nehemiah was in exile, a captive far from his beloved
homeland. He served as the king's cupbearer, having become
a trusted servant. News came from Judah about the terrible
plight of the Jews living there. Nehemiah's heart ached for his
brethren.

His sad countenance alerted the king to Nehemiah's troubled heart. He asked, "What's troubling you?"

Nehemiah sent a quick prayer heavenward. God gave Nehemiah favor in the sight of the king, and he was able to go to
his brethren and help them for a season.

Often I have found myself in a situation where I have needed to offer a quick short prayer Godward. For example:

When listening to a friend pour out her troubles: "Lord,
give me a word of encouragement for her."

When driving: "Lord, get me though the traffic lights so I
won't be late for my appointment."

When working with the young children in my day care:
"Lord, give me wisdom. How do I stop Lexie from scratching
Justin's face?"

When trying to stretch the contents of my wallet: "Guide
my shopping today. You know I have a limited amount of
money to spend."

When you find yourself in a situation as Nehemiah did,
remember to send a prayer heavenward.

Insight

*Remember God is always there. Quick, short prayers reach
Him when you are in trouble.*

Nehemiah 4:6-9

Watch and Pray

"But we prayed to our God and posted a guard day and night to meet this threat" (Nehemiah 4:9).

Nehemiah, the exile, was back in Judah on special leave from the king of Persia. He was guiding the Jewish remnant in rebuilding the wall of Jerusalem. His was a difficult task, for there were enemies in the land strongly opposed to the work that was going forward so rapidly. They threatened to stop the work. First Nehemiah prayed, and then he set a watch. So half the people labored on the wall and half held weapons in readiness to defend the people.

There are times we must do more than pray. Jesus told His disciples in the garden on the night of His arrest, "Watch and pray so that you will not fall into temptation" (Matthew 26:41). Paul told the believers to put on the whole armor of God, then added, "Praying always with all prayer and supplication in the Spirit, and watching thereunto with all perseverance and supplication for all saints" (Ephesians 6: 18, KJV).

We are to be much in prayer, but we are also to be alert and watchful when dealing with the enemy. Our enemy is subtle and will try to trip us up in unsuspecting ways. For this reason, I pray, "Lord, don't let me fall asleep and fall prey to my enemy. Keep me ever alert, prayerful and watchful. Keep my feet from falling into his snares, my thoughts pure, and my hands busy ministering for You."

Insight

Our enemy is ever on the prowl to wreck our work for God. Keep alert. Watch and pray!

DAY 14
Matthew 14:22-32

Desperate Prayer

"But when [Peter] saw the wind, he was afraid and, beginning to sink, cried out, 'Lord, save me!' " (Matthew 14:30)

Jesus had just fed the 5,000. Then, as evening came, He sent the disciples in a boat across the Sea of Galilee. In the night, the waves increased and the wind buffeted the boat, tossing it in the wild seas. Progress was slow as the disciples toiled at the oars.

In the midst of this desperate situation, Jesus came to His disciples, walking on the water. When Peter saw Jesus, he said, "Lord, if it's You, tell me to come to You on the water" (see v. 28).

Jesus said, "Come." Peter confidently walked on the water-until he shifted his focus from Jesus to the tumultuous wind and waves. Instantly, he began to sink. "Lord, save me!" he cried in panic. And Jesus reached out His hand and saved him.

Peter was in a terrifying life or death moment. Some times we find ourselves in similar situations.

Coming home one night, we were alarmed to see the headlights of a car coming straight toward us in our lane of traffic. I'm not aware of what I prayed, but I certainly did cry out to the Lord. Dan did not swerve or hesitate, and the car crossed the road in front of us and ended in the barrow pit. If I had been driving I probably would have panicked, like Peter, and made a wrong decision. As it was, God kept Dan's hands steady on the wheel, and our lives were preserved.

Insight

In the desperate moments of your life, God hears your cries, and He is always there to help you.

DAY 15
Psalm 50: 1-15

Prayer for Deliverance

"Call upon Me in the day of trouble; I will deliver you, and you will honor Me" (Psalm 50:/ 5).

Things were going well for us. My husband Dan was working on a large remodel, and the second installment on the job would soon be paid to us. Then our world fell apart.

Because costs had run so much higher than the estimate, our client went to a lawyer. He told her she did not have to pay the second installment. There was still a lot of work left to do on the house. If she held Dan to finishing the job totally at our expense, we would be in debt for the rest of our lives. If it went to court, our lawyer told us we would lose.

We simply cried out to God for deliverance in our trouble. A week later, the client released Dan from the job, and we were free.

We owed thousands of dollars to the lumber yards and the bank, but we were able to sell our home, pay off our debts, and have enough left to start over.

Our God is there for us in our times of trouble to deliver us and bring praise to His name.

Today I'm also free from any bitterness, because I could see the hand of God in this trauma uprooting and moving us in an entirely new direction. We were beginning prison ministry, driving over 200 miles each weekend. God moved us closer to our ministry so we could be more effective for Him.

Insight

In times of trouble, cry out to God. Then praise Him for His timely deliverance. You will honor Him.

DAY 16
Genesis 24:1-26

Prayer for Guidance

"May it be that when I say to a girl, 'Please let down your jar that I may have a drink, ' and she says, 'Drink, and I'll water your camels too' let her be the one you have chosen for your servant Isaac" (Genesis 24:14).

Abraham's servant had been sent to Abraham's family to find a bride for his son Isaac. It was important to come home with the right girl, so the godly servant offered a prayer for guidance. A short time after he prayed, God did just what he had asked, and the servant was assured that he had found God's choice of a bride for Isaac.

When facing decisions, large or small, we need always to remember to stop and ask for guidance. Sometimes God opens only one door, and the decision is easy.

Other times He allows us to deal with a choice between options.

When the engine burned up in our LeBaron, we were faced with a major decision. Do we junk it? Or do we replace the engine? Would the old Ford stand up to all the driving Dan had to do? Could we get along with one car while we saved to buy another?

When Dan and I seek the Lord's guidance and then agree on a matter, we believe that is what the Lord would have us do. So we prayed, then made the decision to find a used engine in good condition. Soon the LeBaron was running again and providing reliable transportation.

Insight

God is simply waiting to guide you in your decisions. So why not stop and ask? He will direct your steps.

DAY 17
1 Samuel 1:9-18

Pour Out Your Heart

"'Not so, my lord,' Hannah replied, 'I am a woman who is deeply troubled. I have not been drinking wine or beer; I was pouring out my soul to the Lord' " (1 Samuel 1:15).

Hannah was childless. More than anything in the world she wanted a son. Though her husband Elkanah loved her, he did not understand the depth of longing in her heart.

So Hannah went to the Lord and poured out all the bitterness, ache, and longing of her heart. She came away from that encounter with the quiet assurance in her heart that God had heard her prayer and was going to answer.

During an extended time when I was in great physical pain, I would spend every Thursday evening before the Lord. I pled with Him for relief from the pain. I would pour out my discouragement, tell Him that I didn't think I could possibly go on, and the tears would flow. Did God grant instant relief from the pain? No, but somehow from those sessions of pouring out my heart, I would be given the strength to endure yet another day-another week.

No matter what is weighing on your heart, feel free to pour it all out before the Lord. He knows it all, of course, but He waits for you to come and be honest with Him. Pour out the bitterness, anger, and discouragement that burdens you. He will meet you and encourage you to go on.

Insight

You can be honest with God about all the feelings lurking deep within your heart. Pour out your pain. He is listening.

Prayer for Encouragement

"Look, I will place a wool fleece on the threshing floor. If there is dew only on the fleece and all the ground is dry, then I will know that You will save Israel by My hand, as You said" (Judges 6:37).

God had called Gideon to deliver Israel from the Midianites. Now Gideon was not a very courageous fellow, and was certainly not a likely candidate for leadership. In the dead of night, he had obeyed God by throwing down his father's altar to the false god Baal. But a bigger challenge awaited him. He put out the fleece as a prayer for encouragement-not once, but twice. Then God sent him down to the Midianite camp to hear two men talking about a dream. Gideon needed lots of encouragement, and God gave it.

I remember the day when I could identify with Gideon. I had just come home from the doctor with a poor prognosis on my shoulder. I needed three months of physical therapy to regain the use of it. As I thought about the continued pain, the time involved in therapy, and the expense, my spirits were about as low as the soles of my shoes. "Lord," I prayed, "I just need a word of encouragement." Going to my mailbox, I found a letter from an editor saying they were going to buy and publish a piece I had written. It was just the encouragement I needed that day.

Often I utter a prayer for encouragement-not only for myself, but for others who carry burdens.

Insight

The Holy Spirit is your great encourager. He knows just what you need for each day. Look to Him. He won't fail you.

Mark 9:14-29

Honest Prayer

"Immediately the boy's father exclaimed, 'I do believe; help me overcome my unbelief!' " (Mark 9:24)

A deeply distraught father had brought his demon possessed son to Jesus' disciples, but they had been unable to help the boy. An argument broke out between the onlookers and the teachers of the law.

Then Jesus arrived on the scene. He said, "Bring the boy to Me." Turning to the father, he asked, "How long has he been this way?"

In an agony of soul, the father poured out his trouble, crying, "Have compassion on us and help us!"

With deep compassion, Jesus responded to the father's pain. "If you can believe," He said, "all things are possible to him that believeth."

Honestly expressing his doubts, the father cried out, "I do believe; help me overcome my unbelief!" His son was healed that very moment.

God loves and welcomes honest praying. I remember a time when I simply expressed my lack of faith, and instantly faith came. I knew it was from God.

Dare to be honest with God in your praying, expressing your doubts as this father did. Tell Him of your anger, or that you are having trouble forgiving some one who has hurt you. Be open with Him about your feelings of anxiety or your worries about what tomorrow will bring. God will respond to your pain, as He did to a deeply troubled father long ago.

Insight

God welcomes honest praying-even the expression of your doubts or lack of faith. Tell Him all.

DAY 20
Romans 8:26-27

Help in Prayer

"In the same way, the Spirit helps us in our weakness. We do not know what we ought to pray for, but the Spirit Himself intercedes for us with groans that words cannot express" (Romans 8:26).

I am thankful for today's key verse, because so often I simply do not know how to pray for myself or for others. What a comfort to know that the Holy Spirit is my helper in prayer, taking my feeble words and translating them before the throne of God. I know He is praying according to God's will, and His prayers are going to be answered.

Sometimes my heart is so burdened that I cannot find words to express my cries to God. What a blessing to count on the Holy Spirit to read my soul and bring my requests before God! He knows and understands perfectly what I cannot articulate.

When you don't know how to pray for someone in need, ask the Holy Spirit to show you how to pray. If He doesn't, then take the next step. Trust God to take the person you have lifted before the throne and "do exceeding abundantly above all that you can ask or think" (see Ephesians 3:20, KJV).

In other words, God will answer requests you are not even making for that person, because He knows that one's real needs. So pray, even when you don't know what to pray for. God has given us His Holy Spirit to help us in our weakness.

Insight

Sometimes you won't know how to pray for yourself or someone else, but you have a helper in the Holy Spirit who does.

Agonizing Prayer

"He withdrew about a stone's throw beyond them, knelt down and prayed, 'Father, if You are willing, take this cup from Me; yet not My will, but Yours be done' " (Luke 22:41-42).

On the night of His betrayal and arrest, Jesus was in the Garden of Gethsemane with His disciples. Knowing what lay before Him, He drew aside and prayed in agony, "Father, if You are willing, take this cup from Me" (v. 42). God did not answer that prayer by taking the cup of suffering away. Jesus finished His prayed, "Yet not My will, but Yours be done." He submitted to the Father's will for Him, even though it led to the cross.

The Father loved the Son, and if there had been any other way to purchase our salvation, God would have taken it.

There will come a time in all our lives when we are at the place of agonizing prayer-either for ourselves or for a loved one. We too must come to the place of humble submission to God's will.

God loves us dearly, but He knows that we too must go through deep suffering. When our soul cries out in agony, He is there to care and to comfort, to strengthen and help us go on.

Commit yourself to the loving, all-wise God. Commit your loved ones to Him. Submit yourself to Him and pray, "Not my will, but Thine be done." Then find the rest and peace that comes from submission to Him.

Insight

Who are you that you should choose your way when your loving, all-knowing Father has chosen it for you?

Psalm 102:1-17

Answer Me Quickly!

"Do not hide Your face from me when I am in distress. Turn Your ear to me; when I call, answer me quickly" (Psalm 102:2).

Who has not wanted quick, easy answers to their prayers, especially in emergencies and times of deep distress?

I remember a time such as that a few years ago. I had suffered from a sacrum injury for two or three months, and was in intense pain all the time. I could not walk, stand, or sit without pain.

My brother had tried acupuncture for a back problem, and in one treatment he had been relieved of pain. I decided to try that route as well. After several treatments, my husband and I decided to go to the mountains for three days of camping. During a rainy period, I sat in the car with my Bible and was talking to the Lord about my problem. I still remember how He clearly said to me, "You are not going to have a quick, easy answer, but your healing is going to be a long, slow process." Those were not the words I wanted to hear at that time!

Yes, we want relief immediately when we are in distress. Sometimes it comes, and we praise God. Sometimes He doesn't send the relief as quickly as we wish. Sometimes our healing is a long, slow process. Sometimes the turnaround we long for in a loved one doesn't come as soon as we want. But God gives the grace and strength to endure whatever He sends.

Insight

We long for quick answers, but sometimes the only answer God gives is the strength to endure-one day at a time

DAY 23
Isaiah 37:14-20, 36-37

Laying It all Out

"Hezekiah received the letter from the messengers and read it. Then he went up to the temple of the Lord and spread it out before the Lord" (Isaiah 37:14).

Judah had been invaded. Jerusalem was surrounded by the Assyrians. On top of that, they had sent King Hezekiah a threatening note saying, "Surrender. Your God, you are trusting in, will not be able to deliver you out of our hands."

Hezekiah did the only wise thing. He took the letter to the temple and spread it out before the Lord. God read Hezekiah's mail, and honored the king's trust. He took steps to deliver Judah from the Assyrians.

It's always wise, when threatened by the enemy, to simply lay the problem out before the Lord. Begin to pray about every aspect of your problem. Cry out for deliverance. Leave it in God's hands. Let Him bring vengeance and defend you. Stand clear and wait to see what God will do.

A friend of mine was determined to hurt her ex husband as he had hurt her. Wanting to see him suffer, she found it very difficult to keep her hands off, to let God deal with her ex-husband in His own time and way, especially when it seemed as if God was doing nothing. But slowly-yet-certainly, healing and the ability to forgive has come, and my friend has been able to let go her resentment and anger, and let God have His way.

Insight

When threatened by the enemy, lay your problem all out before the Lord and let Him handle it.

2 Chronicles 20

When We Don't Know What to Do

"We have no power to face this vast army that is attacking us. We do not know what to do, but our eyes are upon You" (2 Chronicles 20: 12).

Judah was in grave trouble. A mighty army was coming against them. From a human point of view, they had every reason to be terrified. King Jehoshaphat called the people to seek the Lord in a day of fasting and prayer. In their weakness they turned their eyes to the Lord, and He told them what to do. Judah's army was led by singers praising God, and a great victory was won.

When you are faced with a problem and don't know what to do, seek the Lord. Turn your eyes to Him alone. Wait for Him to give you direction as you focus your attention on Him. We tend to do the opposite. Our problem fills our vision, and we pray from the problem to God.

Remind yourself that God is fully in control, that He is already at work in your behalf, and that absolutely nothing is impossible with Him. Then begin to praise God and give thanks.

Praise frees the power of God to work. Sometimes His answer comes quickly, and sometimes He simply gives strength to go on until the problem is resolved. No matter what, praise frees your spirit.

No matter what you may be facing today, seek God first, pray from God's perspective to the problem, and then lift your heart in praise to Him.

Insight

When faced with a problem, always remind yourself that God is greater than the problem. Take time to praise Him

Don't Give Up

"Then Jesus told His disciples a parable to show them, that they should always pray and not give up" (Luke 18:1).

In my work with women in prison, I am often asked, "Do I keep praying about a matter, once I've brought it to God?" I answer, "Yes, you keep on praying until the answer comes. God has heard your prayer, but He wants you to keep on asking in faith until the answer comes. Then your heart will overflow with praise to Him."

My husband and I have been learning this lesson as we have prayed over a long period for special needs. We prayed for many weeks for a job for Dan after we were forced to leave our business. We waited through months of darkness, months when God appeared to be doing nothing. Then suddenly, in one week's time, the answers all came, and our hearts rejoiced.

Then we prayed for months for the money required for a problem I had with my jaw. Again, we prayed through weeks of waiting, enduring severe ear pain, before I could even begin the long period of treatment. Then suddenly the money was provided.

More recently, we prayed for a retirement job for Dan. We prayed believing that in God's perfect time, He would reveal His plan for our retirement. Once again we offer thanks to Him as He answered by providing Dan with a part-time position as a prison chaplain at Idaho Maximum Security Institution.

Insight

Keep on praying about your need. God has heard, and He will answer in His time and in His way.

1 Thessalonians 5: 12-28

Pray Without Ceasing

"Be joyful always; pray continually; give thanks in all circumstances, for this is God's will for you in Christ Jesus" (1 Thessalonians 5:16-17).

God is always with us. Any moment throughout our day we can just lift our hearts to Him. Billy Graham says, "I pray all the time."

I'm not exactly sure what Paul meant when he tells us to pray continually, but I do know this: I begin and end my day with prayer, and whenever I have a moment during the day, I just lift my heart to God. It can be a cry for help, a simple word of thanks, remembering a verse of praise, or a precious promise.

That 30 minutes of physical therapy can be a time of prayer for me. Driving to an appointment, I pray, thanking God for the doctor who is taking care of me. Washing dishes doesn't take my mind, so I can pray. Brother Lawrence practiced the presence of God as he washed pots and pans. In my day care, when three year-old Lexie attacks two-year-old Justin because she is so frustrated and he is so stubborn, I utter a quick cry for wisdom. As my husband hugs me as he leaves for work, I give thanks to God for this man.

Make it your first impulse in your daily moments to lift your heart to God. He delights in hearing your voice. You may not see an immediate change in your attitudes, but gradually you'll begin to look at everyday events as opportunities to communicate with God.

Insight

Pray at every opportunity during the day and even in your wakeful minutes at night. God is waiting to hear your voice.

DAY 27
1 Chronicles 4:9-10

Keep Me From Evil

"Oh, that You would wonderfully bless me and help me in my work; please be with me in all that I do, and keep me from all evil and disaster!" (1 Chronicles 4:10, TLB)

In the middle of a list of hard-to-pronounce names in I Chronicles is a precious little prayer that is our key verse for today. Jabez bore in his name a reminder that his birth had caused his mother unusual pain. In spite of this, he was more "honorable" than his brothers and he brought his special requests to God. He heard Jabez's prayer and granted all that he asked Him to do.

One of Jabez's requests was to be kept from evil. Later, in the New Testament, Jesus would teach His disciples to pray, "Lead us not into temptation, but deliver us from the evil one" (Matthew 6: 13).

I have not prayed this request often enough, either for myself or for my children. Perhaps if I had, some of the things that have happened might have been prevented.

Our feet are prone to leave the path of obedience, and we have an enemy lurking out there to trip us up.

Asking God to keep us from evil is such an important prayer, so why do many of us forget to pray about it?

God does bless us in all that we do if we are walking obediently. He is always with us and has power to keep us from the evil-both that which lurks within and that which lurks without.

Ask God to remind you to pray this prayer for your self and all your loved ones.

Insight

We live in an evil world, and we have an enemy who has evil intentions, but God will deliver us if we pray.

At the End of Self

"In my distress I called to the Lord, and He answered me. From the depths of the grave I called for help, and You listened to my cry" (Jonah 2:2).

God had given Jonah an assignment to go to Nineveh, but he decided to squirm out of it. He took a ship going in the opposite direction, hoping to escape his sense of the Lord's disapproval. When God sent a violent storm to the Mediterranean, Jonah knew God was after him.

"Throw me into the sea," he told the distressed sailors. If Jonah expected to drown, God certainly had a surprise for him. A great fish swallowed the disobedient prophet. From within his confines, Jonah prayed.

Finally he had come to the end of himself. He gave up. His pride was broken, and he was ready finally to obey the Lord.

When we were in those first years of marriage, I watched my husband begin to drift away from the Lord. Deeply concerned, I prayed constantly for him. Then while we were visiting his sister and brother-in law, a cow kicked Dan in the knee, tearing it badly. Dan had to spend eight weeks in a full leg cast. That accident brought Dan back to the Lord, and he never drifted away again.

God has His ways of breaking our stubborn wills and bringing us into submission to His plan for us. Don't resist His dealings in your life.

Insight

You may not end up in the belly of a fish, but resisting God has its price.

Psalm 37:1-7

The Desires of My Heart

"Delight yourself in the Lord and He will give you the desires of your heart" (Psalm 37:4).

For years I have wanted to understand today's key verse and its deeper meaning. I kept a page in my prayer list with the heading, "Heart's Desires." On this page I listed all the things I wanted to do but lacked the necessary resources. One by one these desires would be fulfilled. Then one day God revealed to me how very shallow was my thinking.

Heart's desires in today's verse go much deeper. I believe they are those deep, soul-felt desires that will please God-like my desire to be a joy-filled person or Dan's desire in his retirement to serve Him more hours in the prison. Dan has to work part-time in retirement for us to make ends meet. He has always planned to find a part-time job, then spend the rest of his day ministering to the men in the prison.

Last fall a prison chaplain position came open at Idaho State Correctional Institution. Dan failed to get a high enough score on the state test, so that door closed. Then a good friend, Harley Brueck, was hired as the chaplain there. Harley had been the part-time prison chaplain at Idaho Maximum Security Institution, so that position came open. Dan was offered the position and went right into training. Today he is doing what he loves- working with the men. Truly God has given him his heart's desire.

Insight

As I put God first in everything, He will grant me those deep down desires of my heart that are in harmony with His will.

Proverbs 15:8

Prayer Delights God

"The Lord detests the sacrifice of the wicked, but the prayer of the upright pleases Him" (Proverbs 15:8).

Prayer is so important. Jesus prayed. Paul prayed.

The Old Testament saints prayed. Do you want to bring delight to the heart of God? Then pray. He is waiting to hear your voice, to have you communicate with Him, and to have you stop and listen to hear what He has to say to you.

Insight

Our prayers bring pleasure to the heart of God.

Romans 8:28-39

Jesus Prays for Us

"Who is he that condemns? Christ Jesus, who died-more than that, who was raised to life-is at the right hand of God and is also interceding for us" (Romans 8:34).

I have much more confidence when I step out in ministry when I know people are praying for me.

When we realize that the Holy Spirit and Jesus are praying for us, we know God's work is going to be done, and miracles are going to happen. We can make it through anything!

Insight

What a friend we have in Jesus, All our sins and griefs to bear. What a priviledge to carry Everything to Him in prayer.

-JOSEPH SCRIVEN

February

2 Timothy 1:1-7

Fear From the Enemy

"Stir up the gift of God, which is in thee, by the putting on of my hands. For God hath not given us the spirit of fear, but of power, and of love, and of a sound mind" (2 Timothy 1:6-7, KJV).

Paul is encouraging young Timothy to use his spiritual gift, to be bold to share his faith and overcome his fear.

I need the same encouragement and boldness. Too often I let fear stop me from saying what I know I should. I give in to the fear of wrong timing, wrong words, and of offending someone. It's easier to say nothing and let the opportunity pass. I need to trust God to empower me to speak, to love others, and to give me wisdom to ask the right questions. When I trust the Lord for boldness to speak out, I am blessed, and a seed is planted in someone's life for eternity. After Adam disobeyed God in the garden, God asked, "Where are you, Adam?" Adam's first recorded words were, "I was afraid" (Genesis 3:8-10). When sin entered our world, fear came with it, and people have had to fight fear ever since.

From Genesis on, God spoke one "fear not" after another to the hearts of men and women in fear producing situations. We will be looking at the "fear nots" of Scripture this month.

Insight

God releases His power in our lives-power to bring peace of heart and to calm our many fears.

Will God Keep His Word?

"After this, the word of the Lord came to Abram in a vision: 'Do not be afraid, Abram. I am your shield, your very great reward'" (Genesis 15:1).

God came to Abraham and made him some great promises. One, that the land in which he was a nomad would one day belong to his descendants; and two, that his children would be as numerous as the stars. But Abraham was already an old man and had no son. So he questioned God, "Is this servant going to be my heir?" "No," God answered, "You and Sarah will have a son."

Many years would pass and no son was born. Finally, Abraham and Sarah took matters into their own hands, resulting in the birth of Ishmael. Then God miraculously renewed their aging bodies and Isaac, the promised son, was born. God was at work behind the scenes all the time, and He kept His promise.

Are you trusting in one of God's promises, but feeling that He doesn't seem to be doing anything? Is there a nagging fear that God may fail you? Keep praying and trusting. God will work things out in His own time and way. He is at work even when it appears He is doing nothing, when all is dark.

Insight

God is a promise keeper. He gives His word and keeps it. He is always at work behind the scenes.

When Cast Out

"God heard the boy crying, and the angel of God called to
Hagar from heaven and said to her, 'What is the matter,
Hagar? Do not be afraid; God has heard the boy crying as
he lies there' " (Genesis 21:17).

Hagar and her son had been cast out of Abraham's community. She had only a sack of food and a canteen of water.
As she wandered in the desert, the food and water was soon
gone. Hot, tired, and thirsty, this desperate mother lay her son
down under a bush, then collapsed herself and began to sob.
She could not bear to watch her son die. At the end of her
resources, alone, with no one to help, she gave in to despair.

Then God spoke to her through the angel. "What is the matter, Hagar? Do not be afraid." Help was near, for she looked up
and saw a well of water.

Do you find yourself in an abusive situation and you have
to decide whether to stay or leave, but being on your own
throws you into a panic? Or have you just come to know
Christ, and your family wants nothing more to do with you?
Perhaps you've just lost your caring husband, and you are
suddenly thrown into widowhood. Whatever your desperate
situation, listen for God's voice and look for His promise. "Do
not be afraid. I will take care of you."

Insight

*God meets us at our point of desperation and gives us the
strength to go on.*

Genesis 46:1-7

When Facing Change

"I am God, the God of your father. Do not be afraid to
go down to Egypt, for I will make you into a great nation
there. I will go down to Egypt with you, and I will surely
bring you back again" (Genesis 46:3).

Jacob was facing a major change in his life. He was having
to leave the land God had promised to him and his children
and make a long trek to Egypt, where Joseph would care for
him and his family. Jacob was an old man. Perhaps he experienced some fear of the unknown, for change is not easy for
the old. How would he adjust to living in a foreign place?

As Jacob worshiped God, he heard God say, "Fear not to go
down to Egypt." Then God promised that his family would be
blessed and would be a blessing, and would come back to the
land again in God's time. It's amazing how often God follows
a "fear not" with a promise.

I hope I never have to move again, but I know someday I
may have to face that change when I grow too old to care for
my house and yard.

Are you facing a major change in your life? God says, "Don't
be afraid. I will bless you in this change, and I will make you
a blessing, wherever I put you."

Insight

*God is always there in the major changes in life to bless you
and make you a blessing.*

DAY 5
Genesis 50:15-21

Will He Forgive Us?

"But Joseph said to them, 'Don't be afraid. Am I in the place of God? You intended to harm me, but God intended it for good to accomplish what is now being done, the saving of many lives' " (Genesis 50:19-20).

Jacob was dead, and Joseph's brothers were afraid Joseph would now take revenge on them for selling him into slavery. Deciding they needed a face-to-face talk, they pleaded, "Joseph, will you forgive us?"

What an emotionally-charged moment as Joseph's brothers humbled themselves before him! With tears in his eyes, Joseph said to them, "Don't be afraid. I forgave you long ago. God has taken what you intended for harm and turned it around for good to the saving of many lives." With kindness and encouragement he assured them he would take care of them.

How could Joseph be so kind when his brothers had been so cruel? Because he could finally see how God was working out His plan for the Children of Israel.

Perhaps we each need to say to more than one person, "Don't be afraid," and then assure them they are loved and forgiven. We can do this, even though we can't yet see how God is working out His plan through the hurts.

Insight

Forgiveness frees you to offer words of encouragement to those who have hurt you.

DAY 6
Exodus 14:10-31

When Facing a Red Sea

"Do not be afraid. Stand firm and you will see the deliverance the Lord will bring you today . . . . The Lord will fight for you; you need only to be still" (Exodus 14:13-14).

The Israelites had fled Egypt and were camped by the Red Sea, as God had instructed Moses. Suddenly a cry of alarm went through the camp. On looking back toward Egypt, they saw Pharaoh's entire army in pursuit. They could not go forward because of the Red Sea, and they could not go backward. They were terrified and began to accuse Moses of bringing them out in the desert to die.

Moses' response was, "Be not afraid. Be still and watch God's deliverance." That night God performed a miracle and made a way through the Red Sea.

We all face "Red Sea" places in our lives. God has led us into an impossible situation and unless He chooses to intervene, we are lost. Our first response may be overwhelming fear. Then God speaks, "Fear not." With the "Fear not" comes His promise, "I will make a way through this impossible place in your life. Be still and trust Me. Watch Me work in your behalf and give Me the glory."

Will you let God quiet your fears? Will you be still and trust Him to do the impossible for you?

Insight

*When facing a "Red Sea," we can be terrified or we can trust,
be anxious or be still and watch God work in our behalf.*

DAY 7
Numbers 13:26-14:9

When Facing a Challenge

"Only do not rebel against the Lord. And do not be afraid of the people of the land, because we will swallow them up. Their protection is gone, but the Lord is with us. Do not be afraid of them" (Numbers 14:9).

The Israelites were camped on the border of land God had promised to give them. Men had been sent to spy out the land. Ten of the spies saw only the obstacles. Their report discouraged the hearts of the people. Caleb and Joshua counseled the people, "Do not be afraid. The Lord is with us, and He will give us the land."

Some years ago the Lord called my husband Dan and me into prison ministry. In the beginning, I always ministered beside my husband, and only to men. It was a joy-filled experience. Then one day I was asked to minister to the women in prison. I was afraid, for Dan would not be at my side. How could I relate to these women when my life had been so different?

I wanted to tell the Lord, "You've called the wrong person." Yet I faced the challenge He had given me. His love replaced my fear and His joy filled my heart as I accepted His call.

Are you facing a new challenge? Fear not! God will equip you for what He calls you to do.

Insight

Those God calls, He enables. Don't be afraid of new challenges. Obey Him, and do what He asks of you.

Deuteronomy 20:1-9

When Facing Battle

"Hear, O Israel, today you are going into battle against your enemies. Do not be fainthearted or afraid; do not be terrified or give way to panic before them" (Deuteronomy 20:3).

Moses is giving some last instructions to Israel before they go into the Promised Land. He told them, "You will be going into battle. The enemy will outnumber you, and they'll be better equipped. Do not be afraid, though, for the Lord God goes with you to fight for you and give you the victory. If you're afraid, go home. You will only discourage your brethren. The fainthearted have no place in God's army."

Have you ever been numbered among the faint hearted? I have. I'm afraid to witness to people who do not know the Lord. I let opportunities to speak a word for the Lord simply slip by, then I'm ashamed. When I do have the boldness to speak a word or give a New Testament, I am blessed. Then why am I so afraid? Is it become I'm sure I will be rejected?

My prayer these days is for boldness, to speak that word for the Lord that does not come naturally. I am trusting the Spirit of God to give me opportunities and then to help me take advantage of them. How about you?

Insight

The fainthearted have no place in Gods army. Trust Him for holy boldness to do what He asks you to do.

Will He Reject Me?

"And now, my daughter, don't be afraid. I will do for you all you ask. All my fellow townsmen know that you are a woman of noble character" (Ruth 3:11).

Ruth, a Moabite widow, had come to Israel with Naomi, her mother-in-law. Since they were two poor widows, Ruth had gone to glean in the barley harvest to sustain herself and Naomi. She just happened to glean in the fields of Boaz, a near kinsman, and she had come to his notice. At the end of barley and wheat harvest, Naomi gave Ruth some strange instructions. She was to go to the threshing floor and lay herself down at Boaz's feet and ask him to be a kinsman redeemer to her.

Ruth may have gone with a certain amount of fear and trembling. She was a foreigner. What would Boaz think? She may have felt she was throwing herself at Boaz. After all, she was proposing marriage. She may have been afraid of rejection. Nevertheless, she obeyed Naomi, and Boaz received her proposal, saying, "Do not be afraid. I will be your kinsman redeemer and will marry you. Just rest and wait until I settle things."

Insight

It is never wrong to do what God tells you to do. Don't let fear of rejection stop the blessing God in tends to give you.

1 Samuel 23:15-18

Pursued by the Enemy

"Jonathan went to David . . . and helped him find strength in God. 'Don't be afraid,' he said. 'My father Saul will not lay a hand on you. You will be king over Israel, and I will be second to you' " (1 Samuel 23:16-17).

David had been anointed king in Saul's place, but Saul was still king and had become David's bitter enemy. He pursued David all through the land of Israel. Even people David trusted betrayed his hiding places to Saul. Yet God was with David and protected him from falling into the hands of Saul.

On one occasion. Jonathan, Saul's son and David's good friend, came to David and encouraged him in the Lord. "Don't be afraid," he said. "You will be king someday." I'm sure Jonathan's encouragement came just when David needed it most, when David may have been tempted to be afraid he would never live to be king.

We each need a friend like Jonathan, someone to speak the very word of encouragement we need in a moment of fear and to remind us of God's sure promise. We need also to be that kind of friend to others in their moments of distress. We need to remind them that God is there, He has heard, He has seen, and He will surely help. Our God is faithful to keep His promises to His children.

Insight

We each need a friend, an encourager in times of fear and doubt Ask God to give you that friend. Then be that friend to someone else.

1 Kings 17:7-16

The End of Your Resources

"Don't be afraid. Go home and do as you have said. But first make a small cake of bread for me from what you have and bring it to me, and then make something f or yourself and your son" (1 Kings 17:13).

God's prophet, Elijah, was in danger from the wrath of Israel's evil king. When the brook dried up in the place where Elijah hid, God sent him to an unlikely source of supply-a poor widow who had only a handful of meal and a little oil. As she gathered a few sticks to prepare her last meal, Elijah asked her for a drink of water. Then he added, "Could you also bring me a piece of bread?"

She told Elijah she was at the end of her food. "Don't be afraid," he assured her. "Feed me first, then feed yourself, for there will always be enough."

She may have thought, Can I trust this stranger's word? Nevertheless she obeyed, and God stretched her resources.

I remember a winter when we drew unemployment. It would not stretch around our needs, yet we gave God His portion first and trusted Him to take care of us and our children. Somehow the bills were always paid and there was food on the table. We learned that when we reach the end of our re sources, God steps in to provide.

Insight

You can always give to God. He pays wonderful interest on His loans, and He has promised to meet every need.

1 Chronicles 28:19-21

A Mammoth Task

"Be strong and courageous, and do the work. Do not be afraid or discouraged, for the Lord God, my God, is with you. He will not fail you or forsake you until all the work is finished" (1 Chronicles 28:20).

David was instructing his son Solomon in the gigantic task before him-the building of the temple. Solomon was young and had never directed a building project. To help him, David said, "Here is the plan and here are the materials I have gathered, and here are the skilled craftsmen to help you. Also, God is with you and will help you. Don't be afraid or discouraged."

A young woman once asked me to make her wedding dress. She had an idea of what she wanted, but could not find a pattern. We decided to take parts of two patterns and put them together. She was afraid the dress might look like a glorified sheet. I worried that I could not make the dress she visualized and that it would be a total failure! However, when she came for the fitting, it fit perfectly, and she was delighted with the way the dress turned out.

Are you afraid to tackle a project because it seems overwhelming? God often challenges us with a mam moth task so we will have to depend on Him, and He receives the glory for its success.

Insight

God stretches our faith by making the task bigger than we are. Then we give Him the glory when we succeed in it.

2 Chronicles 20:1-30

We Don't Know What to Do

''This is what the Lord says to you: 'Do not be afraid or discouraged because of this vast army. For the battle is not yours, but God's' " (2 Chronicles 20:15).

The enemy was massed on Judah's border, far out numbering God's people. Instead of calling a council of war, King Jehoshaphat called for a day of fasting and prayer. He began his prayer with his focus on God-who He is and what He had done for His people. Then he prayed about the problem, ending with, "We do not know what to do, but our eyes are upon You" (v. 12).

God's first words were, "Do not be afraid. Go out and face the enemy. Stand firm and see the deliverance of God." When the people of Judah began to praise God, the enemy destroyed each other.

There are going to be times in your life when you simply don't know what to do. The problems you face are overwhelming. Turn your eyes to God and look to Him alone. Pray from His character to the problem. Remind Him of His power to help, that He is in control, that He loves you, and has promised to meet your needs. Begin to praise Him for the answers even before they come. Then wait expectantly for Him to act in your behalf.

Insight

When problems come---and they are sure to come sometime-turn your eyes to God alone. Trust Him to meet your need. Then praise Him for His answer.

Isaiah 43:1-7

When Troubles Come

'This is what the Lord says-He who created you, O Jacob, He who formed you, O Israel: 'Fear not, for I have
redeemed you; I have summoned you by name; you are
Mine' " (Isaiah 43:1).

Today's "fear not" comes to a people in trouble and is
followed by a wonderful promise: that God will be with us
whatever troubles come and that those troubles will not over-
whelm us.

One spring we experienced a series of troubles. First, both
cars went in the shop the same week. A week later, the engine in our good car burned up and had to be replaced. The
next week our refrigerator died on a Sunday morning. Then
in quick succession, my husband had to have a wisdom tooth
pulled, the good car needed a brake job, and a week later, developed a serious oil leak. The food program lost my atten-
dance sheet, and I had to work out a new one in order to receive my food check for my day care business. I began to fear
what would happen next.

I knew God was in control, but I started to wonder what
He was doing. Then God turned things around and began to
bless in double measure.

Whatever trouble you are facing, God is with you. He
promises those troubles will not drown you, even though it
feels like it.

Insight

*God promises to be with us and make a way through what-
ever troubles He allows in our lives.*

Bad News

"Blessed is the man who fears the Lord, who finds great delight in His commands . . . . He will have no fear of bad news; his heart is steadfast, trusting in the Lord" (Psalm 112:1, 7).

My brother rarely calls me, but when our father died suddenly of a heart attack, my brother was the one who called and broke the news to me. He still rarely calls, but when he does, usually his first words are, "This is not bad news." He knows my heart almost stops now when I hear his voice.

Do you fear bad news, that unexpected phone call in the night? The Psalmist assures us that the one who is trusting in the Lord is secure. His heart is steadfast. His feet are firmly set on the rock, Christ Jesus.

We do not need to be afraid, because God prepares us for the surprises of life. He is there to catch us and hold us and keep us from falling. Nothing can touch us except it comes through His love.

God prepared me for my father's death before it happened. Some time before, I had a conversation with a grief specialist in an airport, and she recommended a book to read that would help a person through grief. God's amazing love was reaching out to me before I knew I needed it. God's love was there to cushion the blow.

Insight

As we learn to trust Gods rich promises of grace, those promises will be fulfilled in our lives.

My Salvation

"Surely God is my salvation; I will trust and not be afraid. The Lord, the Lord, is my strength and my song; He has become my salvation. With joy you will draw water from the wells of salvation" (Isaiah 12:2-3).

Are you afraid of what will happen when you die? Where you will end up? You can have the assurance of being with Jesus for eternity by simply receiving Him as your Saviour. You see, He died on the cross to pay the penalty for your sins and mine. He died the death we deserve so that we could have the gift of eternal life. By simply accepting the free gift of salvation, we can have the assurance of being with Him forever.

When I trust in Jesus, He chases away my fears. He becomes my confidence, my comfort, my peace, my joy, my security.

Salvation is a free gift. It can't be earned by any amount of good works we do. It is all of God's grace. You can settle the matter of eternity today.

Fear and faith cannot dwell together. It will be one or the other. Tell God your fears. Tell Him that you need Him and want to be sure that you will go to heaven. Make your decision today so you can say with Isaiah, "I will trust and not be afraid because God has become my salvation" (v. 2).

Insight

Will it be fear or faith? It is a choice only you can make. Make that decision today.

His Presence

"Even though I walk through the valley of the shadow of death, I will fear no evil, for You are with me; Your rod and Your staff, they comfort me" (Psalm 23:4).

Are you afraid of death? I don't think I'm as afraid of death as I'm afraid of the suffering that may precede it.

David says so much in this psalm. Even though he may be facing death, he will not be afraid. Why? Because God will be with him. God's loving presence will never be taken away from us, even as we go through the valley of death. We will not face it alone. I find comfort that it is also called "the valley of the shadow." There can be no shadows without light, so we are assured there is the light of His presence there also. It will never be total darkness, only a shadow.

My grandmother had been quite ill. After she recovered, she wrote me in a note, "It would have been so easy for Him to pull the curtain and let me through." There was no fear, only an expectancy of going to sleep and waking up in the arms of Jesus.

Similarly, when we face the day of our death, we need not be afraid. Again His promise comes, "Surely, I will be with you and will bring you safely home to Myself."

Insight

Death holds no fear for God's children, for Jesus has taken away its sting (1 Corinthians 15:55-57).

DAY 18
Luke 5:1-11

When God Calls

"Then Jesus said to Simon, 'Don't be afraid; from now on you will catch men.' So they pulled their boats up on shore, left everything and followed Him" (Luke 5:10-11).

Peter and his partners had just been part of a miraculous catch of fish. Now Jesus was calling them to leave everything and follow Him. It can be scary to be called to leave what is familiar and do something entirely different. Again, we hear the encouraging words, "Do not be afraid."

Two women asked me separately to visit them when they moved from prison to the work center. Permission was granted for me to visit both women, but I was afraid to go. I was just coming out of two years of depression and I wasn't sure I could even carry on a conversation. In spite of my fear, I knew I had to obey God and trust Him for the words I would need. My fears were groundless. Both women simply poured out their stories as I listened.

Is God calling you into a special ministry? Or is He asking you to reach out to a neighbor or friend who needs Him? Don't be afraid. Whom God calls, He enables. He has already prepared you for the task He is calling you to perform. The job is always bigger than we are, so that we will trust in Jesus' help.

Insight

Obey God and step out You will be blessed. When God calls you to minister to others, He prepares and enables.

Mark 4:35-41

In the Storm

"He got up, rebuked the wind and said to the waves, 'Quiet! Be still!' Then the wind died down and it was completely calm He said to His disciples, 'Why are you so afraid? Do you still have no faith?'" (Mark 4:39-40).

Jesus and His disciples had entered a boat and were crossing the Sea of Galilee. Exhausted, Jesus had fallen asleep when a furious squall came up and waves were breaking into the boat. In a panic, the disciples woke Jesus shouting, "Don't You care if we drown?" Then Jesus spoke to the wind and the waves, "Quiet. Be still," and immediately there was a great calm. Turning to His disciples, He asked, "Why are you so afraid?   Can't you trust Me?"

How often Jesus must ask me the same two questions, and I'm so ashamed. Some storm in my life is about to inundate me, and I panic, forgetting Jesus is right there. He is not asleep but perfectly in control of the circumstances. If I will only look for Him, I will see His hand, experience His mercies poured out, and hear His voice speaking to still the storm in my heart.

Are you in a storm today? Is the water pouring into your boat? Are you sure you will drown? Cry out to Jesus, the One who stills the storms of life.

Insight

In the storms of life you can panic or you can trust the One who gives peace in the midst of the storm.

Luke 8:40-56

When Death Strikes

"Someone came from the house of Jairus. . . . 'Your daughter is dead,' he said. . . . Hearing this, Jesus said to Jairus, 'Don't be afraid; just believe, and she will be healed'" (Luke 8:49-50).

A crowd met Jesus as He arrived in the city. A man named Jairus stepped forward, begging Jesus to come to his house, for his daughter was dying. But the pressing crowd and a sick woman delayed Jesus. Then word came from Jairus' home that his daughter was dead. Jesus was too late. "Don't be afraid," Jesus comforted Jairus. "Just believe and she will be healed." Jesus went on to Jairus' house and raised his daughter to life again.

My father died suddenly of a heart attack. There was no warning. He was just gone. For months afterward I lived with the fear that God would take my husband as unexpectedly. As time went by, the fear quieted, but it can still raise its ugly head when I least expect it.

Are you afraid of losing someone precious to you? God prepared me for the loss of my father. Everything was in place to see me through that time. God can still be trusted. Our loved ones are safe in His arms.

Insight

God will see us through whatever loss we must suffer. He has prepared a way through those times. Trust Him and do not be afraid.

Acts 27:13-26

When Shipwrecked

"Last night an angel of God ...stood beside me and said, 'Do not be afraid, Paul. You must stand trial before Caesar; and God has graciously given you the lives of all who sail with you'" (Acts 27:23-24).

Paul was in a dangerous situation. The crew had set sail, though Paul had warned them not to leave port. Now they were caught in a violent storm. When the ship had been driven before the storm for 14 days and all hope of being saved was gone, an angel had appeared to Paul, saying, "Don't be afraid. Your life will be saved and all those on the ship with you." Paul had to go through storm and shipwreck to reach Rome, but God was with him and brought him through it all.

I have never been shipwrecked, but I have watched the shipwreck of our construction business. As things fell apart around us, my husband feared we would lose everything we had worked so hard for over the years. We sold all the large tools we had accumulated. Our home had to go to pay business debts, but God graciously left us enough to start over. He provided a job for my husband and a down payment on a home.

Are you facing storm and shipwreck in your life today? Listen for God's voice and direction. Look for His mercies and do not be afraid.

Insight

When everything falls apart, God will still be there to hold things together. You can count on Him.

The Terror by Night

"I will say of the Lord, 'He is my refuge and my fortress,
my God, in whom I trust' . . . You will not fear the terror
of night nor the arrow that flies by day" (Psalm 91:2, 5).

Mark Bowman, a missionary in Cambodia, had taken a
truck to a distant town to pick up some equipment that had
been donated to his orphanage. By the time the truck was
loaded, there was only one hour of daylight left for the three-
hour drive home. The country was full of bandits, and it was
not safe to travel after dark. Yet Mark and his driver decided
to head for home. They had not gone 20 kilometers when they
saw a group of men with guns blocking the road in front of
them. The leader, with gun in hand, came up to the truck.
Mark and the driver were afraid and silently cried out to God
for help. The terrified driver called out, "You win!" Inexplica-
bly, the leader lowered his gun, turned around, and the bandits melted away into the darkness. Mark and his driver drove
on and reached home safely. God had carried them through
the terror by night.

God is still God, even in the darkness. He is still saying,
"Don't be afraid."

Insight

*God sees what terrifies us at night and is able to calm our
troubled hearts and bring peace.*

The Fear of Man

"When I am afraid, I will trust in you. In God, whose word I praise, in God I trust; I will not be afraid. What can mortal man do to me?" (Psalm 56:3-4).

I have lived by a neighbor for 13 years and had never spoken to the wife. I was acquainted with other members of the family, but not Sherry. I'm ashamed to admit this. What was I afraid of? Rejection? That's no excuse for not making some effort to get acquainted. I had made some effort to be friendly when I first moved in, but when I didn't meet with success, I gave up.

When God began to speak to me about reaching out to all my neighbors, I began to pray for a way to break the ice. Then one day several women in the neighborhood gathered across the street at a yard sale. I prayed for an opportunity to talk to Sherry, and God opened the door to invite her family to dinner.

Later, Sherry sent over some apples, which we turned into apple crisp and shared with them. Then the children in my day care helped me make cinnamon rolls. Together we shared them with the neighbors on both sides, hoping to build relationships. The ice has been broken. Now we share a friendly wave whenever we see each other.

Insight

The fear of man handicaps our witness. When we trust in the Lord, we overcome our fear and enjoy the freedom God has for us.

DAY 24
Luke 22:54-62

Afraid for His Life

"Peter replied, 'Man, I don't know what you're talking about!' . . . Then Peter remembered the word the Lord had spoken to him: 'Before the rooster crows today, you will disown Me three times'" (Luke 22:60-61).

Fear can make us do things we never intended to do and say things we never dreamed of saying. Peter found this true. A devoted follower of the Lord, he swore he would never deny Jesus. Yet when Jesus was taken before the high priest, Peter followed at a distance, fearful of being associated too closely with his Lord. While Peter warmed himself by the fire in the courtyard, a servant girl pointed him out. "This man was with Him." Peter denied it firmly, "Woman, I don't know Him!" Twice more, fearful for his own life, Peter denied he even knew Jesus. When reminded by the rooster crowing, Peter was broken and heart sick. He wept in repentance for what he had done.

How like Peter I am! I'm certain I won't deny Jesus, yet when given a wide open opportunity to share my faith, I sometimes bite my tongue and say nothing. I fear a hostile response. Peter was afraid he would die with Jesus. The boldness that comes from the Holy Spirit was the only cure for Peter-and the same is true for you and me.

Insight

When we trust the Holy Spirit, He chases away our fears by giving us spiritual boldness, wisdom, and sensitivity.

You Are Precious to Me

"'Are not two sparrows sold for a penny? Yet not one of them will fall to the ground apart from the will of your Father. . . . So don't be afraid; you are worth more than many sparrows" (Matthew 10:29-30).

Am I afraid of what God will allow to happen in my life? Are you? To be truthful, I am afraid, because some things that can happen are very painful, and I want to avoid pain at all costs. Some things are very earth shaking, and I hate having things out of control.

But there is a God in heaven who is in control of every detail of my life. Jesus says, "Even the very hairs of your head are all numbered" (v. 30).

A sparrow is a very common bird. They are so numerous that they are treated as inconsequential. Yet not one falls without God taking note. Jesus tells us to take heart and not be afraid, because we are of more value to God than many sparrows.

Nothing can touch my life except it comes through God's all-encompassing love. My heart needs to believe and rest in God's control, even when my feelings say that everything is spinning wildly and it doesn't appear God is in control at all.

God says, "Trust Me, my child. I can take you through anything that can happen in this world."

Insight

We need not carry fear in our hearts. The God who numbers the hairs of our heads can take us through any trouble.

DAY 26
Proverbs 31:10-31

Prepared for Winter

"A woman of noble character who can find? She is worth
far more than rubies. . . .When it snows, she has no fear
for her household; for all of them are clothed in scarlet"
(Proverbs 31:10, 21).

Being prepared for something helps take away much of
our fear. Obviously we cannot be prepared for everything
that happens in life, but we can prepare for some things. The
woman in Proverbs 31 had prepared warm wool clothing for
her family, so she was prepared for snow. She was not afraid.

My first winter in Idaho caught me unprepared. After that,
I learned to can and freeze fruits and vegetables to carry us
through the cold months. We tried to put money in savings
to carry us through the weeks of no construction work. Still, I
grew to dread winter and getting behind on our bills. I began
providing day care for young children so that there would always be some in come, even if my husband was not working.
I discovered that the more prepared I was to face winter, the
less I dreaded those slim months.

Our best preparation for hard times is to have our feet
firmly on the rock, Christ Jesus, and our faith placed in the
God who cannot fail.

Insight

*Be prepared to face the surprises of life by placing your faith
today in the God who cares for you.*

Proverbs 3:19-26

Sleep in Peace

"When you lie down, you will not be afraid; when you lie down, your sleep will be sweet ... For the Lord will be your confidence and will keep your foot from being snared" (Proverbs 3:24, 26).

When my husband is gone and I am home alone I am usually relaxed. So long as I hear only the familiar sounds of the night around me, I am calm and peaceful. However, if an unusual sound jars me, my heart starts to pound and I search for what could have caused the commotion.

One evening I was watching Disney's Old Yellar when in the climax of the movie, I heard a loud clang of metal on metal. It sounded like someone had hit my car in the driveway. Cautiously I peeked out the door, but even in the darkness I could see that nobody was there. I was puzzled about what had caused the noise. When my husband came home later that night, he discovered that the spring had broken on the garage door. The loud clang had a simple explanation.

Our confidence is in the God who cares for us and sets His angels to watch over us. We do not need to be afraid. God works the night shift. He does not sleep, but keeps watch over us-even when strange noises disturb us.

Insight

God is always watching over us--even when things go bump in the night. We can trust His loving care.

1 John 4:13-21

Casting Out Fear

"There is no fear in love. But perfect love drives out fear, because fear has to do with punishment The one who fears is not made perfect in love" (1 John 4:18).

God is in the business of casting out our fear, and He does it by convincing us that He loves us.

What do I do when something very painful enters my life? Do I really believe God loves me, so I continue to trust Him? Do I live one day at a time and let Him remove all dread of the unknown future? Do I let Him mature me through all of the trial and give Him the glory, whatever happens?

God is more interested in building our characters than in our comfort. The painful events of life can be the times of greatest growth for us, if we let them. If there were no tests in life, we would have no testimony to God's power at work in us.

It is better to go through pain and learn from it than to have an easy road and grow complacent. It is better to learn to live in dependence on God than to think boastfully that we can get along without Him. It is better to rely on God's love for us than to fear that He is sending trials to punish us.

Let God convince you of His love today and cast out any fear that lurks within.

Insight

When we are sure God loves us, we will not live in dread of the unknown. No matter what happens, we can rest in the fact that He loves us and cares for us.

John 14:1-6

An Untroubled Heart

"Do not let your hearts be troubled. Trust in God; trust also in Me. . . . Peace I leave with you; My peace I give you. . . . Do not let your hearts be troubled and do not be afraid" (John 14:1, 27).

Fear and faith cannot dwell together. If you want an untroubled heart, you are going to have to trust God.

The disciples were troubled because Jesus said He was leaving them. To calm their fears, He assured them that He was only going to prepare a place for them and that He would return to bring them to that prepared place. Our future is certain. Someday we are going to be with Jesus forever.

Is it possible to go through life with an untroubled heart? Yes, through the power of the Holy Spirit, who makes the truths of Christ real to us. He can lead us from panic to peace, from fear to faith. Certainly, we have our fears, but over and over this month we have seen in fear-producing situations where God came in Bible times and said, "Fear not." He speaks the same to us today.

The Lord can help us face our fears head on and truly trust His Word to us. We can listen for His voice assuring us that He loves us and is in control of all things for our good.

Insight

An untroubled heart is a sign of our faith in God, who loves us and has only our good in mind.

Fear or Faith

"When I am afraid, I will trust in You. In God, whose word I praise, in God I trust; I will not be afraid. What can mortal man do to me?" (Psalm 56:3-4)

Fear entered our world in the Garden of Eden through the sin of Adam and Eve. Fear has pursued every person since that day. Even the bravest of our heroes have had to face it.

David, whom God chose to rule over His people (Psalm 78:70-72), was not immune to fear. Once when King Saul was hunting him down as his enemy, David escaped to the Philistine city of Gath. He was recognized by the king's servants and was immediately in grave danger. Today's psalm was wrung out of his heart when he was seized by the Philistines. He had every reason to be afraid for his life, and he did not deny his fear. Rather, he told God by faith, "When I am afraid, I will trust in You." He committed himself to trust whatever happened to him.

For every fear-producing situation David experienced, he deliberately chose to move from fear to faith. He then could testify, "I sought the Lord, and He answered me; He delivered me from all my fears" (34:4).

Insight

Moving from fear to faith brings praise to God and peace to our troubled hearts.

March

Matthew 11:25-30

Jesus, Gentle and Humble

"Take my yoke upon you and learn from me, for I am gentle and humble in heart, and you will find rest for your souls. For my yoke is easy and my burden is light" (Matthew 11:29-30).

The only time Jesus gave a verbal self-portrait, He described Himself as gentle and humble in heart. He was never arrogant or proud. He knew who He was-the eternal Son of God. He knew where He had come from and where He was going. Throughout His life on earth, he lived in total dependence on His Father. He never did anything on His own initiative.

And He says to us, "Come, learn of Me. Let go of your pride and independence. Be teachable. Take My yoke and we will walk together in gentleness and humility. You will find that My yoke is easy and My burden is light. Cease your striving. Find heart-rest in walking with Me."

I see too much striving and not enough rest in my life, too much pride and not enough humility. Too often I fight my way through the frustration of my days instead of letting the gentleness of Jesus take over. Too often I grow impatient and angry and raise my voice. My heart cry is, "Lord, help me change. I long to rest in Your easy yoke."

Insight

Are you struggling in your heart today? Take the easy way out. Walk with Jesus in gentleness and humility, laying your pride in the dust.

Proverbs 6:16-19

How God Views Pride

"There are six things the Lord hates, seven that are detestable to him: haughty eyes, a lying tongue, hands that shed innocent blood, a heart that devises wicked schemes, feet that are quick to rush into evil . . . ." (Proverbs 6:16-18).

Andrew Murray, in his classic, *Humility*, challenges us to take a month and pray only one thing-that God would take from our hearts every kind and degree of pride, and that He would give us the deepest understanding of that humility which can make us capable of walking in His light and in fellowship with His Holy Spirit.

When I first read that challenge, my soul shrank from engaging in such an exercise. It would be painful to have my blind spots revealed and my pride exposed to God's searchlight. Then I thought of how much God hates pride. Did I want to be offensive to God? Well, no. I had no choice but to submit my heart to God's humbling process, trusting Him to reveal the subtle pride which needed exposure. So I began a rather timid prayer for humility, hoping that it would not be answered in too large a dose.

What about you? Are you willing to let God humble you and make you that much more usable in His service?

Insight

God opens the door to heart-rest when we let Him begin the process of exposing our pride and bringing true humility to our hearts and lives.

The Root of Sin

"He that is of a proud heart stirreth up strife: but he that putteth his trust in the Lord shall be made fat" (Proverbs 28:25, KJV).

Adam and Eve wanted to be like God, so they yielded to Satan's temptation and ate of the tree God had forbidden them.

In arrogance of heart, a man will continue in crime, thinking, I'll never get caught. Then suddenly everything goes wrong, and he finds him self in prison. Simply thinking, I can do it myself and I don't need God in my life, can lead to a person's downfall.

Why do we get angry? Because someone has violated our rights. In response, we rise up to assert ourselves. How often do we take matters into our own hands, pay back others for the pain they have caused in our lives?

The way of pride leads to strife and every kind of unrest. The way of humility leads to peace and joy and God's blessing.

Are you going your own way or God's way? Have you chosen the path of pride or of peace? Self-centered independence or submission to God? Let God bring true humility into your life.

Insight

At the root of every sin is selfish pride. Turn to the selfless one, Jesus Christ, and let Him give you His humble spirit

DAY 4
Proverbs 16:16-24

Where Pride Leads

"Pride goes before destruction, a haughty spirit before a fall. Better to be lowly in spirit among the oppressed than to share plunder with the proud" (Proverbs 16:18-19).

Today's key verses give us a warning. Whenever we think we are doing great and are ready to break our arms patting ourselves on the back, watch out!

I was very busy serving God in our church directing a children's church ministry, building a church library from scratch, and teaching a Sunday School class. I thought I was walking with the Lord in my personal life as well. I kept a personal quiet time daily, reading my Bible and praying.

Then my pastor called me into his office and began to point out to me where I had hurt the feelings of one person after another, not so much by what I had said but by the tone of voice I used. I was crushed. What a painful coming down for me! I had to recognize that my tongue was out of control. While I thought I was doing so well, it was nothing but foolish pride and that pride had taken a devastating fall. God used my pastor's confrontation to bring me to a new dependence on the Holy Spirit within.

Insight

Be on alert for the obstacle that pride places in your path. You may be about to trip and fall flat on your face.

Why Would We Forget God?

"And when your herds and flocks grow large and your silver and gold increase and all you have is multiplied, then your heart will became proud and you will forget the Lord" (Deuteronomy 8:13-14).

Moses was preparing the Israelites to enter the Promised Land. They were going to experience prosperity and God's blessing once they entered the land. But Moses warned them against forgetting God. He knew they were going to be tempted to say, "Look how well we've done. Our herds are growing and the crops are bountiful." They had been forced to depend on the Lord while they traveled in the wilderness, but Moses knew that in the time of prosperity they would begin to forget God, taking the credit for the good times instead of humbly thanking God.

We do the same. When we are poor and needy, we have to depend on God. The test of prosperity is much harder, and here we often fall. We relax when things are going well and forget God is the source of all our blessings. We no longer depend on Him but on our resources. My husband Dan al ways reminds me, "God never allowed us a savings account because we would depend on it rather than on God." On what are you depending today?

Insight

Pride is forgetting that God is the source of our prosperity. It is being self-sufficient rather than depending on God.

DAY 6
Daniel 4:28-37

Falling from the Top

"Now I, Nebuchadnezzar, praise and exalt and glorify the King of heaven, because everything he does is right and all his ways are just. And those who walk in pride he is able to humble" (Daniel 4:37).

God is able to humble even the mightiest of kings. Nebuchadnezzar, King of Babylon, had a dream. It was a warning that God was going to humble him. He would become insane and be driven from his kingdom for seven years until he acknowledged that God ruled in the kingdoms of men.

The prophet Daniel warned the king to change his ways. Instead, Nebuchadnezzar looked at all he had done and boasted in the things he had built. Then the dream was fulfilled. After seven years, his sanity returned and his kingdom was restored, and he gave God the credit for it all. He came to realize that God is able to humble every one who walks in pride.

God is in the humbling business. When we reach that pinnacle of success or win a great victory, God is able to put us in our place. The elation of victory is short-lived. Then it is back to the nitty, gritty of life. Without God, the top of the ladder can be an empty, hollow place.

Insight

Beware of taking credit for the successes in your life. Give God His rightful place and let Him receive the glory.

DAY 7
James 4:1-10

Grace for the Humble

"That is why scripture says: 'God opposes the proud but gives grace to the humble.' Submit yourselves, then, to God. Resist the devil, and he will flee from you" (James 4:6-7).

I am a fighter. When God allows something traumatic to come into my life, my first impulse is to fight God on the issue and cry out, "Why?"

Years ago when I became pregnant with our third child, I fought God for months. I did not want to be pregnant. The timing was all wrong. It was a financial hardship. My doctor tried to comfort me by saying this unplanned child could be a great blessing. Finally, I submitted myself and this unplanned baby to God. When I quit resisting Him, He poured out His grace on me.

I like to think that over the years the battles have become shorter as I have walked with the Lord. I believe I have learned to submit to Him much quicker than in those early years, for I have seen that God will battle with us until our pride is broken and we bow in submission to His will, whatever it is.

Do you tend to fight God when He allows something traumatic to happen to you?

Insight

The proud find themselves in opposition to God, and He always wins the battle. We find His grace when we submit to His will in the beginning.

Matthew 23:1-12

Humility Before Honor

"The greatest among you will be your servant. For whoever exalts himself will be humbled, and whoever humbles himself will be exalted" (Matthew 23:11-12).

Sitting in a prison chapel one day, Chuck Colson discovered God's upside down kingdom. When he lost everything that he thought made Chuck Colson a great guy, he discovered his true self. The humbling had taken place; the real honor would come much later.

Jesus tells us that we are never to seek honor, but rather, to be humble. If honor is to come, then God will bring it in His time. As the disciples gathered around Jesus, it was obvious that He was the greatest in His group. Yet on the night of His betrayal, He took up the basin and the towel, becoming the lowliest servant as He washed His disciples' feet (John 13).

No matter how high we go, we should never lose our servant attitude of being willing to be the servant of all.

The ground is level at the foot of the cross. The men and women Dan and I minister to in prison are our brothers and sisters in the Lord and have much to teach us.

Insight

Do you desire honor? Then seek the lowest position of all, a humble servant. Should honor come, never lose your servant spirit.

Matthew 18:1-14

Like a Little Child

"Therefore whoever humbles himself like this child is the greatest in the kingdom of heaven. And whoever welcomes a little child like this in my name welcomes me" (Matthew 18:4-5).

I love little children and enjoy working with them every day in my day care. They are so open and trusting. They are natural believers. They love and accept me as I am and are quick to forgive me when I fail them. Their reactions are spontaneous and honest. They are easy to comfort when they are hurting.

One day the disciples asked Jesus, "Who is greatest in the kingdom of heaven?" They must have been surprised when He set a child in their midst. He told them, "Unless you come with child like trust, you will never enter the kingdom of heaven."

We need to come to the Lord with the openness and honesty of a young child. We will never become children of God unless we do. He requires no effort on our part, just acceptance of all Jesus has done for us by dying on the cross.

Have you come in childlike trust to Jesus just as you are? Come today. He waits to welcome you into God's forever family.

Insight

We have new vigor when we realize that the ground at the foot of the cross is level. Inevitably this insight over flows in our relationship with others.

Isaiah 57:14-21

Where God Dwells

"For this is what the high and lofty One says . . . 'I live in a high and holy place, but also-with him who is contrite and lowly, in spirit, to revive the spirit of the lowly'" (Isaiah 57:15).

God is so high and lifted up, He stoops to be hold His creation. Yet He chooses to dwell with those who have humble hearts.

With whom did Jesus choose to associate when He walked this earth? The rich, the rulers, the religious leaders? No. With the tax collectors, prostitutes, the working man and housewife, the common people, and sinners. And I am so glad He did! He touched the leper, healed the blind beggar, and welcomed little children when the disciples would have turned them away.

I often imagine Jesus sitting with us in our Bible study with the women at the prison work center. Though they probably consider themselves great sinners, He is so at home there, and so are we. We are able to share our hearts with these women and they with us. We pray for one another, and I long to see them make it on the outside.

Yes, God is at home with the lowly, for His kingdom is made up of the poor, the weak, and the despised.

Insight

Not many wise, noble, or mighty are called, but rather the foolish, weak, and despised make up God's kingdom.

God Guides the Humble

"Good and upright is the Lord; therefore he instructs sinners in his ways. He guides the humble in what is right and teaches them his way. . . . He will instruct him in the way chosen for him" (Psalm 25:8-9, 12).

Have you ever tried to guide two-year-olds in a new task? Usually they insist, "I can do it myself!" If assured of the children's safety, you must stand back, take your hands off, and let them try on their own. Finally, when they are totally frustrated, they may allow you to help.

How often must God stand back and let us make a mess of things because we, in pride, insist, "I can do it myself!" Then when we are completely humiliated, we turn to Him admitting we need His help.

God cannot guide the proud, for they will not respond to His direction. But He promises to guide the teachable and humble. Humility is admitting that we cannot handle our problems ourselves, that we need to rely on God's help. When we reach that point, God steps into our lives and shows us the way to go.

Are you teachable today, willing to let God direct you in His way? Or are you insisting, "I can do it myself"?

Insight

The proud go their own way and fall. The humble follow God's way and live in His blessing and with His guidance for their lives.

God Sustains the Humble

"Great is our Lord and mighty in power; his understanding has no limit The Lord sustains the humble. . . . The Lord delights in those who fear him, who put their hope in his unfailing love" (Psalm 147:5-6, 11).

Whatever you need, God will meet it if you truly depend on Him. If you think you can get along without Him, He will let you.

I began 1999 with chest pain which I chose to ignore for a few days until I could see my doctor. I was quite confident I wasn't having a heart attack, as I had no shortness of breath.

Doctors take chest pain very seriously, so the following morning I had an echo cardiogram. It was a great relief to find that there was nothing wrong with my heart. I had simply pulled a rib cartilage picking up a very heavy baby in my day care. But through it all, God had sustained me, keeping me from peace-shattering anxiety about my health, and about the needs of my day care if I had been unable to continue the work.

Whatever your need, God is there to meet it, to keep, hold, guide, nourish, and make provision for you. There is nothing too hard for God. He promises to sustain those who are humble enough to lean on Him.

Insight

There is no need God cannot meet, but we must come to Him in humility and dependence. He will sustain us and keep us.

God Blesses the Humble

"Humility and the fear of the Lord bring wealth and honor and life. In the paths of the wicked lie thorns and snares, but he who guards his soul stays far from them" (Proverbs 22:4-5).

Jesus said, "I am come that they may have life and have it to the full" (John 10:10). The path to that life is the pathway of humility. This involves

* admitting our need and coming to Jesus to have that need met,

* giving up our pride of independence and being willing to live entirely dependent on Him,

* guarding our hearts so that we do not fall into the snares of the enemy,

* having a grateful heart for all God does for us,

* giving Him the credit for our successes,

* thinking of others first,

* realizing that God loves us in spite of our imperfections,

* trusting God to keep us from stumbling over the rocks in our path.

Do you really want God's blessing? Then be humble, trusting, submissive to what God wants to do in your life. Give up anger or bitterness, forgiving those who have wronged you. God will bless you and bring honor in His time and way.

Insight

God blesses the humble and keeps their feet from the snares of the enemy, while the proud go on and stumble and fall.

God Hears the Humble

"You hear, O Lord, the desire of the afflicted; you encourage them, and you listen to their cry, defending the fatherless and the oppressed, in order that man, who is of the earth, may terrify no more" (Psalm 10:17-18).

The prayers of the proud go no higher than the ceiling, but the cry of the humble reaches the heart of God, and He is moved to help.

Remember the leper who came to Jesus and said, "Lord, if you will, you can make me clean." Jesus replied immediately, "I am willing. Be healed" (see Matthew 8:1-3). He didn't make God do anything through his prayer, but simply laid hold of His willingness to act in his behalf.

It is a comfort to know God hears me when I cry out to Him, even when I can't put into words what I'm feeling. He knows just what I need to encourage me when I'm down. When I'm simply too tired to pray, He reads the names on my heart. As I carry a prayer burden through my busy day, His Spirit prays through me for that loved one.

If our hearts are humble, God hears those thought prayers we do not put into words, and we can be confident He is at work behind the scenes doing so much more than we can think or even imagine.

Insight

The proud feel no need of God, but are confident they can handle things. The humble cry of the needy reaches Gods heart, and He acts.

The Humble Glorify God

"My soul will boast in the Lord; let the afflicted hear and rejoice" (Psalm 34:2).

"The poor will see and be glad--you who seek God, may your hearts live" (Psalm 69:32).

The proud boast, saying, "Look what I have accomplished. See the degrees hanging on my wall. Take note of the many honors that have been bestowed on me." They are always climbing the ladder, reaching for the power at the top, but are never satisfied.

In contrast, the humble boast in the Lord, saying, "See what God has done in my life." And all who are watching rejoice and give God the credit also.

My favorite part of our church service is our praise and prayer time. From the youngest to the oldest, we share how God has worked in our lives in the past week, and we rejoice together as we see what God is doing. This is often followed by a prayer request. We all feel part of a very special family-the family of God. We pray for one another and give glory to God as we acknowledge how He is working.

Give God the credit for what He is doing in your life, so others may rejoice with you.

Insight

The proud boast in their own accomplishments but the humble boast in the Lord and what He is doing in their lives.

2 Chronicles 7:11-16

God Forgives and Heals

"If my people, who are called by my name, will humble themselves and pray and seek my face and turn from their wicked ways, then I will hear from heaven and will forgive their sin and will heal their land" (2 Chronicles 7:14).

I want you to know that if you ever wander from God, there is a way back. I can assure you of this, because of what God has done for me and for countless others, He will do for you.

If God has brought you low, fall on your face before Him, admitting, "Lord, I have sinned. I need You." Turn to God, and earnestly seek His face. Determine to go in the new direction God is pointing you. Then come God's wonderful promises. "I will hear. I will forgive. I will heal" (v.14).

Speaking of the temple Solomon would build, He added, "My eyes will be open and my ears attentive to the prayers offered in this place" (v. 15). Today you come to the very throne of Grace and find the same is true for you. God sees, He hears, His heart is there. You can get up from your knees and walk on with the Lord, confident that He will keep His word.

Perhaps you have wandered from God. Will you come back? Will you humble yourself and know His forgiveness and healing? He is waiting for you.

Insight

No matter how far you have wandered from God, there is always a way back where His forgiveness and healing await you.

2 Chronicles 34:14-28

God Is Merciful

"'Because your heart was responsive and you humbled yourself before God when you heard what He spoke against this place and its people . . . I have heard you,' declares the Lord" (2 Chronicles 34:27).

King Josiah had sent men to clean and repair the temple. While they were cleaning, they found the book of the law. It was brought to the king and read to him. Josiah's heart was broken as he realized how he and the people had sinned and that consequences were certain. God saw Josiah's humble attitude and his tears for his people. In mercy, God granted a reprieve, putting off the punishment until after Josiah died.

God has not changed. When we turn to Him, He is merciful. A dear friend is discovering this truth. She was deeply concerned about the years she had spent in drugs and was fearful for her children. I shared with her God's promise, "I will restore to you the years that the locust hath eaten" (Joel 2:25, KJV). It's true, she will reap the harvest of those years, but God will temper it with His mercy so long as she walks with Him. He is able to bring good out of the most evil circumstances, redeeming her mistakes. What He is doing for my friend He will surely do for all who turn to Him.

Insight

When we humble our hearts before God, confessing our sin, He pours out His mercy, and purifies us from all our unrighteousness (1 John 1:9).

Deuteronomy 8:1-5

Why Troubles?

"Remember how the Lord God led you all the way in the desert these forty years, to humble you and to test you in order to know what was in your heart, whether or not you would keep his commands" (Deuteronomy 8:2).

Have you ever taken a long look back over your life and strolled through your memories? What stands out the clearest? For me it is the troubles, the most painful experiences along the way. However, surrounding those experiences are the memories of how God brought us through and how He provided for us-His faithfulness. Then there are the lessons I learned from it all.

Why does God test us? To humble us. To knock our pride in the dust. To see what is really deep in our hearts. To see if we are going to continue to trust and obey Him even when the going gets really tough.

Oh, it's easy to say we are trusting God when things are going well. It is also easy to forget Him and begin to depend on ourselves. But when it's dark and we don't understand why God is allowing tests to come, will we trust Him then? Will we believe He will bring us out safely to the other side? Will we look for the blessings in the trials? Lord, help us to do so!

Insight

The testing of our faith builds endurance and reveals what is really in our hearts, whether we will trust God or not.

Philippians 2:5-11

A Servant Attitude

"Made himself nothing, taking the very nature of a servant, being made in human likeness. And being found in appearance as a man, he humbled himself and became obedient unto death-even death on a cross!" (Philippians 2:7-8)

Jesus is our example of a truly humble person. He is the Son of God, yet He laid aside His glory, coming to earth and taking on a human likeness. And as a man, He became the servant of all. He spoke of Himself as one who came not to be served but to serve, and He literally laid down His life for us (Matthew 20:28; John 10:15).

Now where does that leave us as His followers? Do we have a servant spirit? Are we willing to lay down our lives for others without asking what benefit will come to us?

Have you noticed that it is hard to find a servant spirit among people today? I searched and searched for someone to care for my 83-year-old mother with alzheimers so we could go on vacation. Then my neighbor offered to take her, and she treated Mother with Jesus' sweet love.

A truly humble person is the servant of all in the spirit of Jesus. I ask myself how I measure up to that standard. Am I willing to serve others in Jesus' name and with His attitude?

Insight

Jesus laid aside His glory and became the servant of all. How dare we not have a servant spirit when He set the example for us?

Two Men who Prayed

"I tell you that this man, rather than the other, went home justified before God. For everyone who exalts himself will be humbled and he who humbles himself will be exalted" (Luke 18:14).

Two men went up to the temple to pray. One very religious, the other was labeled a sinner. The self-righteous man prayed with himself and for the ears of those around him. He puffed himself up with pride and said, "I'm thankful I'm not like other men." Then, because he could see out of the corner of his eye, he added, "or even this tax collector." Then he proceeded to point out his good points.

The tax collector, on the other hand, stood afar off and bowed his head in shame, and from his heart cried out, "God, be merciful to me, a sinner."

Jesus pointed out that the tax collector went home forgiven because he humbled himself, while the religious man went on in his sin because he thought he didn't have any.

We each need to take that step of humbling ourselves before God and crying out for mercy. God waits to forgive us and make us part of His forever family. Let's not let pride stand in our way.

Insight

The sinner's plea for mercy is never turned away, while the proud go on their own way and are lost, unless they turn back.

Be Real!

"For by the grace given me I say to every one of you: Do not think of yourself more highly than you ought but rather think of yourself with sober judgment, in accordance with the measure of faith God has given you" (Romans 12:3).

How are we to think about ourselves? We are not to have too high or too low of an opinion of ourselves. Both are forms of pride, because both are self-centered. We are to be real, having an honest opinion of who we are and how we can contribute to others. We are all members of Christ's body, the church, and we each have different work to do. We belong to each other, and we need each other.

Each of us has been given the ability to do certain things well. We need to use that ability for the glory of God and to serve others. One ability is not more important than another, though one may be more visible.

When I was a young mother, I was given charge of teaching a department of young children. At first, my helper did not want to work with me because she felt I had an attitude of superiority. I am sorry that is how I came across to her. God still had a lot of humbling to do in my life. When we learned to know the real person beneath and could value each other, we became good friends and worked well together.

Insight

Be real! See yourself as God sees you. He gave you your abilities. Thank Him for them and use them to serve others.

Associate with the Lowly

"Live in harmony with one another. Do not be proud, but be willing to associate with people of low position. Do not be conceited . . . . If it is possible, as far as it depends on you, live at peace with everyone" (Romans 12:16, 18).

Who wants to spend time with a know-it-all? Most of us shrink from individuals whose attitude screams, I know I am better than everyone else. God warns against pride. Rather, He tells us to be willing to associate with the lowly, the poor of this world, those of another race, and the prisoner.

I suppose working with men and women in prison has taught me that the ground is level at the foot of the cross. They are my brothers and sisters in Christ and have much to teach me.

The kingdom of God is made up of the lowly. Jesus spent time with outcasts. He touched lepers and had a conversation with a despised Samaritan. It is the troubled who realize they need a divine touch, the poor and needy who are ready for a Savior, the burdened who are looking for rest.

May God preserve us from a know-it-all attitude. May we realize that the newest babe in Christ has something to teach us. May we never be afraid to associate with people who are looked down on by others. Instead, let's lift them up as valued by God.

Insight

We all have our own gifts and we all need each other. God can use even our weaknesses to bring glory to His name.

Service with an Attitude

"You know how I lived the whole time I was with you. . . . I served the Lord with great humility and with tears, although I was severely tested by the plots of the Jews" (Acts 20:18-19).

We can serve the Lord with an attitude of arrogance, but we will offend people right and left, and God will have to step in and humble us. I know! I offend people often enough with my tongue and tone of voice.

Recently my husband and I have had to go through our volunteer training again for the prison ministry. At first I complained. Why? After all, I went through 40 hours of training 14 years ago. But it has been helpful to go through it again because we forget, and there have been changes. Also, being a prison volunteer means a great deal to me and I will do anything to keep my badge.

Last summer I inadvertently broke a rule at the work center by taking an inmate's children into my day care. The social worker told me that what I had done was a very positive thing, yet she had to terminate our work with the women until the children were moved away. It was a humbling process to be reinstated, but we did what was required, and God has blessed.

Insight

To serve the Lord effectively, we need to serve as Paul did—with tears and humility. A prideful spirit will only undo Gods work.

Ephesians 4:1-13

Showing Jesus' Patience

"Be completely humble and gentle; be patient, bearing with one another in love. Make every effort to keep the unity of the Spirit through the bond of peace" (Ephesians 4:2-3).

Humble and gentle are the two words Jesus used to describe Himself (Matthew 11:29). If we are to be like Jesus, we too will be gentle and humble.

In his book, *Just Like Jesus*, Max Lucado challenges us with the thought of spending a day with Jesus' heart instead of our own. How would I react all day if I had Jesus' heart? I'm sure I would be more patient with the children in my day care, wiser in dealing with them and their little problems. I would be more loving and gentle. I probably wouldn't raise my voice at them when they frustrate me. I have two four-year-olds who never run out of ideas for mischief. Praise God for nap time when one of them is out of circulation!

As I review my day, I see too much of Earline and not enough of Jesus. We can thank God that His Spirit is at work in us. We can look to Jesus and draw from His limitless supply of the traits we need to reflect His beauty. He will not fail us when we depend on Him.

Insight

Christ enables a truly humble person to be patient with others, making allowances for their faults, and to be loving and accepting with realistic expectations.

Special Consideration

"Though the Lord is on high, he looks upon the lowly, but the proud he knows from afar. Though I walk in the midst of trouble, you preserve my life.. . . . The Lord will fulfill his purpose for me" (Psalm 138:6-8).

Some people are drawn to a proud person, hoping, perhaps, that some of the aura will rub off on them. In time, they recognize that the proud person thinks only of self and how to use others.

Christ's followers are drawn to a truly humble person, noting that he or she is a giving, serving person who is willing to help them toward success.

God looks on the humble with respect. He gives the humble special consideration, concerning Himself with them, caring for them, paying attention to them, and honoring them. He keeps a distance from the proud.

Until the proud are humbled, they do not come to God's attention. They cannot come near to God until there is a change of attitude.

Do you want God's special consideration? Then humble yourself. Do you want His respect? Then humble yourself. Do you want God to esteem and honor you? Then humility comes first. Bow your head and heart before God. If you hold on to pride, be prepared for God to humble you in time.

Insight

The proud serve themselves and use others, but the humble serve God and enjoy His undivided attention and special blessing.

2 Corinthians 12:1-10

Why This Pain?

"To keep me from becoming conceited because of these surpassingly great revelations, there was given me a thorn in my flesh, a messenger of Satan to torment me" (2 Corinthians 12:7).

Paul had some kind of physical affliction. Though he pleaded with God for relief, healing was refused. Instead, God gave Paul grace to live with the pain and discomfort. Paul would always have a physical reminder to depend on God daily. It's called being humble.

When I sustained a sacrum injury several years ago, I too pleaded with God for relief from the constant intense pain. I still do not know how I got through those days and cared for my day care children. Today I still must do my stretches and endure the pain that comes from sitting for any length of time. I have to depend on the grace of God, and that in itself is cause for rejoicing.

Do you live with a constant physical affliction? It may be there to keep you dependent on God. He still chooses to display His power through our weaknesses, for it is in our weakness that His power is magnified. Dependence on God, no matter how it comes, leads to true humility and ultimately to honor.

Insight

Do you want God's power in your life? Then be willing to be weak. Do you want God's honor? Then be willing to be humbled.

1 Corinthians 13

At the Heart of True Love

"Love is patient, love is kind. It does not envy, it does not boast, it is not proud. It is not rude, it is not self-seeking, it is not easily angered, it keeps no record of wrongs" (1 Corinthians 13:4-5).

I once knew a man who kept a little black book in which he listed everyone who had ever wronged him. I wonder if he went about thinking of ways to get back at each person recorded there. He would never know true freedom and genuine love until he burned his record of real or imagined offences.

True love is humble, dedicated to making another successful, and truly concerned about the needs of others. It is encouraging, patient, and kind. If we are truly loving persons, then we will be truly humble, unselfishly seeking the welfare of others.

My love is really tested in my day care. It seems God has always given me at least one child who needs an extra measure of love, and that one usually gives me the most challenge. Often I need to remind myself, God sent me this child!

Let God love others through you, even the difficult and unlovely. He can do miracles in you and in that other person!

Insight

Loving others with God's love saves us from the trap of self-centeredness and moves us into outgoing concern for others and a loving treatment of their needs.

An Attitude of Gratitude

"And bove all these virtues put on love, which binds them all together in perfect unity. Let the peace of Christ rule in your hearts, since as members of one body you were called to peace. And be thankful" (Colossians 3:14-15).

While still a teenager, our son, who is now a pastor, preached his first sermon. The title, "An Attitude of Gratitude." I probably still have the tape. Being thankful to God for who He is and all He does is so important.

If at any time we begin to pat ourselves on the back and think, Look how well I've done, we are headed for a fall. If we have a humble, grateful attitude, we will thank God that He has seen fit to use us to touch someone else or has carried us successfully through a frustrating day.

For a week now, as I write this, I have prayed, "Lord, help me be slow to anger." Friday was especially stressful in my day care. In one incident after another my patience was challenged and stretched. We all have days like that. God kept my exasperation under control. With His help I could smile and calmly finish my day. As the children left to go to their homes, I lifted my heart with gratitude to the Lord and offered Him praise and thanksgiving.

Insight

Humble people are grateful people, always giving God the credit for their victories in life's frustrating circumstances.

1 Corinthians 1:26-29

A Healthy Mindset

"Do nothing out of selfish ambition or vain conceit, but in humility consider others better than yourselves. Each of you should look not only to your own interests, but also to the interests of others" (Philippians 2:3-4).

Who do you invite to dinner? Only the people you really enjoy being with, or others further down on your list? Some time ago my husband and I decided to invite them all, one couple or family at a time. It took us a year to get through the list and in that time we discovered some rich blessings along the way.

On occasion I've been guilty of thinking I'm better than someone else, and God has had to work in my heart and humble me. He has reminded me that His family is basically made up of the poor and needy. The apostle Paul notes that not many wise or famous are called into God's family. Jesus welcomes all who are willing to admit their sin. They recognize their need of a Savior, while the rich trust in their wealth and the wise rely on their wisdom.

As we learn from Jesus we will develop a humble mindset and stop assuming we are better than others. Jesus will help us look for the good points in others and teach us how to encourage them in their walk with the Lord.

Insight

Jesus can give us a healthy mindset, turning around our natural tendency to look down on others and exalt ourselves.

Welcome Suffering

"Although he was a son, he learned obedience from what he suffered" (Hebrews 5:8).

"Man looks at the outward appearance, but the Lord looks at the heart" (1 Samuel 16:7).

No one welcomes suffering, yet it comes to all of us. And in each painful thing that happens to us, God has some lessons for us to learn. It is important that we do not lose faith, that we endure the test, and that we cling to God. The way we react to suffering can bring great glory to God and help turn others to the faith, or it can bring shame on God's name.

If Jesus had to learn obedience through suffering, how much more do we!

When I went through TMJ treatment several years ago, my dentist had to sharply rebuke me. I had not been out of pain in 30 days, and I developed a long face. The treatment did not go well for me. I thought my dentist was going to give up on me. I greeted him with a complaining attitude and disappointment. I deserved the dressing down he gave me, and I determined that with God's help I would smile when I entered his office, no matter how much pain I was in. My changed attitude helped both of us.

Insight

Let's submit to the lessons God has for us in pain and suffering and let His joy shine through our tears.

Walk Humbly

What does it mean to walk humbly with my God? Use a few questions to help you evaluate what you have been learning from Christ about humility.

* Am I learning to welcome trials, knowing they will reveal what is in my heart and whether I will obey God?

* Am I living in complete dependence on God, not assuming I can handle everything on my own?

* Am I becoming less self-seeking and more willing to unselfishly reach out to others?

* Do I have a growing sense of being loved by God, in spite of my many imperfections?

* In my relationship with others, am I showing more patience and gentleness?

* Am I grateful to God for all He does in and through me?

* Do I have a realistic opinion of myself in the sight of God?

Which will it be: pride or humility? Christ invites us, "Come, learn humility of Me."

Insight

Would you like your life to over flow with God's grace? While He opposes the proud, He lavished His grace to the humble (1 Peter 5:5).

April

Proverbs 12:18-28

An Anxious Heart

"An anxious heart weighs a man down, but a kind word cheers him up" (Proverbs 12:25).

"Do not be anxious about anything, but in everything, by prayer ..." (Philippians 4:6).

Who among us has not had anxious moments when our peace fled and our minds chewed on thoughts, like a dog worrying a bone? Those anxious thoughts keep us awake, and we simply can't turn them off.

When I'm hurting or deeply troubled about a matter, I walk a mile through my neighborhood. As I walk, I talk to the Lord, laying the matter all out before Him. By the time I return home, things look and feel much better.

I have always been an encourager, but there are times when I'm in desperate need of encouragement. As I cry out to God, He meets me at that point of desperation. He may bring to my mind the words of a hymn or point me to a Scripture verse, or He may simply speak through a comment in a phone conversation with a friend.

I'm still learning to let go of a matter and place it squarely in God's hands. I'm still learning to run into His presence when I'm hurting and let Him calm the fears and fill my heart with His gift of peace.

Insight

At the center of anxiety is a core of fear. But there is One who can calm your troubled heart. His name is Jesus.

DAY 2

1 Peter 5:5-11

Daily Anxiety

"Humble yourselves, therefore, under God's mighty hand, that he may lift you up in due time. Cast all your anxiety on him because he cares for you" (1 Peter 5:6-7).

I don't remember what I was worried about, but as I had my morning devotions I was pointed to today's Scripture by three different devotional writers. I knew I had better listen to these very familiar words and do exactly what they said.

"Cast"- It would take concentrated effort to literally throw my anxiety on Jesus.

"All"- I dared not keep even one portion to try to handle by myself. That would mean total freedom from worry.

"On Him"-I needed to throw it all on Jesus, the only One who could truly carry my burden.

Why? "Because He cares for me." Jesus really loves me and will take care of me, no matter what happens. He is still in control of my anxiety-producing situation and will bring great good out of it in my life and in the lives of those I love.

My part is to believe and obey, to stand back and watch Him work.

Too simple? you ask. Yes, but sometimes difficult to do.

Insight

Simple obedience to God's Word brings freedom from the cares which would drag us down. Easy to say-hard to do. But it is the key to enjoying Jesus' gift of peace.

Future Anxiety

"Do not let your hearts be troubled. Trust in God; trust also in me. In my Father's house are many rooms; if it were not so, I would have told you. I am going there to prepare a place for you" (John 14:1-2).

Trust and anxiety cannot abide in the same place at the same time. We are either trusting or worrying. The Psalmist said, "When I am afraid, I will trust in you" (Psalm 56:3).

Something which can cause us deep anxiety is our fear of the future. I recall worrying about how we would get through the teenage years with our three sons. More recently I have worried about retirement. Would we have enough income to continue to live in our home? My husband's Social Security would not even begin to meet our needs. Now I am faced with his diagnosis of early Alzheimers. How long will I be able to take care of him? When do I take the car away? What will I do for income when I have to give up my day care? So many questions! I dare not look to the future and try to carry its worries.

Jesus tells us that we must live one day at a time, trusting the uncertain future to our Father in Heaven. When we do that, we enjoy His provision of peace.

Insight

What a glorious certainty! Jesus is preparing a place for us and He will see that we get there in His perfect timing. So kiss worry about the future good-by!

Depression and Anxiety

"Why are you downcast, O my soul? Why so disturbed within me? Put your hope in God, for I will yet praise him, my Savior and my God. My soul is downcast within me" (Psalm 42:5-6).

When my father died suddenly of a heart attack, I was plunged deeply into depression. I despaired of ever getting through the grief process. I wondered if I could ever look forward to life again. My zest for living was gone, and I simply endured the days. That was a dark, hopeless time.

During those days I memorized Psalms 42, 43, and 51. Every day I prayed those verses back to God, especially the plea that God would restore his joy (see 51:12). God answered those desperate cries for help. After a year of counseling with a godly pastor, l was back on my feet. I became an encourager again instead of being the needy one.

One day I looked more closely at today's verses and noticed that depression and anxiety often go together. We are disturbed, we hurt, we withdraw. Hope hangs by a slender thread.

Begin to look up and praise God for who He is. Lift your eyes off yourself and your problems and look to the only One who can really help. As you praise Him, He will fill your heart with His peace.

Insight

Praising God, even when you don't feel like it, begins to chase away the black clouds of depression and anxiety

DAY 5
Luke 10:38-42

Anxious Martha

"Martha, Martha . . . you are worried and upset about many things, but one thing is needed. Mary has chosen what is better, and it will not be taken away from her" (Luke 10:41-42).

I wonder if Martha was a perfectionist, insisting that everything be just so. We know she was concerned about all the details of serving a special meal. After all, Jesus was a special guest. Then with all the disciples, she had a crowd to feed. She surely needed help in the kitchen. There was no way she could relax-not with the house full of company.

One summer all our family came home-sons, wives, and grandchildren. There were 13 of us in our small house. Just figuring out where everyone would sleep was a challenge in itself. Then there were the meals to prepare for us all. I could sympathize with Martha.

But Martha evidently took Jesus' words to heart, because later she would host Him and the disciples again. This time Jesus did not rebuke her.

I often serve guests one of my hearty soups with a simple dessert. I've learned that a meal does not have to be fancy and that conversation around the table is more important. The main thing is to keep Jesus in the center of our home.

Insight

Anxiety can make us irritable when things go wrong. Better a relaxed hostess more concerned for the people she serves than for perfection.

Where To Turn in Trouble

"O our God, will you not judge them? For we have no power to face this vast army that is attacking us. We do not know what to do, but our eyes are upon you " (2 Chronicles 20:12).

Israel was in trouble. Three different armies were massed on their border, so they did the only wise thing. They sought the Lord in fasting and prayer. God answered and gave them specific instructions. When they began to praise the Lord, the battle turned in their favor, and a great victory was won.

Some years ago my husband's remodeling job was in trouble. Dan turned to our pastor, who recommended we see a lawyer. After the lawyer told us we would lose if it went to court, we simply turned to the Lord alone. He delivered us from a situation that was totally beyond our control.

Do you find yourself in a situation where you don't know what to do? The wisest thing to do is simply turn to the Lord and look to Him alone. Begin to praise and thank God, as Israel did long ago. Praise releases God's power. He may choose to act in your behalf or He will enable you to go on, even though the situation does not change. Over it all, He will let His gift of peace fill your heart.

Insight

When you don't know what to do, look to the Lord alone. He has the power to help you He will enable you to endure.

DAY 7
Philippians 4:10-23

Learning Contentment

"I am not saying this because I am in need, for I have learned to be content whatever the circumstances. I know what it is to be in need, and I know what it is to have plenty" (Philippians 4:11-12).

Contentment is not an automatic response. It is something we each must learn. When the apostle Paul was working for a living and preaching on the side, I'm sure he enjoyed a time of plenty. Then came the prison years when he was in need. He went from one extreme to another, but could say, "I've learned to be content whatever the circumstances."

While my husband Dan was a prison chaplain, we were in a time of plenty and were able to do a number of things with the extra income. But when he was suddenly relieved of his post, we had to do some real belt tightening. Knocking a full-time income out of the monthly budget is no small item. We sold the second car, dropped my health insurance, and increased the day care license to 6-12 children so we could take a sixth child. It has been an adventure living week to week, watching God make the money go around even in high expense months. Am I content? Well, I am learning, and through it all, I have found Jesus to be a kind and patient teacher.

Insight

The Lord is going to bring one situation after another into your life so you can learn contentment. Thank Him and go on.

1 Peter 3:1-7

A Gentle and Peaceful Spirit

"Your beauty should be that of your inner self, the unfading beauty of a gentle and quiet spirit, which is of great worth in God's sight" (1 Peter 3:4).

Dan and I recently had some communication breakdowns. One occurred when we were headed to the community work center to hold a church service. Dan packed in his briefcase all I would need to teach the women. However, we ended up at the work center with only the box of songbooks. Dan said, "I told you to pick up the brief case." I raised my voice and replied, "You didn't say anything to me!" (There was no gentle spirit expressed.) I went in to lead singing with the women while Dan went home for the missing briefcase.

A few mornings later, he left at 7:30 to get gas and didn't return until after 10. I kept my cool, believing there must be a good explanation why he was gone so long. On his return, he explained he had been putting an inmate on the bus. I was thankful that I had not hit him with an accusing, "Where have you been?" My anxiety over the missing briefcase had made me lash out at Dan, but later a gentle spirit kept me from saying something I would regret. That gentle spirit came as I allowed Jesus' Spirit to fill my heart.

Insight

An anxious spirit may lash out in unkind words and actions. But a gentle spirit smooths things out for others.

Matthew 6:25-34

Anxiety About Tomorrow

"Therefore do not worry about tomorrow, for tomorrow will worry about itself. Each day has enough trouble of its own" (Matthew 6:34).

Look at today's troubles like a bundle of sticks. There is no problem if we carry only that bundle. But if you add yesterday's sticks and tomorrow's sticks to your load, it becomes unbearable.

I have watched my mother deteriorate through Alzheimers and have cared for her at various times. When I think of losing my husband through the same disease, the emotional pain is nearly unbearable. I dare not look down the future and try to carry tomorrow's load today. I must live only for today. I can easily bear the amount of forgetfulness I see in Dan today, and I will trust God for tomorrow.

When I realized Dan might have Alzheimers, l cried out to God, "Lord, I need to hear from You!" The next morning as l awoke, the first words in my mind came from the old hymn, "The clouds you so much dread will break with blessing on your head." What a comfort that was to me, and how I have clung to it over these last months!

Our Lord has special grace for us as we trust Him one day at a time.

Insight

Tomorrow will have its own share of troubles and trials. Live one day at a time with your eyes fixed on the Lord.

Do Not Fret

"Be still before the Lord and wait patiently for him; do not fret when men succeed in their ways, when they carry out their wicked schemes" (Psalm 37:7).

There's nothing harder than waiting, especially when a situation seems to demand action and God appears to be taking entirely too long to rescue us. We fret when we agitate in our minds, allowing our thoughts to gnaw or wear away. We just can't quiet those troubling thoughts. But God's command is to stop fretting and to be still, to be at peace as we wait patiently. God is at work. In His perfect timing, our need will be met.

In my day care work, I've experienced God filling two openings immediately, and I've experienced long waits. At one point I wanted only a full-time child, so turned down all part-timers. I also did not feel ready for a newborn with my two very active four-year-olds. When I finally made up my mind to accept an infant, the right call came. When the Lord fills a day care opening, He brings the right child at the right time, even if we have to wait.

God had promised to give David the throne of Israel—but not right away. David needed to learn to keep his heart still while he waited God's timing.

Insight

To fret is to waste energy in a useless pastime. To rest in the Lord shows that you trust Him to meet your need in His perfect timing.

Know My Anxious Thoughts

"Search me, O God, and know my heart; test me and know my anxious thoughts. See if there is any offensive way in me, and lead me in the way ever lasting" (Psalm 139:23-24).

When our middle son, John, graduated from high school, he prepared to leave home. He loaded his saddle and belongings into his pickup and struck out for Montana to be a cowboy. Within a month he was home again. Later he left again to find a ranch job in Oregon. He went with a friend who was not a good influence.

Weeks went by with no word of any kind-no letters, no phone calls. We had no idea where he was or what he was doing. My mother's heart yearned to hear something. If I had prayed, "Lord, know my anxious thoughts," I'm sure He would have pointed out several that were tumbling around in my mind. When word finally came from John, the world was a brighter place.

Whatever our situation, God looks deep in our hearts and puts His finger on our anxious thoughts. As Warren Meyers writes, "God is seeking to bless you through whatever He allows to happen in your life." When we let go our anxiety, He brings peace to our hearts.

Insight

Anxious thoughts do not come from God. Let Him point out what makes Him sad and follow Him as He leads you in the path of peace.

Jeremiah 17:1-10

Rooted in the Divine

"He will be like a tree planted by the water that sends out its roots by the stream. It does not fear when heat comes; its leaves are always green. It has no worries in a year of drought and never fails to bear fruit" (Jeremiah 17:8).

The prophet Jeremiah contrasts two ways of life, trusting in man or trusting in God. The choice is ours.

We cheat ourselves when we put our full trust in human resources, for disappointment awaits us. Government programs get bogged down. Products do not live up to their advertised benefits. Promises are broken, and rewards are given to the less worthy. Even trusted friends and loved ones let us down. Jeremiah says that when we put our trust in man, we are like a bush in a parched land.

When we trust in the Lord, we do not have the visible props that would seem to justify our trust. But Jeremiah says we are like a tree with its roots nourished by a constant source of water. God never fails us. He is always available with a listening ear and a word of comfort.

Let the problems in your life today cause your roots to go down deep into God's love. Count on Him. He is a never-failing source of all you will need to flourish in hard places.

Insight

Where are you placing your trust? In friends who may fail you, or in the unfailing God, whose ear is always open to your cry?

2 Timothy 4:1-8

Calm and Steady in Ministry

"But you, keep your head in all situations, endure hardship, do the work of an evangelist, discharge all the duties of your ministry" (2 Timothy 4:5).

Has God given you a ministry? Do you need encouragement? Have you suffered rejection? Paul encouraged young Timothy to keep on teaching and preaching even though many would turn away from the truth.

As my husband Dan and I minister in the prison and community work center for women we are never concerned about numbers. If only one woman comes to our Bible study, she usually opens up and shares when she would keep silent in a larger group. We've had very meaningful times with two or three and with ten.

When we started our prison prayer group, we asked the Lord for three men. He gave us 13 that first day, which quickly jumped to 25, then 35-40. Now our room is at capacity and all for a prayer meeting.

God just asks that we be faithful and leave the results to Him. We have peace knowing our labor is never in vain (1 Corinthians 15:58). The true rewards for faithful service will be given out in glory.

Insight

Minister with the gifts God has given you. Be steady and faithful, willing to suffer rejection, for great is your reward in heaven.

A Quiet Soul

"Come to me, all you who are weary and burdened, and I will give you rest. Take my yoke upon you and learn from me, for I am gentle and humble in heart, and you will find rest for your souls" (Matthew 11:28-29).

Most of us experience a stressful day, at least once in a while. Mishaps occur and frustration builds. Equipment breaks down. Customers complain. Children quarrel. The weather causes traffic delays. Coworkers thoughtlessly add to our load. Family members take us for granted. Someone speaks harshly to us and we wilt.

For some, though, every day is stressful. Many people feel as if their plates are full to overflowing. They cannot cope with one more problem.

Are you stressed out by life? Would you like a calm and peaceful spirit within even while you cope with difficult circumstances? Jesus invites you to come to Him today. Just lay down your pride and the burden of trying to do everything on your own. Give your load to Him. Put on His yoke by giving the controls of your life to Him. The results will be blessed peace. You'll discover a quiet freedom from being tyrannized by the pressures in your life. Jesus promises that His yoke is easy and His burden is light.

Insight

The only way to real peace is through Jesus, who died and rose again to make it possible. Stop your striving and rest in Him.

DAY 15
Isaiah 41:1-10

The Promise of His Presence

"So do not fear, for I am with you; do not be dismayed for I am your God. I will strengthen you and help you; I will uphold you with my righteous right hand" (Isaiah 41:10).

God's promise in today's verse is for all time, for whatever happens in our lives. It is steady as a rock, for it is God Himself speaking.

When my husband Dan was first diagnosed with Alzheimers, he went around sharing the news with everyone. I could talk to no one about it. I may have been in denial. During that time, Truit Ford of Haven Ministries called us. As we talked, I finally broke my silence and shared with him about Dan. One word from our conversation that day has stuck with me-endurance.

God will enable us to endure whatever the future holds for us. He will make a way and send whatever help is needed. There is nothing that we will go through in this life that lies outside the promises of God. He will be present in our trials. He will be our strength. He will be our perfect peace. He will be our wisdom. He will be our comfort and our encouragement. He will give grace.

So lay aside your fear, worry, and anxiety. Cling to the promise of your never-failing God.

Insight

When you have a need, cash in the promises of God. They are like money in the bank-and much more precious.

DAY 16
Philippians 4:1-9

A Cure for Anxiety

"Do not be anxious about anything, but in everything, by prayer and petition with thanksgiving, present your requests to God, and the peace of God . . . will guard your hearts and your minds" (Philippians 4:6-7).

God has given us a formula that works. I've tried to live by it down through the years whenever I have been tempted to worry.

When I shared in the prison that I was writing about anxiety and God's perfect peace, a young man came up to me saying that he was so anxious that he had not been able to eat. I asked, "What are you worried about?"

He poured out his story, adding that he had been praying but it had not helped. I then asked, "Did you pray with thanksgiving?"

"What do you mean?" he responded.

I explained that we have to make an effort to quell anxious thoughts, to literally refuse them, then to pray about our concerns with thanksgiving. We need to lay it all out before the Lord and begin to thank Him for everything we can think of in the situation. It works! God's perfect peace does keep our minds and emotions.

I hope that young man was able to find peace. We prayed with him, then left.

Insight

Worry leads to agitation of mind and heart, while prayer with thanksgiving leads to peace of mind and heart.

DAY 17
John 14:15-31

An Untroubled Heart

"Peace I leave with you; my peace I give you. I do not give
to you as the world gives. Do not let your hearts be troubled and do not be afraid" (John 14:27).

Can we go through life with an untroubled heart? Jesus
says we can, because one of His most precious gifts to us is
His peace. This means we can put up the barricades and refuse to let those troubling thoughts gain entrance.

Lately when my husband or I have faced medical tests, I've
refused to think of all that could be wrong. In the past, my
thoughts would jump to the worst conclusions with worry
about cancer or need for heart surgery. I'd think of the loss of
work and the medical bills. When the results came in, I found
I had worried about things that were not going to happen. All
my worry was for nothing! Now I'm learning to resist those
troubling thoughts.

Jesus gives peace that will last, not the fragile, easily broken
peace the world gives. In the troubled times of life we can refuse to listen to the whispers of the enemy, but choose instead
to believe God. At that very moment a wonderful peace will
come over our spirits.

Insight

*A believing heart is an untroubled heart. Peace is the legacy
of the Comforter Jesus has sent to be with us.*

With Heart and

"Trust in the Lord with all your heart and lean not on your own understanding; in all your ways acknowledge him, and he will make your paths straight" (Proverbs 3:5-6).

Obeying today's Scripture is really hard to do! I'm always trying to figure things out and make specific plans for the future. I'm a real goal-setter and doer. I plan a budget and am disappointed when I can't make the money do what I want. Yet I've watched God overrule my plans again and again, working things out and meeting our needs in spite of my inability to reach my goals. His ways are so different from ours. Our puny plans must make Him chuckle as He prepares a miracle in our behalf.

He is waiting to say to us, "My child, when are you going to trust Me with all your heart and mind, and quit trying to figure things out?"

We can answer, "Okay, Lord. I won't get uptight when my plans don't work out. I'll do the best I can but trust You to overrule whenever necessary. Lord, there are times when I don't understand what you are doing in my life, but I know it's for the best, and I'm going to trust You. But you're going to have to remind me often not to ever lean on my own understanding!"

Insight

God is still – and will always be – the Blessed Controller of all things for your good and for His glory. Lean hard on Him.

Psalm 4

Safe in Jesus

"I will both lie down and sleep in peace, for you alone
Lord, make me live in safety" (Psalm 4:8).

Even when my children were small and my husband would
be gone overnight on the truck, I never had trouble sleeping
alone. Now in these retirement years when he is gone to a
men's retreat, the same is true.

Yet I've known nights when my thoughts were so troubled
that sleep eluded me for hours.

I wonder what David's circumstances were when he penned
this psalm. Was he fleeing from Saul? Still he was able to say,
'I'm at peace. God is watching over me.' His heart was also
filled with joy because God's presence was real. Joy and peace
often go together like twins.

When we lose our peace and joy we probably have lost our
focus. We are looking at our needs and problems, not at the
Lord.

We need to pray from God to the problem, not from the
problem to God. Our focus is key to experiencing the peace
and joy only God can give. Where is your focus today? Is it on
God or on your problems?

Insight

*The higher our focus the greater our joy and peace. Turn
your eyes upon Jesus. He alone can meet your soul's deep
needs.*

Psalm 119:161-176

A Love for God's Word

"Great peace have they who love your law, and nothing can make them stumble. . . . May your hand be ready to help me, for I have chosen your precepts" (Psalm 119:165, 173).

The Word of God is vitally important in our lives. It reveals God's ways and character to us. It is filled with great and precious promises which we can take to the bank of heaven. It is filled with examples of men and women who did great things for God, and it is filled with warnings of the wrong way to go.

Love the Word of God. Spend time in it. Memorize it, thus giving the Holy Spirit portions to bring to your mind when you need them. Some time ago when I was troubled by depression, I memorized entire psalms. They built a buffer zone between my conscious and subconscious mind.

There is great comfort in the Word of God, and the Holy Spirit is faithful to make it real in our lives. It is a source of strength and peace. We can literally pray the words of Scripture back to God, knowing we are praying according to God's will. Those prayers are sure to be answered.

Insight

The Word of God is essential to our growth in Christ. Neglect it and you will grow weak and unstable. Be filled with the Word and be filled with peace.

Anchor Your Mind in God

"You will keep in perfect peace him whose mind is stead-fast, because he trusts in you. Trust in the Lord forever, for the Lord, the Lord, is the Rock eternal" (Isaiah 26:3-4).

No matter what you are facing in life, it can be accepted with a peaceful heart. How? By maintaining your focus. That is by keeping your mind and your heart's eyes stayed on God.

Do you remember how Peter actually walked on water? He could do so as long as he kept his eyes on Jesus. But when he began to look at the tempest around him, he began to sink. When he cried out in terror, "Lord, save me!" Jesus rescued him. He lovingly chided Peter, "You of little faith, why did you doubt?" (Matthew 14:22-33).

So long as we maintain our focus on God and His promises, we can live with difficulties. But the minute we focus on the situation, we begin to sink. May we have Peter's wisdom to immediately cry out to the Lord for help and get our eyes back on Him. Otherwise, we are in danger of sinking down into hopelessness. It's our choice: trust or sink.

No matter what is troubling you today, ask yourself, "Where is my focus?" Keep your eyes on the Lord, even as you are being buffeted by a storm.

Insight

Maintain your focus on the only One who can really help in the storms of life and you will be at peace.

God Leads in Peace

"You will go out in joy and be led forth in peace; the mountains and hills will burst into song before you, and all the trees of the field will clap their hands" (Isaiah 55:12).

I remember clearly the day this promise became real to me. God had uprooted me and was moving me to a new home and a new town. I had packed the last of our possessions in our little blue pickup, cleaned the house for the last time, and left the keys for the new owner. As I took down the calendar, I found Isaiah 55:12 was the verse for that day.

As I drove from the foothills to the valley, I asked God to help me embrace His promise. Tears were streaming down my face as I left my home and friends of 19 years, but my heart was at peace because I knew in my heart that God was leading me.

The adjustment ahead would be difficult, but I would soon take root once again and have the joy of being close to the state prison where God had called us to minister.

Is the Lord asking you to leave your comfort zone, to launch out for Him? Don't be afraid to follow His leading.

Insight

Our Heavenly Father never lets us get too comfortable. He stirs up our nest and encourages us to fly.

Plan of Hope

" 'For I know the plans I have for you,' declares the Lord,
'Plans to prosper you and not to harm you, plans to give
you hope and a future' " (Jeremiah 29:11).

God gave this precious promise to Israel while they were in
captivity far from their homeland. They were there because
they had sinned and refused to turn back from their wicked
ways even though He had warned them again and again. Now
He promised that after 70 years he was going to take them
back to the land of promise. He had not forsaken them but
was planning great blessing for them.

What are God's plans for you, for me? We know one thing:
He plans to make us like Jesus, whatever it takes. He plans to
make us witnesses for Him. He plans to make us comforters
to those who hurt. He plans to make us victorious. He plans
to redeem our mistakes and bring great good out of them for
ourselves and others. And that is only the beginning!

God promises that His plans are to bless us through whatever He allows to come into our lives. Our place is to look for
those blessings and not miss them entirely.

Insight

*God's purposes are always good, never evil, no matter what
He allows to happen. His thoughts and ways are much higher than ours. We can trust Him fully.*

DAY 24
Mark 4:35-41

Jesus Calms the Storm

"He got up, rebuked the wind and said to the waves, 'Quiet, be still!' . . . He said to his disciples, 'Why are you so afraid? Do you still have no faith?'" (Mark 4:39-40).

It is dark and a fierce storm has suddenly come up. The boat is in danger of swamping. Jesus is asleep, oblivious to the emergency. The disciples wake him with the question, "Don't you care? We're about to drown."

How many times have we been in a storm and accused God of not caring? In the darkest hour we call out, "Lord, I'm really hurting and You appear to be doing nothing!" He hears our desperate cries and moves to still the storm in our lives, calming our hearts and minds with His peace.

Then He often rebukes us. "Why did you panic? I've been in the boat with you all the time. I've felt every wave and the pressure of the wind."

Jesus is the great stiller of storms, bringing calm and peace in the midst of turmoil. Jill Briscoe says, "Jesus can see in the dark." Even if you lose the sense of His presence, He is still there, for His promise is "'Never will I leave you; never will I forsake you.' So we say with confidence, 'The Lord is my helper; I will not be afraid'" (Hebrews 13:5-6).

Insight

When the storms of life rock our boat, Jesus is near. He meets you at your point of desperation and calms the storm.

John 16:19-33

Our Peace Is in Jesus

"I have told you these things, so that in me you may have peace. In this world you will have trouble. But take heart! I have overcome the world" (John 16:33).

The world rejected Jesus. Should we be surprised that it rejects us today? Jesus said, "If the world hates you, keep in mind that it hated me first" (John 15: 18).

I've been doing a neighborhood survey, looking for people interested in a home Bible study. I did not have real freedom in going until I faced the fact that 90 percent of the people I contacted would likely reject me.

I'm not "a people person," so it has been very difficult to go. I've learned a lot about my neighborhood, and God has led me to a few receptive people around me. But I would not know if I didn't go and ask.

On Saturday I attended a workshop on life style evangelism. Our leader said, "God is calling out someone in your neighborhood." I thought, "I've knocked on a lot of doors, but I haven't found that person yet." Then on Sunday I met a young couple eager to study God's Word. "Lord," I prayed, "I've found them. Thank You, Lord, for sending me out."

Insight

God is calling people in the world to Himself. Let's do our part to find them, knowing our peace is in Jesus and the world may reject us.

Blood Bought Peace

"He was pierced for our transgressions, he was crushed for our iniquities; the punishment that brought us peace was upon him, and by his wounds we are healed" (Isaiah 53:5).

Our peace was bought at a terrible price-the precious blood of Jesus Christ. God visited the punishment for our sins on His own beloved Son. Jesus was a lamb without spot and without blemish, a perfect sacrifice (see 1 Peter 1:19).

While we are going our own way and living our self-centered lives, peace is a fleeting thing or nonexistent. The burden and turmoil of living in sin exacts its price.

God invites us, saying, "Come to Me. I will give you rest and peace. Accept the sacrifice of My Son in your behalf. Give Him the control of your life."

Jesus lifts the heavy burden, grants rest to the weary, strength to the faint hearted, peace to the troubled, and forgiveness of sin to the wandering ones.

If you are thirsty, come and drink. If you are hungry, come and be satisfied. If you are troubled, come, find peace and rest. He is waiting. He invites you. He has paid the price.

Insight

Jesus purchased your peace on Calvary. The invitation is always open. You only need to make the decision to come to God on His terms.

John 20:19-31

Fearful and Hiding Disciples

"When the disciples were together, with the doors locked for fear of the Jews, Jesus came and stood among them and said, 'Peace be with you!'" (John 20:19)

Picture the scene. Jesus has died. The disciples are rudderless without their teacher and leader. We find them hiding behind locked doors. Suddenly Jesus stands in their midst and speaks peace to their fearful hearts.

Later, after Jesus endowed them with the Holy Spirit, He sent them forth to witness for Him. We find them in the Book of Acts speaking with great boldness. If God can change cringing, fearful disciples into bold witnesses for Him, then there is hope for me.

When I determined to knock on every door in my neighborhood, I prayed for boldness. However, I was still afraid. Once I stopped on the sidewalk outside a home and could not make myself go up to the door. I turned and walked on home.

My efforts have not become easier, but a few warm receptions have encouraged me to keep going and leave the results with God. I have peace when I remember Jesus is walking my neighborhood with me.

Insight

God asks us to come out of hiding and leave our comfort zone and love the people around us. He replaces our fear with peace when we obey Him.

A Spirit Controlled Mind-Set

"The mind of sinful men is death, but the mind controlled by the Spirit is life and peace; the sinful mind is hostile to God. It does not submit to God's law, nor can it do so" (Romans 8:6-7).

Where does fear come from? Not from God, for He "did not give us a spirit of timidity, but a spirit of power, of love and of self-discipline" (2 Timothy 1:7). Fear is really self-centered. We want to be liked and accepted. We don't want people to reject us. Our pride gets in the way.

It's better to be focused on God. If He asks us to do something, He is going to empower us by His Spirit to do His will.

When I first started in prison ministry, I was afraid to go to the women. I had been on a team with my husband working with men. Once when I was asked to visit a woman, I actually refused to go since I would have to talk with her alone. Thank God for His patience with us! Thank God for His Spirit who uses such weak vessels of clay!

Remember that the spirit of fear is not of God. Be willing to be stretched, and dare to do what God lays on your heart. As you step out in faith, He will give you the spirit "of power, of love and self-discipline," and His peace will be yours.

Insight

God has given us His Spirit to empower and give us boldness. Refuse fear. Accept the gift of His peace.

Fruit of the Spirit

"The fruit of the Spirit is love, joy, peace, patience, kindness, goodness, faithfulness, gentleness and self-control. Against such things there is no law" (Galatians 5:22-23).

When I cared for my mother, who had Alzheimers disease, I had opportunity to grow in patience, gentleness, and kindness. Evidently God has a lot more gardening to do in my life, now that my husband is going to need care.

At times it seems easy to get frustrated and upset with him. I need to develop a sense of humor so I will smile more at the mistakes and communication glitches.

Our Lord is very adept at putting us in a situation when we must grow in one area or another. He tailors our circumstances to give us opportunities to learn from Him so that we can be come Christlike. He brings people into our lives who challenge us to grow in love.

Is there an area in which you sense your need to grow? God will design the special circumstances to help you develop that fruit of the Spirit. He is faithful to teach. Your part is to be faithful to learn from Him, and as you do, the Holy Spirit will produce fruit in you.

Insight

God is in the gardening business. He is growing the fruit of the Spirit in the lives of His children.

Called to Peace

"Over all these virtues put on love, which binds them all together in perfect unity. Let the peace of Christ rule in your hearts . . . and be thankful" (Colossians 3:14-15).

One of two things is going to rule in our hearts: anxiety or peace, self or the Holy Spirit. We have a constant choice to make. We can let fear rule; or we can let peace rule.

We find ourselves in troubled circumstances-will it be anxiety or peace? A major storm breaks over our lives-will we trust or be afraid? It's dark and we have lost the sense of Christ's presence-will we reach out to Him in faith or sink in despair?

God hears every cry of our hearts, even the ones we can't put into words. He comes to us walking on the stormy waters and we don't recognize Him because He looks different. But He is there and He is about to speak to our hearts, calming the storm of fear.

So many things come into our lives to disturb us, and these can produce anxiety. Refuse those anxious thoughts. Go to prayer. Lay it all out before the Lord with thanksgiving. He will surround your heart with His gift of peace.

Insight

God has called His children to peace. Their peace in troubled circumstances speaks of Christ to the world that looks on.

DAY 31
Romans 15:1-13

Overflowing Peace

"May the God of hope fill you with all joy and peace as
you trust in him, so that you may overflow with hope by
the power of the Holy Spirit" (Romans 15:13).

Hope is an effective antidote for anxiety. I went with my
husband to see the doctor after his diagnosis of Alzheimers
disease. I told the doctor, "I just need to hear from you what
you told Dan." The doctor assured me that with medication,
Dan could continue to drive and do all the things he has been
doing. I walked out of that office with tremendous hope. My
spirit was much lighter. I trust God will give Dan and me a
few more months, even years, to serve the Lord together.

If we are going to be filled with joy and peace, we are going
to have to trust God with all our hearts. We will need to refuse
anxious thoughts. We dare not look down the road, but live
one day at a time.

We can remember to carry only what God gives us to carry
today. We need not pick up yesterday's load or add tomorrow's. It would be too much to bear.

Comfort and encouragement come from the most unexpected sources. May you be filled with joy and peace as you
trust in God.

Insight

*God's way is the way of peace. Anxiety comes from the old
self. Live in the new life in Christ and be filled with peace
and joy today.*

May

Matthew 5:1-12

Blessed Are the Poor

"Blessed are the poor in spirit, for theirs is the kingdom of heaven. Blessed are those who mourn, for they will be comforted" (Matthew 5:3-4).

When Jesus looked out on the crowds, He saw the richly dressed Pharisees, proud of heart. He saw the common working people, poor and needy, looking for hope. He saw them as sheep without a shepherd and had compassion on them.

He pointed out that the humble in heart will become part of God's family. The proud reject Him because they are self-sufficient. The humble, knowing they need the Lord, turn to Him for help. Jesus says they are the blessed ones.

The single parent is blessed even as she struggles to raise her children and make ends meet. She has greater opportunity to exercise her faith in God and watch Him work to meet her needs.

We will be going to Scripture in the month ahead to see the people God used to do great things for Him. We will see how He worked through weakness so He would receive the glory.

Do you feel you are not very important in God's plan? Everyone has a special place and special task. God wants to bless others through you.

Insight

God bypasses the proud and chooses to work for the humble in heart that He might bless others through them.

2 Corinthians 8:1-9

Though He Was Rich

"For you know the grace of our Lord Jesus Christ, that though he was rich, yet for your sakes he became poor, so that you through his poverty might become rich" (2 Corinthians 8:9).

How does a king come? He is usually born of royal parents in a palace and his birth is announced to the world with a 21-gun salute.

In contrast, the Son of God left the riches of heaven to enter very humbly this world which He had made. He was born to a simple village maiden, and the only room made for Him was a corner of a stable. His first bed was a manger filled with hay. The royal announcement of his birth was made by angels to shepherds in the hills surrounding Bethlehem, men who were on the bottom of the social scale.

Instead of bursting on the world as a mighty conqueror, He came as a helpless baby, needing nurturing and protecting. He grew up in a humble home in an obscure village, and He experienced human life to the full so He could understand all that you and I go through. He knew what it was to have no money, to be tired and hungry after a long day. Yes, truly though He was rich, He became poor so we could enter heaven's gates someday.

Insight

God chose to clothe the divine Son of God in the weakness of human flesh so that we could be saved from our sins and enter God's family.

Luke 5:1-11, 27-32

A Bunch of Losers

"After this, Jesus went out and saw a tax collector by the name of Levi sitting at his tax booth. 'Follow me', Jesus said to him, and Levi got up, left everything and followed him" (Luke 5:27-28).

When Jesus began His public ministry, He chose twelve men to walk with Him and learn from Him. They became His inner circle. Now we probably would have gone to the Hebrew University and chosen the men with the best grades and greatest potential for leadership.

Instead, Jesus chose a despised tax collector; four rough-and-ready, unlearned fishermen; a zealot ready to overthrow Rome; a betrayer who would not remain loyal; and a doubter who would have a hard time believing-all common men. There was not one who was highly educated, but they would learn to love and follow Him.

God does not think as we think. His ways are often totally the opposite of the world's ways. He lets the proud follow their independence and chooses the poor to become rich in faith. They have faith and know they need Him to redeem their mistakes and help them start over. He will bless the world through those who are weak in their own estimation but are strong in the Lord.

Insight

God continually turns things upside down. He chooses the weak and despised to accomplish His plans on earth.

DAY 4

Mark 11:1-11

Enter, the King

"When they brought the colt to Jesus and threw their cloaks over it, he sat on it. Many people spread their cloaks on the road, while others spread branches" (Mark 11:7-8).

When Jesus entered Jerusalem that day, He did not come as a mighty conquering hero on a white charger. Instead, He chose to ride on a lowly donkey surrounded by the poor who acclaimed Him gladly. Children shouted "Hosanna!" echoed by their parents.

Every year my husband and I attend the "No Greater Love" Easter production performed by a large church in our valley. Each time something new moves me to tears as the life of Christ is depicted. I especially love the scene in which the children come running barefoot down the aisles waving their palm branches and joyfully singing "Hosanna." I think it captures a little of what that first entry into Jerusalem was like-the great joy of the moment when Jesus, the humble itinerant healer-teacher, triumphed for a little while.

The day of the white charger is yet to come when Jesus will rule with a rod of iron. But on this day so long ago He was the humble One choosing the way of weakness.

Insight

We can identify with this Jesus so gentle and humble, yet so very much the Son of God, strong and true.

The Lowest Servant

"So he got up from the meal, took off his outer clothing, and wrapped a towel around his waist. After that, he
poured water into a basin and began to wash his disciples'
feet" (John 13:4-5).

Jesus and His disciples were preparing to eat last Passover
meal together. Evidently one thing had been overlooked-a
servant to wash dusty feet, a common courtesy.

Jesus got up from the table, poured water in a basin, and
began to wash His disciples' feet. They were astonished that
their Teacher and Lord had assumed the task of the lowliest
servant.

When he sat down again, He explained that He had set
them an example. As He had served them, they ought also to
serve one another.

Sometimes we have to look long and hard to find someone
with a servant spirit, but it should not be so in God's family.
Our Lord came to serve. Can we do any less? Let's be willing
to take the lowly place of a servant. Most of us are in jobs in
which we serve other people. Few of us are the top boss, and
even then we would be accountable to God. Let's serve with
a joyful, thankful spirit, knowing that God has promised to
reward us with His "Well done."

Insight

*Jesus is our example of a true servant attitude. He served
not for thanks but out of love.*

DAY 6
Luke 23:1-25

Like a Lamb

"He was oppressed and afflicted, yet he did not open his mouth; he was led like a lamb to the slaughter, and as a sheep before her shearers is silent, so he did not open his mouth" (Isaiah 53:7).

When we are falsely accused, we are quick to let it be known and to defend ourselves. Yet when Jesus was on trial on trumped-up charges, we read that He did not defend Himself. He simply let his accusers do their worst, even bringing in false witnesses. We are so quick to vindicate ourselves, but Jesus did and said nothing.

Have you ever watched sheep being sheared? The shepherd tosses the sheep onto its back and clips until the fleece is off. It never fights or bleats. When the shearing is done, the sheep trots away.

Recently I heard of a father falsely accused by his teenage daughter. I was not at the trial, so I do not know what he said in his own defense. The court believed the daughter, and her father will spend ten years in prison. His mother will finish raising his sons. How could God let this happen to one of His children? We don't know, but He let it happen to His own Son, and God's purpose was fulfilled. We can't see how, but God will work in this situation also.

Insight

We are so quick to defend ourselves. We need to remember that Jesus was silent before His accusers, yet God was in control.

The Way of the Cross

"The soldiers also came up and mocked him. They offered him wine vinegar and said, 'If you are the king of the Jews, save yourself'" (Luke 23:36-37).

When Jesus came the first time, He chose the path of suffering and death. He became the Godman, totally God yet totally human, yet without sin. He experienced being totally human, even experiencing death. When He hung on the cross, it looked as if the enemy were winning. But God turned dark Friday into triumphant Sunday with a victorious resurrection from the dead.

All of our sin was nailed to that cross when Jesus hung there. He paid the price of death for me, so I don't have to die for my sins. By accepting Jesus Christ as personal Savior, I have eternal life and become part of God's forever family.

Philip Yancy writes, "God made Himself weak for one purpose, to let human beings choose freely for themselves what to do with Him. The cross redefined God as One who was willing to relinquish power for the sake of love."

Jesus loves you so much, enough to die for you. What are you going to do with Him? Make your decision today. Don't put it off!

Insight

God let the human race do their worst so that He might give us His best-eternal life in His Son.

DAY 8
Luke 24:13-35

On the Road to Emmaus

"He said to them, 'How foolish you are, and how slow of heart to believe all that the prophets have spoken! Did not the Christ have to suffer these things and then enter his glory?'" (Luke 24:25-26).

Their dreams lay shattered at the foot of a cross and locked behind the stone door of a tomb. They were so sure Jesus was the long-promised deliverer who would free them from Roman oppression to rule and reign in righteousness.

Sadly they walked along the way to Emmaus, pondering the events of the past week. As they talked, a stranger joined them and asked, "Why the long faces?"

Astonished, they responded, "Where have you been? Don't you know what has happened in Jerusalem these last days? Also some women have reported He is alive."

Then Jesus explained to them how He had to die and then be glorified. When they broke bread together, their eyes were opened and they believed. God's way was so different from the way they were thinking, and isn't it the same for us today? We lean on the world's way of thinking and lose our way. We need to get back to seeing things God's way and let Him show us His perspective.

Insight

There is a time to shift gears and let God be God in our lives, to get His point of view on our circumstances. Perhaps that time is right now!

DAY 9
1 Corinthians 1:26-31

God Chooses the Weak

"Brothers, think of what you were when you were called. Not many of you were wise by human standards; not many were influential; not many were of noble birth" (1 Corinthians 1:26).

Who does God choose to serve Him? Those with a willing heart. Who does He choose to make a blessing to others? Those who have faith in Him and are faithful. He chooses the weak of this world to confound the mighty. He chooses the foolish of this world to amaze the wise with their insights.

A friend went through cancer treatment. He was probably as weak as he had ever been in his life. Yet what did people comment when visiting him? "O his faith!" His trust in the Lord was shining brightly to all who cared for him even in his weakness.

God chooses to take our weaknesses and work through them so that He receives the glory. Some time ago I wrote an issue of Anchor on the theme of suffering. It came out of a period of deep depression, yet it brought an outflow of reader response. What I considered a time of great failure in my life, God used to touch the hearts of others.

Are you weak today? Do you feel that you've failed or made a major mistake? Give it to God. He delights to work through weakness.

Insight

God chooses to work through weakness and what men consider foolishness, so He receives the glory.

Exodus 4:1-17

A Speech Problem

"Moses said to the Lord, 'O Lord, I have never been eloquent, neither in the past nor since you have spoken to your servant I am slow of speech and tongue'" (Exodus 4:10).

God called Moses to deliver the Children of Israel out of Egypt and lead them to the Promised Land. But when God assigned the task, Moses began to make excuses. "I can't talk very well." God's answer for his excuse, "I will help you speak and will teach you what to say." Did Moses trust God? No, he asked God to send someone else.

One summer we attended a family camp out in Billings, Montana. Our main speaker was an evangelist who had a speech impediment, requiring us to listen closely. This man had obeyed Gods calling and did not let his speech problem stop him. Isn't that just like God, choosing to work once again through a man's weakness?

Have you made excuses when God has called you to step out and. do something for Him? Has there been a time in your life when you asked God to choose someone else? I have, but God ended up sending me. What a blessing I would have missed if I had not obeyed!

Insight

When God calls you to a task, He will enable you to do it. You need not be afraid. If you trust Him and do what He asks, He will supply what you need.

Judges 6:1-24

Excuses, Excuses

"'But Lord', Gideon asked, 'How can I save Israel? My clan is the weakest in Manasseh, and I am the least in my family.' The Lord answered, 'I will be with you'" (Judges 6:15-16).

God chooses some very unlikely people to do His will. When the Midianites were totally overrunning Israel, God called Gideon to save the people. But Gideon said, "God, I'm a nobody. I'm not a great leader or warrior. You'd better look for someone else." This young man did not have much courage or confidence. His first assignment was to throw down the altar of Baal. He was so fearful that he did it at night.

Then he needed a great deal of encouragement to pursue the task God had given him. He set a fleece out, not once, but twice, seeking God's guidance. Finally Gideon ended up saving Israel from the Midianites, and God received the glory.

Are you fearful today because God is asking you to step out and do something for Him? Be encouraged. Gideon was afraid too, but God used this fearful young man. He sent the right encouragement at the right time to infuse him with confidence in his God. You may be a nobody, but God will encourage you and use you for His glory.

Insight

God is our encouragement and confidence. He delights in using nobodies - so get going!

DAY 12
1 Samuel 16:1-13

The Runt of the Litter

"Do not consider his appearance or his height. . . . The Lord does not look at the things man looks at. Man looks at the outward appearance, but the Lord looks at the heart" (1 Samuel 16:7).

Samuel had been sent by God to anoint a king among Jesse's eight sons. As the eldest, Eliab, tall and good looking, passed before Samuel, he thought, Surely this is the Lord's choice. Yet God rejected him, warning Samuel that He looked at the heart. Seven of Jesse's son were rejected.

"Is there another?" Samuel asked.

"Only the youngest out with the sheep," Jesse replied. David wasn't even considered important enough to call in to the feast honoring God's prophet. His brothers looked down on him, and he was given the lowliest job in the family. Yet it is this shepherd boy, with a heart of faith, that God chose to be the next king of Israel.

How easy it is for us to judge people by outward appearances instead of seeing the love and faith shining through their lives. God often chooses the most unlikely people to be used to bless others or to have a special ministry. When God helps us see others as He sees them, we can appreciate the blessing they share with others.

Insight

It's not outward appearances that count but what God sees and knows about one's heart attitudes. He sees and will reward in His time and way.

Only a Boy

"He looked David over and saw that, he was only a boy, ruddy and handsome, and he despised him. He said to David, 'Am I a dog, that you come to me with sticks?'" (1 Samuel 17:42-43).

Goliath, the Philistine giant, shouted to Israel's army, "Send a man to fight me!" Young David heard the challenge, but when he inquired about the matter, his brothers became angry with him. Jesse had sent him to see how the brothers fared in the battle. They bitterly resented his bold questions. Yet David was brought before King Saul and volunteered to fight the giant.

When David went down in the valley to meet Goliath, he was armed only with a staff and a sling. When Goliath saw he was only a boy, he threatened to make mincemeat of him and feed him to the wild animals. Cursing David, Goliath advanced to carry out his threats. David, fearless and full of faith in God, ran to meet him, slinging a stone into Goliath's forehead and felling him, then cutting off his head with his own sword.

Others were much taller and stronger, but useless through fear. A young shepherd boy whose confidence was in God alone became the instrument in God's hand for Israel's victory.

Insight

God constantly chooses those whom others consider too young or inexperienced or not talented enough to do great things for Him.

Esther 2:5-18

An Orphan Girl

"This girl, who was also known as Esther, was lovely in-form and features, and Mordecai had taken her as his own daughter when her father and mother died" (Esther 2:1).

Esther was an orphan girl carried away from her home to a foreign land. She probably had lost her parents when Nebuchadnezzar captured Jerusalem. Her uncle Mordecai had raised her and she had grown up to be a beautiful woman.

After King Xerxes deposed his queen and began to look for another, Esther was taken into the royal harem. When Esther's turn came to go before the king, he chose her to be the next queen. Esther went from being an orphan in exile to queen of a kingdom, but her hardest test was yet to come.

Wicked Haman conceived a plot to destroy all Jews. Would Esther take her life in her hands and plead with the king for her people? She rose to the challenge Mordecai laid before her. After three days of fasting and prayer, she appeared before the king, and he showed her favor and mercy.

The Jews were saved by the unselfishness and courage of a young woman whom God had placed in the right place at the right time.

Insight

What counts with God? Is it having the right background or the right parents and a cultured upbringing? No, He is looking for a willing, courageous heart.

Genesis 18:1-15

Too Old

"Sarah was past the age of childbearing. So Sarah laughed to herself as she thought, 'After I am worn out and my master is old, will I now have this pleasure?'" (Genesis 18:11-12).

If we were planning to build a nation, we would choose a young couple in the prime of life and give them a large family. But God called a man, Abraham, whose wife is barren, and promises them a son. Yet the years go by. Both of them grow old. Sarah was not only barren, she was now past the age of childbearing. Then, when all looked hopeless, God announced, "Sarah will bear a son next year." How Abraham and Sarah laugh-he in faith and she in doubt. But baby Isaac, whose name means laughter, was born right on time, and the promised nation began.

God's ways-how they astound us-and the people He uses! He may choose individuals we call senior citizens and set aside as being too feeble or "out of it" to contribute to His work.

You are never too old to be used of God. Determine now to serve Him until your last breath. "Too old" isn't in God's vocabulary, only in ours. If you doubt that, just remember what God did with Abraham and Sarah.

Insight

God chooses to work through the people we consider too old and accomplishes His purposes through circumstances we consider hopeless.

1 Kings 17:7-15

Too Poor

"I don't have any bread-only a handful of flour in a jar and a little oil in a jug. I am gathering a few sticks to . . . make a meal for myself and my son, that we may eat it-and die" (1 Kings 17:12).

During the drought Elijah predicted, God hid His prophet by a brook and sent ravens to bring him food morning and evening. One day the brook dried up, and God sent Elijah to the poorest of the poor, a widow down to her last meal.

Elijah had been fed by unclean birds and then sent to a Gentile widow about to die. We would at least have sent him to a family with a cellar full of supplies to last out the drought. When God gets ready to do a miracle, He often lets us get down to the end of our resources.

Because the widow obeyed Elijah and fed him first, her oil and meal lasted until the drought ended and the rain came. Imagine her sense of wonder after having used all her meal to make a cake then going back and finding there was enough for one more cake day after day.

Again God chose to use someone we would call weak and to work through unusual circumstances. God is not limited, no matter how inadequate you feel or how difficult your circumstances may be.

Insight

You are never too poor to give to God. What you give to Him, He will return to you many times over.

2 Kings 5:1-14

A Jewish Captive

"Naaman was commander of the army of the king of Aram
. . . Now bands from Aram had gone out and had taken
captive a young girl from Israel, and she served Naaman's
wife" (2 Kings 5:1-2).

A young girl, torn away from family, friends, and home and
carried to a foreign land, became the slave of Naaman's wife.
Now Naaman was a great soldier, but he was a leper in a day
when there was no cure for the disease. This young slave knew
about the prophet Elisha and the miracles God had enabled
him to perform. She spoke boldly to her mistress, saying, "If
only my master would see the prophet who is in Samaria! He
would cure him of his leprosy" (v. 3).

This is all we know about the girl, but her words and faith
set a miracle in motion. Naaman went to see the prophet,
eventually obeyed him, and was healed. Not only that, he
came to worship the true God. This child became God's messenger to impact a foreign military leader for Him.

Young children can be used by God. More than one child
has been the key that turned an entire family to the Lord. Too
young, too old, too poor God uses them all, working through
weakness that He may be glorified.

Insight

*Jesus had a special place in His heart for young children.
Their hearts are open to Him. They have much to teach us,
so let's observe and learn from them.*

DAY 18

Exodus 19:1-6

A Slave Protest

"I carried you on eagles' wings and brought you to myself. Now if you obey me fully and keep my covenant, then out of all nations you will be my treasured possession" (Exodus 19:4-5).

The nation that God promised would come of Abraham grew until, in the days of Joseph and widespread famine, the family went down to Egypt. Seventy souls arrived, and 400 years later, some two million slaves would leave Egypt for the Promised Land.

The years of slavery did not appear to have taught them faith in God. Camped by the Red Sea and pursued by Pharaoh, they complained to Moses, "Have you brought us out in the desert to die?" They grumbled when there was no water, and later when there was no bread, they wailed, "Have you brought us out here to starve?"

Yet God promised them, "If you will obey me, you will be to me a treasured possession, a holy nation" (see vv. 5-6).

What a merciful, forgiving God! He chose a doubting and complaining crew to be His special people. He had power to take them from slaves to become a holy nation which would show His glory to a sinful world.

Insight

What is so special about you and me? Nothing, except that God has chosen to use us and make us a blessing to others.

Amos 7:10-16

A Common Herdsman

"I was neither a prophet nor a prophet's son, but I was a shepherd. . . . But the Lord took me from tending the flock and said to me, 'Go prophesy to my people Israel'" (Amos 7:14-15).

Amos was a simple shepherd and farmer. His only qualification for service was God's call. He did not claim to be a prophet, or even the son of a prophet. But he obeyed God, left Judah and traveled to Israel to proclaim God's words.

There, he was not well received. Crowds did not gather to hear him. Instead, they stopped their ears against his warnings and told him to go back home to do his preaching.

Amos did not let the opposition stop him, and eventually his words came even to the king.

Has God called you to a ministry for Him? When God called my husband Dan and me into prison ministry, we went, though I felt God was calling two very unlikely people to serve behind prison walls. After all, we had never been where they are. People are very effective who have been in prison and get out, then go back to serve God there. But who was I to question Him? We obeyed and went, and God has blessed us beyond anything we could have dreamed.

Insight

Has God called you to a ministry for which you don't feel qualified? Obey and go. God knows what He is doing, even if you don't. He will go with you and help you.

Matthew 18:15-20

Where Two or Three

"If two of you on earth agree about anything you ask for, it will be done for you by my Father in heaven. For where two or three come together in my name, there am I with them" (Matthew 18:19-20).

It takes only two or three believers praying together to multiply the power of God in the lives of others, and it is not just doubled.

I don't concern myself with numbers. If only one woman shows up for my Bible study at the work center, I know God has something special to say to her. If there are only two or three, they tend to open up and share more than they would in a larger group. I've watched God minister in a special way in the life of only one or two. Of course I love to see eight or ten come, but I would be there for one.

Often our Sunday evening prayer group has only three of us. Then I am reminded of today's scripture. We will never know this side of heaven what God has done through those faithful prayers for others.

It's not numbers but individuals that count with God. Always Jesus singled out one person in the crowd. He healed a woman who touched the hem of his garment, though the crowd pressed Him.

Insight

God doesn't deal with crowds but with individuals. What counts is the work God does in a single heart.

DAY 21
Isaiah 42:1-9

A Bruised Reed

"A bruised reed he will not break, and a smoldering wick he will not snuff out. . . . He will not falter nor be discouraged till he establishes justice on earth" (Isaiah 42:3-4).

The symbol of Prison Fellowship Ministries is a bruised or broken reed. It speaks of how God doesn't throw away persons who are broken and bruised, but rather heals and restores them. He trims the smoldering wick so that it burns brightly again.

One of our most prized possessions is an old oak chest. It was given to us after a neighbor left it when she moved. I set about to refinish it, spending hours with paint remover and sandpaper to remove its coating of layers of black varnish. Eventually I gave it a new, clear finish. Today its warm oak beauty draws comments of visitors in our home. What one person discarded as useless has become for us a piece of value and beauty.

That's how God works to redeem broken, discarded lives, restoring them to beauty and usefulness. Nothing is wasted with God, not even our mistakes, our brokenness, and pain. When we give God the broken pieces of our lives, He puts us back together again.

Insight

God is first and foremost a Redeemer. He treasures and restores the most broken of us and makes us useful in His service.

Romans 8:26-39

Help for Our Weakness

"In the same way, the Spirit helps us in our weakness. We do not know what we ought to pray, but the Spirit himself intercedes for us with groans that words cannot express" (Romans 8:26).

Have you ever struggled, not knowing how to pray for someone? Do you sometimes groan, unable to express in words the cry of your heart? Be encouraged. You have a helper in prayer-the Holy Spirit.

When I don't know how to pray for an individual, I trust the Holy Spirit to pray through me for that person. Because He prays according to God's will for that one, I know those prayers are going to be answered. We are weak humans, and we fall short of what God wants us to be. But He helps and works in our behalf, even through those weaknesses.

I find it helpful to pray Scripture back to God for ourselves and for others. For example, for a man just out of prison, I pray, "Lead him in the paths of righteousness for Your name's sake. Don't let him get off the path you have for him."

I believe that every cry of the human heart is found somewhere in the Psalms. Find your heart cry and express it to God in the words of Scripture. God will hear.

Insight

Human beings are weak, but God has sent us a helper in the person of His Holy Spirit. His prayers are always right on target.

2 Corinthians 4:1-12

Vessels of Clay

"God . . . made his light shine in our hearts. . . . But we have this treasure in jars of clay to show that this all-surpassing power is from God and not from us" (2 Corinthians 4:6-7).

I love the song, "Ordinary People, God Uses Ordinary People." It's based on Paul's teaching that God has chosen to entrust ordinary humans with the glorious light of the Gospel. We carry this treasure in the common clay pots of our humanity. Why? So when the glory shines through, people can see it's God's power at work, and He gets the glory.

We have been entrusted with something very precious, and we need to let it shine through. One of my prayers for a friend in cancer treatment is, "Let his faith shine brightly so all who see it will see Christ. May he touch many lives by the way he goes through this time of weakness and suffering."

God could have chosen a spectacular way to share His Gospel, but He chose you and me, ordinary human beings, to share His truth. He has taken us, weaknesses and all, to carry around this glorious light and let it shine forth.

Are you willing to be a common clay pot to be used every day? Or do you want to be fine china brought out only occasionally for company?

Insight

God chooses ordinary people for His work. He chooses to bless the world through them so that He will receive the praise and glory.

He Remembers

"As a father has compassion on his children, so the Lord has compassion on those who fear him for he knows how we are formed, he remembers that we are dust" (Psalm 103:13-14).

Our Heavenly Father does not expect the world of us. He understands us, for He made us. He knows the strengths and weaknesses He has built into each of us. Those weaknesses keep us depending on Him.

When I fall flat on my face, I remember I am dust. Thank God, He remembers I am too, picks me up, dusts me off, and sets me on my feet again. We hurt when our children go through difficult times. We would bear the pain and confusion for them if we could. Likewise, our Heavenly Father hurts with us when we are suffering.

Our Father allows us to go through a myriad of experiences so He can build compassion in us. We would avoid the grief of losing a loved one, physical pain, financial worries, problems with our children, and rejection, but God uses these to tenderize our hearts toward Him and toward others. Every day He is at work transforming us into the image of Christ, making us more sensitive to the needs of others.

Insight

God understands our weaknesses for He made us and remembers always that we are dust. He chooses to use ordinary people.

1 Corinthians 2:1-15

Coming in Weakness

"I came to you in weakness and fear, and with much trembling. My message and my preaching were not with wise and persuasive words, but with a demonstration of the Spirit's power" (1 Corinthians 2:3-4).

The apostle Paul was an educated man. He had an impressive list of qualifications, but he laid them all aside to simply preach Christ. He did not rely on his religious training, but in weakness and much trembling, on the Spirit of God. He did not use his persuasive power of speech, but depended on the Spirit to persuade men to believe God's truth.

My husband Dan is in the early stages of Alzheimers. I watch him struggle with speaking and reading, yet he never turns down an opportunity to serve the lord in our prison ministry. I'm reminded that God works through our weakness not our strength. He has been invited to help with the death row services on Sunday. The men love him because he is gentle and compassionate, and he cares about them. The year he was the Maximum Security Prison chaplain, he won their hearts, and they are delighted to see him again.

The Spirit of God persuades men to believe not our eloquence or education. God loves to work through weakness so that His power can be seen.

Insight

God worked through the confidence of a David, a shepherd boy, and through the fear and trembling of the apostle Paul. He can work through you.

1 Corinthians 4:1-21

Fools for Christ

"We are fools for Christ, but you are so wise in Christ! We are weak but you are strong . . . Up to this moment we have become the scum of the earth, the refuse of the world" (1 Corinthians 4:10, 13).

Have you ever been called foolish by the world when you knew you were doing what God wanted you to do? We have.

We left a secure ranch job and a nice house in Salmon, Idaho to move to Weiser, Idaho, to teach in an evening Bible school. As we prepared to leave, our boss said, "You're crazy to move with no place to live and no job." We made the move anyway because we knew God was calling us. The job and house were soon provided.

Later when we lost our construction business and owed so much money, people asked us why we didn't go through bankruptcy. We knew we could sell our home and pay our debts. It was the right thing to do, and God graciously left us enough money to start over.

God is faithful when we obey Him and do things His way. Yes, the world may call us foolish, but it is never foolish to do what God calls us to do. Our job is to obey and let Him take care of the consequences.

Insight

Be willing to be a fool for Christ's sake for the foolishness of God is far stronger than the wisdom of men.

1 Corinthians 1:18-25

No Boasting

"Since in the wisdom of God the world through its wisdom did not know him, God was pleased through the foolishness of what was preached to save those who believe" (1 Corinthians 1:21).

The message was simple, "Christ died to save you," but people in all their brilliance and wisdom stumbled over the simplicity of the good news. God was making sure that the way to Him would not be through human wisdom. The humblest of individuals could come to Jesus simply by believing in His death, burial, and resurrection.

"This so called 'foolish' plan of God is far wiser than the wisest plan of the wisest man, and God in His weakness-Christ dying on the cross-is far stronger than any man" (1 Corinthians 1:25, TLB).

Over and over God has chosen to work through weakness-not strength; through foolishness-not wisdom. Why? So not one of us can boast in His presence. None of us can say; "I did it myself. Look how smart I am." No, all of us have to admit that it is only through God and His power that anyone is saved and can enter heaven. The wise depend on their wisdom, the rich on their wealth, the celebrities on their talent, but those who are saved put their full trust in the Lord.

Insight

To some, the way of the cross is foolishness; to others it is a stumbling block; but to those who believe, it is the power and wisdom of God.

DAY 28
Hebrews 11:32-40

Out of Weakness

"Who through faith conquered kingdoms, administered justice, and gained what was promised. . . . Whose weakness was turned to strength " (Hebrews 11:33-34).

Carol Cymbala was ready to flee the city and the work to which God had called her and her pastor husband. Their oldest daughter Chrissy had forsaken the family and the God they served. They had no idea where she was, and their hearts cried out in an agony of prayer for her. Then Carol had to have surgery. During her recovery, she became very depressed.

At this low point and time of weakness, Carol went to the piano and wrote the song, "He's Been Faithful to Me." That song has been used of God to minister to thousands-more than anything else Carol has written.

God came to Carol in her weakness and gave her those words of encouragement, making her a blessing to many.

Are you at a weak point in your life? Do you feel that God is indifferent to your desperate need? He is faithful. When we so desperately need a word from the Lord, He comes with His comfort and encouragement.

Insight

Don't despise your weakness. God delights in taking what we consider failure and using it for His glory.

2 Corinthians 13

Crucified in Weakness

"For to be sure, he was crucified in weakness, yet he lives by God's power. Likewise, we are weak in him, yet by God's power we will live with him to serve you" (2 Corinthians 13:4).

The cross stands at the focal point of history. God took the worst that man could do to His own dear Son and made it the best that God would do for man-his salvation. God took the hatred and cruelty of men and caused it to fulfill His divine purpose. The weakness of God Christ dying on a cross-would be stronger than men.

Jesus could face the terrible suffering of the cross with joy, knowing it would bring many sons into glory.

God would have us realize our weakness so that we may serve in His strength. Even though my husband Dan is in the early stages of Alzheimers, God has opened the door so he can return to the Maximum Security prison where he once was chaplain. He continues to teach two classes at the Medium Security prison. He also counsels men on Saturday afternoons. God is literally working through a weak vessel who is willing to serve Him in God's power.

Insight

When we serve God in our weakness rather than in our human strength, others realize that the power comes from God.

Mustard Seed Faith

"The apostles said to the Lord, 'Increase our faith!' He replied, 'If you have faith as small as a mustard seed, you can say to this mulberry tree, "Be uprooted and planted in the sea," and it will obey you'" (Luke 17:5-6).

I have often wanted to pray, "Increase my faith," but Jesus says this is the wrong request. Rather, He says, we should put the faith we have to work. It's not the size of our faith that counts but the person in whom we place that faith.

Remember that Jesus chided His disciples, "You of little faith, why did you doubt?"(Matthew 14:31). Remember the father who said, "I do believe; help me overcome my unbelief!" (Mark 9:24).

Is God asking you to step out in faith for Him? That first small, trembling step of faith may lead you to opportunities of ministry you never even dreamed possible.

I'll never forget the first time I stepped into a county jail and heard the door clang shut behind me. I was obeying the Lord's leading, but I did so as a step of faith. Now every Sunday Dan and I step through the gates of a state prison to guide a prayer group of prison inmates, and great is our joy to serve the Lord in this way.

Insight

Remember, it isn't the amount of faith you have. It's the great God in whom that faith is placed.

2 Corinthians 12:1-10

Power Made Perfect

"He said to me, 'My grace is sufficient for you, for my power is made perfect in weakness.' Therefore I will boast all the more gladly about my weaknesses, so that Christ's power may rest on me" (2 Corinthians 12:9).

Don't despise your weaknesses. That's the very channel through which God works. When others observe Him working through your weaknesses, they glorify Him as they see His power.

Delight in the difficulties that come your way, for then you have the opportunity to see God work, and your heart will be filled with joy. When you have to do something you are sure you can't do, throw yourself on the grace of God, and you will find it sufficient. God is faithful; He will not fail you.

Paul said, "I am going to boast only about how weak I am and how great God is because He chooses to use such weakness for His glory."

I trust you have been encouraged this month to see how God chooses to work through our weaknesses. We may be common clay pots, but we hold the glory and power of God. Let's let it shine through, for God's power shows up best in weak people. May He be glorified in your life and mine-even in our weakness.

Insight

The less we have, the more we depend on God. The weaker we are, the greater others see God's power at work in our lives.

June

Lamentations 3:22-30

Waiting on God

"I say to myself, 'The Lord is my portion, therefore I will wait for him.' The Lord is good to those whose hope is in him . . . it is good to wait quietly for the salvation of the Lord" (Lamentations 3:24-26).

Waiting! It is probably one of the hardest things we do in life. Waiting in line. Waiting at a stop light. Waiting for a loved one to come out of surgery. Waiting for a letter. Waiting after a job interview. Waiting for a check to come in the mail. Waiting for my appeal to go through the courts and the judge to rule in my favor. Waiting while it appears God is doing nothing in the darkness and prayers remain unanswered. Waiting, trying to keep my focus on God alone and trying not to become discouraged.

God is not absent. He is doing very important things in our lives during waiting periods. He strips away our props so that we lean on Him alone. He teaches us patience as we learn to rely on Him. He sends just the word of encouragement we need. He remains near and holds us close to His loving heart. We may beg and plead for it to end, but He strengthens us to go on. No, waiting is never easy, but it is a necessary part of growing up in the Lord.

Insight

Waiting is never easy for us, but when we wait on God it brings great rewards. Place your hope in Him and wait with quiet trust and expectation.

Wait and Renew Your Strength

"They that wait upon the Lord shall renew their strength; they shall mount up with wings as eagles; they shall run, and not be weary; and they shall walk, and not faint" (Isaiah 40:31, KJV).

God has a special heart for the weak and weary. Jesus would invite all those who are weary and burdened to come to Him and rest, to take His easy yoke and light burden (Matthew 11:28-30). Then they would walk and not faint, for Jesus would be carrying most of the load.

When we wait on God, we are placing our hope in Him alone, acknowledging that we can't make it without Him. To wait, we need to spend time in His presence, laying out our needs before Him.

I remember when I was once in so much physical pain, I would fall on my knees by my bed and beg for healing. With tears I would plead my cause. God did not touch me and heal me instantly, but He did give me strength to endure. I was able to go on-to walk and not faint. As I look back now, I am amazed at how I got through those days.

Are you so weary today that you feel you can not cope? Come to Jesus. Wait on Him. Let Him renew your strength and enable you to go on. He pours out His grace to the weak, not the strong.

Insight

God gives more grace when the burdens grow heavier. He gives more strength when the demands on us increase. Wait on Him and be renewed.

Wait for Encouragement

"I am still confident of this: I will see the goodness of the Lord in the land of the living. Wait for the Lord; be strong and take heart and wait for the Lord" (Psalm 27:13-14).

We can be confident of two truths as we wait on God: He is good and He is working in our behalf. Though it may appear that God is doing nothing, He is always at work behind the scenes engineering circumstances to accomplish His plans. So wait on Him and resist taking matters into your own hands and running ahead of Him.

Our part is to wait and be of good courage, keeping our eyes focused on God. His part is to strengthen our hearts in the waiting. When Peter walked on water, he was safe until he took his eyes off the Lord and saw the raging waves. Then he began to sink (Matthew 14:22-33).

It's tough to keep our eyes on Jesus. It takes real effort, especially when the income drops and the bills come due. Or the lab report comes back, and it is cancer. Or the parole board says, "Come back in a year." We focus on the invisible, not the visible. Paul said, "We don't lose heart because inwardly we are being renewed day by day" (see 2 Corinthians 4:16-18).

Insight

Don't wait in a vacuum. Wait on the Lord alone, fixing your eyes on Him. He will send the encouragement you need.

Wait Expectantly

"My soul, wait thou only upon God; for my expectation is from him. He only is my rock and my salvation; he is my defense; I shall not be moved" (Psalm 62:5-6, KJV).

Twice, when we were in need, friends in the church gave us a large check. How easy to look to them again when God tells me to wait only on Him. Most months my sister sends a healthy check. In low income months that check has seen us through. How easy to look for her check in the mail and not look to God alone to meet our needs for the month.

God is so creative that He can use totally unexpected sources to meet our needs-and He has done this.

The greater the need the greater the miracle. God has a generous heart, and He loves to do wonders for His children. Our part is to trust Him completely, to look up, and expect God to act in our behalf.

In my child care work, one mother's employment was unexpectedly cut to four days a week. She would be keeping her child home with her when she did not work. God immediately sent me a two-day-a-week child, keeping our income even. Before we knew our need, God planned to meet it.

Insight

Don't look to those around you to meet your needs. Look to God alone. He is full of surprises.

DAY 5
Psalm 37:1-7

Wait Patiently

"Rest in the Lord, and wait patiently for him: fret not thyself because of him who prospereth in his way, because of the man who bringeth wicked devices to pass" (Psalm37:7, KJV).

We all go through waiting periods, but often we don't wait very well because we're filled with anxiety, fretfulness, and impatience. I find myself tapping my foot and saying, "Hurry up, God. I've waited long enough!"

In our prison ministry, one of our prayers for men is that they will have the patience and endurance to serve their time. We pray that while they wait they will be busy serving the Lord and sharing their faith, for prison is a dark place.

Rest: Stop, be quiet, breathe deeply and let God work in His time and His way.

Wait patiently: Refuse to grumble or complain because God is taking His time.

Fret not: Do not agitate, don't allow troubled thoughts to control your mind. Let the peace of God take over.

Once when I was struggling in waiting for God to fill my day care openings, God led me to today's verse. God handpicks the children, if I will only wait for Him to work.

Insight

God's way is one of peace and rest. Our way is one of fretfulness and anxiety. May we choose God's way over ours.

DAY 6
Psalm 69:1-18

Waiting in Darkness

"I will wait for the Lord, who is hiding his face from the house of Jacob. I will put my trust in him" (Isaiah 8:17). "I am weary of my crying . . . mine eyes fail while I wait for my God" (Psalm 69:3, KJV).

Our construction business was gone. Our home was for sale. Every week Dan traveled to Boise in search of work. He made the rounds of construction sites, but no one would hire a man in his fifties. God was hiding His face while we waited for Him.

We kept praying through the months of darkness. Winter in Idaho shuts down much construction. Not even a maintenance job opened for Dan. In the spring, Dan packed his suitcase and went to Boise to stay and hit the streets, looking for work. One day he answered an ad in the paper for a job in a door factory. He was hired on the spot and went to work at noon that day. The darkness and waiting were over. Our prayers of many months were answered.

God is faithful. He keeps His promises to His children. Cling to Him. Cry and plead with Him. One day He will come out of hiding, and all those prayers will be answered according to His good plan for you.

Insight

There's no darkness where God is. He can be trusted, even though you can't discern the working of His hand.

Wait for Needs

"The eyes of all look to you, and you give them their food at the proper time. You open your hand and satisfy the desires of every living thing" (Psalm 145:15-16).

God meets our needs on a daily basis. Jesus taught His disciples to ask their Father in heaven, "Give us this day our daily bread." Today maybe you need strength, or wisdom, or a friend, or healing, or grace. God will meet your need for today.

When our income drops below budget, I start living from day to day. I look up and thank God for meeting the needs of that day. I pay the bill that is due that day with the money I have, and trust God for tomorrow. Amazingly, even in high expense months, every need has been met as it has come due. I don't know how God always sees us through; He just does.

Trust God to meet your need today and trust Him for tomorrow, even though you don't see how it will be done.

As you wait on God, you'll discover that His timing is always perfect for meeting your needs, or giving you an opportunity to serve Him, or bringing someone into your life.

Insight

God is a present tense God, meeting our daily needs, whatever they are. Trust Him for your need today.

Isaiah 30:15-18

God Waits to Bless

"Yet the Lord longs to be gracious to you; he rises to show you compassion. For the Lord is a God of justice. Blessed are all who wait for him!" (Isaiah 30:18)

Do you believe God is waiting to bless you right now? As you wait on Him, He will begin to pour out His blessings and fill your cup to overflowing.

One day, as I looked to the future, I visualized being pretty much confined to my home, caring for a husband with Alzheimers. I knew that one day Dan and I would have to leave our active prison ministry. When that day came, I planned to start corresponding with men in prison.

Soon after those moments of reflection into our future, I received a letter from a young man in a Florida prison asking for someone to write to him. That began a correspondence that has been pure joy for me and a blessing to him. Next, my son put me in touch with a man in a Wisconsin prison. Then I joined the Prison Fellowship pen pal program. As of today, I'm writing eight men regularly.

Amazingly, God has put me in this ministry now, before Dan becomes a care. When God blesses, it is an overflowing cup!

Insight

God loves to bless His children, for He is a totally giving God. Pray for His blessing. You'll be amazed at what He will do.

DAY 9
Romans 12:9-21

Wait, Let God Take Revenge

"Do not say, 'I'll pay you back for this wrong!' Wait for the Lord, and He will deliver you" (Proverbs 20:11). "'It is mine to avenge; I will repay,' says the Lord" (Romans 12:19).

When my friend went through her divorce after 20 years of marriage, all she wanted to do was hurt her ex-husband as he had hurt her. She was not willing to let God take her revenge.

She has had great difficulty letting go of her anger and bitterness, and as a result she has suffered deep depression. She really wanted to take matters into her own hands because God didn't appear to be doing anything in her behalf. It has taken her many months to "let go and let God," and thus find healing for her broken heart and let God deal with the one who has wronged her.

Yes, it is hard to forgive someone who has deeply wounded you. Perhaps you could begin by asking God to help you even want to forgive. Allow time, for forgiveness is a process. Ask God to enable you to forgive. Then do something loving for that person.

Wait for God to act, even if He seems slow. Don't take your own revenge. Bitterness imprisons you, while forgiveness frees you.

Insight

Two wrongs never will make a right. God is much wiser than we are. Let Him take any revenge: Wait. Don't take matters into your own hands.

DAY 10
Psalm 123

God, My Salvation

"But as for me, I watch in hope for the Lord, I wait for God my Savior; and my God will hear me" (Micah 7:7). "So our eyes look to the Lord our God, till he shows us his mercy" (Psalm 123:2).

Mercy is God not giving us what we deserve. We've all disobeyed God, taken the controls of our lives in our own hands and gone our own way. Sadly, we discover we only get hurt and bring on ourselves a bundle of trouble. Our way is a way of death.

How do we get on the right track in life? By casting ourselves on the mercy of God. He visited our punishment on His Son on the cross so He could extend grace to us. Our part is to accept what Jesus has done for us and give Him the controls of our lives. Then God becomes our salvation.

Grace is God giving us what we don't deserve-forgiveness and eternal life in Him.

God is extending His grace and mercy to you today. What is your response? You can tell Him, "Please forgive me. I accept Your Son today as my Savior. Take my messes and make some thing beautiful out of them. Thank You for Your mercy and grace so freely given.

Insight

God's salvation is a free gift bought with the blood of His Son. When you come to Him, God accepts you just as you are.

Noah Waited

"By faith Noah, when warned about things not yet seen, in holy fear built an ark to save his family. By his faith he . . . became heir of the righteousness that comes by faith" (Hebrews 1.1:7).

God gives us many examples of waiting in Scripture; Noah was one of the first. God instructed him to build an ark because He was going to judge the earth with a flood. For 120 years Noah was a preacher of righteousness with a hammer, but in the end, only his family believed his warnings.

When the animals and food were on board, God said it was time. Noah and his family entered the ark, and God shut the door. Then they waited. One day and no rain. Would God keep His word? Two days . . . three days . . . four days . . . On the seventh day, the rain came just as God said it would.

God keeps His word to His children. He kept His promise to Noah and He will keep His promises to you. He won't disappoint or fail you. Keep trusting while you wait, no matter how long it takes.

You can say, "Father, You are my confidence. You have never failed me yet. Even when everything goes contrary to my way of thinking, I will trust You while I wait."

Insight

God is the God of His word. What He says, He will do, and He has the power to carry it out.

Genesis 18:1-14; 21:1-6

Abraham and Sarah

"Why did Sarah laugh and say, 'Will I really have a child, now that I am old?' Is anything too hard for the Lord? I will return to you at the appointed time next year and Sarah will have a son" (Genesis 18:13-14).

God had chosen Abraham to be the father of His people and to bless the world through him. Yet the years went by and the promised son did not come. Abraham and Sarah remained childless.

As the wait grew long, Abraham and Sarah took matters into their own hands. Abraham had a son by Sarah's Egyptian maid Hagar. It led to disaster, and that son eventually had to leave. Then, when Sarah became too old to have children, God renewed the promise of a son. Twenty five years had gone by. Sarah was 90 and Abraham 100 when Isaac was born.

For years Dan and I had wanted to serve the Lord. Two mission boards rejected us. Then we were asked to run a ranch for juvenile delinquents. A year later, we were asked to leave. Then 25 years later, God fulfilled our dream by putting us into a prison ministry, where we are still active today. The wait was long, but the blessing is great.

Insight

Keep trusting. The longer God waits, the greater the need, and the greater the need, the greater the miracle.

Genesis 37:1-10; 44:41-46

When Dreams Are Fulfilled

"Joseph was the governor of the land, the one who sold grain to all its people. So when Joseph's brothers arrived, they bowed down to him... Then he remembered his dreams" (Genesis 42:6, 9).

God had given Joseph a dream that he would one day be a ruler, and his brothers would bow down to him. His brothers hated him and sold him into slavery in Egypt. When his master's wife enticed him to sin, he would have nothing to do with her. She cried "Rape" and Joseph was thrown into prison. Where were his dreams now?

When Pharaoh's butler and baker were thrown into prison, Joseph interpreted their dreams. "Please remember me," Joseph pleaded, but the butler promptly forgot him.

When Pharaoh had puzzling dreams, the butler remembered Joseph. Once Joseph interpreted Pharaoh's dreams, he was immediately promoted to be a ruler in Egypt. During a famine, his brothers arrived to buy food and bowed down before Joseph. Then Joseph remembered his dreams.

Things kept going from bad to worse during the many years before God kept His promise to Joseph. Yet God came through for this young man as he clung to God's promises and his faith.

Insight

Throughout your bad times, cling to all you know of God. He rewards those who have faith in Him.

Exodus 3:1-12

Waiting and Training Time

"'So now go. I am sending you to Pharaoh to bring my
people the Israelites out of Egypt. . .I will be with you. . .
You will worship God on this mountain'" (Exodus 3:10,
12).

Moses' life was spared Pharaoh's death decree when he
was a baby, and miraculously God arranged for him to grow
up in Pharaoh's court. As a young man, he realized God had
preserved his life for a purpose. He tried in his own way to
begin to rescue his people from slavery, and then had to flee
Pharaoh's wrath. For the next 40 years this privileged prince
of Egypt endured God's humbling process, working as a shepherd on the backside of the desert. Finally, after 80 years of
preparing His leader, God called Moses to deliver His people
Israel.

It is hard to be patient when you are in a waiting and training time. Beware of running ahead of God and beware of
doing things your way instead of His. Our waiting times are
often humbling times. We are always in a hurry, but God isn't.

God did not lead Dan and me into prison ministry until we
were in our fifties. We've been told that is the perfect age. God
always knows best.

Insight

*Be patient! Waiting periods are often humbling times in our
lives as God prepares us for future service for Him.*

When Desires Are Thwarted

"O Lord Almighty, if you will only look upon your servant's misery and remember me, and not forget your servant but give her a son, then I will give him to the Lord for all the days of his life" (1 Samuel 1:11).

Hannah longed for children, but God had denied her desire for years-how many, we do not know. At the annual feast, Hannah went to the tabernacle and poured out her sorrow and longing before the Lord. She asked God for a son, promising to give him back to the Lord to serve Him all the days of his life.

Somehow, God spoke comfort to Hannah's heart, assuring her that she would have the son she had requested. And the next year young Samuel was born. Hannah kept her word to the Lord and brought him, as a young child, to serve in the tabernacle.

The waiting period for Hannah had been a time of sorrow and suffering, but when it was ended, her joy was great.

Perhaps you are going through a period of suffering. These times of trial purge the dross from our faith and purify us like gold. We cry for relief-now, but God says, "Hang on a little longer. I'm not done with you yet."

Insight

Sometimes waiting periods are times of trial and suffering. God will not end it until His purpose is accomplished.

DAY 16

1 Samuel 16:1-13; 2 Samuel 2:1-4

When Promises Remain Unfulfilled

"So Samuel took the horn of oil and anointed him in the presence of his brothers, and from that day on the Spirit of the Lord came upon David in power" (1 Samuel 16:13).

David was anointed as king over Israel while he was a young man, but he would wait many years before he reigned over all Israel. He never doubted God's promise. He served King Saul until Saul turned against him and David became a fugitive with a price on his head. At least twice Saul was at David's mercy. Though David's men urged him to take matters into his own hands by killing Saul and becoming king, David refused.

Saul was eventually killed in a battle with the Philistines, and David became king over part of Israel. He reigned in Hebron seven years before becoming king over all Israel (2 Samuel 5:1-5).

David waited for God's timing to make him king. Unlike others before him, he did not run ahead of God and try to work things out. He cooperated as God continued to groom him for the throne through all the trials that befell him.

Suffering precedes glory. Our momentary troubles are working for us eternal glory. Let's not give up in the waiting.

Insight

God will not waste our trials. What we go through in this life helps prepare us to reign with Christ forever.

1 Kings 17:1-15

Elijah by the Brook

"Leave here, turn eastward and hide in the Kerith Ravine, east of the Jordan. You will drink from the brook, and I have ordered the ravens to feed you there" (1 Kings 17:3-4).

Elijah is in the waiting room. God has hidden him from King Ahab. While Elijah sits and waits by the brook, ravens bring him bread and meat morning and evening. Imagine-meals on order from God Himself!

As a drought progresses, Elijah watches the brook get smaller and smaller until it dries up entirely. Did Elijah worry and fret? God had sent him there. God would tell him what to do next. Elijah simply trusted as he waited.

When it was time for the next step, God gave him specific instructions. "Go to a widow in Zarapath and she shall sustain you."

Someday when my husband Dan becomes a care because of Alzheimers, we will be forced to close the day care. I'm trusting God to direct us to the next step in our lives. We will need some sort of income to supplement the Social Security.

God did not leave Elijah guessing. He cared for His prophet throughout difficult, life-threatening times. He will care for us.

Insight

God is the God of detailed instructions in the waiting periods, even in the most difficult times.

2 Chronicles 20:1-29

When Facing the Enemy

"O our God, will you not judge them? For we have no power to face this vast army that is attacking us. We do not know what to do, but our eyes are upon you" (2 Chronicles 20:12).

The enemy army was massed on the border, poised to wipe-out the little nation of Judah. King Jehoshaphat did the only thing he could he proclaimed a day of fasting and prayer. As all God's people waited before the Lord, He gave them specific instructions. "You will not have to fight, for the battle is the Lord's. March down, stand still, and watch. God will deliver you." Praise won a great victory that day.

One summer both our college boys were home, but because of a recession, neither my husband nor the boys had work. Our only income was the day care. We set aside an evening for fasting and prayer. We came to the table with our Bibles and a simple outline for the evening which included telling stories of God's past faithfulness to each of us. That evening ended in spontaneous praise to God as we sang as a family, "How Great Thou Art." Work still did not come, but a check from our church saw our boys back to college.

Insight

Look to God alone when tough- even impossible-problems assail you. Wait on Him. Praise Him. He will give you directions for your life.

Esther 5:1-14

Esther Waited Overnight

"If the king regards me with favor and if it pleases the king to grant my petition . . . let the king and Haman come to-morrow. . . I will answer the king's question" (Esther 5:8).

God's people, the Jews, had been destined for slaughter by wicked Haman. Queen Esther, took her life in her hands and went before the king to intercede for her people. She invited the king and Haman to a banquet. At that banquet she didn't answer a question the king had raised, but invited them back the next day.

Now the king was troubled. What would be so important that Esther would risk her life for it? There was no sleep for him that night, so he had the daily records of his reign read to him. As those records were read, he discovered that Esther's uncle Mordecai had saved his life. Next morning, Haman was ordered to take Mordecai through the town and honor him. Later at the banquet, Haman's wicked plot was exposed and the Jews were saved.

Because Esther wisely waited, God worked in her behalf. Too often we rush into things. We simply don't give Him the room to work out things for us in His way-always the best way.

Insight

God is always at work behind the scenes engineering our circumstances for our good and His glory, even in life and death situations.

Habakkuk 2:1-14

Pour Out Your Complaints

"I will stand at my watch and station myself on the ramparts; I will look to see what he will say to me, and what answer I am to give to this complaint" (Habakkuk 2:1).

Israel had forsaken God, and He was using the godless Babylonians to punish them. When He revealed this to Habakkuk, the prophet had a hard time understanding what God was doing.

He complained, "How long must I call for help and You turn a deaf ear?" Everywhere I look there's destruction and violence. Why are You silent while the wicked devour the righteous?" Simply put, Habakkuk asked, "God, why don't You step in and do something?"

Habakkuk poured out his complaint to the Lord. Then he sat down to wait and see what God would answer.

You and I have the same privilege. We're welcome into God's presence to pour out our complaints. Once, when calamity struck us, I cried out in panic to God, "If You're in control, then why did you allow this to happen to us?"

He answered, "Wait and see. I am working out My plan for you, and I'm going to bring great blessing out of this seeming disaster." And He has!

Insight

We're free to bring our complaints to God. Then wait and see what He says. He may explain Himself - or simply ask us to keep trusting Him.

DAY 21
Luke 2:21-39

Anna and Simeon

"Now there was a man in Jerusalem called Simeon, who was righteous and devout. He was waiting for the consolation of Israel, and the Holy Spirit was upon him" (Luke 2:25).

The wait was long. Simeon was an old man, but God had promised he would not die until he had seen the Christ. When one day Mary and Joseph brought the baby Jesus to the temple, God said, "Simeon, this is the one." Simeon took that tiny baby in his arms and blessed God.

At that moment Anna stepped up and prophesied over this child. She also was very old and had waited a long time for God to send His Son.

The wait was long but the promise was sure. God kept His word to send His Son to secure us our salvation.

You wait and you pray earnestly, and still someone you love has not turned back to the Lord. The time grows long, years go by, and that wayward one appears to be doing fine without Him. Why is God taking so long to deal with the indifference and answer your prayers? Keep waiting and praying. God sees, hears, and knows. The answer may come even after He has called you home to Himself.

Insight

Don't give up! God is very patient, longsuffering, and kind. His ways are not our ways, but His promises are sure.

John 11:1-43

When God Comes Too Late

"Jesus loved Martha and her sister and Lazarus. Yet when he heard that Lazarus was sick, he stayed where he was two more days. Then he said to his disciples, 'Let us go back to Judea'" (John 11:5-7).

Lazarus was deathly ill. Mary and Martha sent an urgent message to Jesus, "Come quickly. He whom you love is sick."

But Jesus did not rush to their side. While they waited anxiously, Lazarus died and was buried. Their hope for healing was gone.

When Jesus did arrive, the sisters each cried in their grief, "Lazarus wouldn't have died if only You had been here. You're too late!"

Was Jesus too late? Not according to God's plan, for He would raise Lazarus from the grave and turn their grief to joy.

Have you ever felt that God was too late? As you waited and prayed, did things go only from bad to worse? Did you cry out, "Where are You, God? Don't You hear me? Why don't You help?"

Mary and Martha knew Jesus as a healer, but they were going to experience Him as the Resurrection and the Life, and their joy would be far greater. He may be waiting to do the greater miracle for you.

Insight

Stand on tiptoe with expectancy. The longer the wait, the greater the need, and the greater the need, the greater the miracle.

John 20:1-22

Waiting in Fear and Trembling

"On the evening of that first day of the week, when the disciples were together, with the doors locked for fear of the Jews, Jesus came and stood among them and said, 'Peace be with you!'" (John 20:19)

Their hopes lay shattered at the foot of a cross and locked in a tomb. Who would be next? Would the authorities strike out at Jesus' followers and kill them? The disciples gathered together and waited behind locked doors. While they waited, fearful, and afraid, Jesus appeared to them and said, "Peace be with you!"

In the waiting period you may be full of fear. What if that lab report comes back with bad news? What if I get laid off? What if I can't find a job? What if no one hires me? How will we pay the bills? What if my son continues on his self-destructive course? What if my daughter becomes pregnant while living with her boyfriend? What if my health fails and I can't work anymore?

Whatever your "what if," let Jesus come and speak those words of peace to your heart. Yes, sometimes waiting periods are fraught with fear, and we must cling close to Jesus. "Hold me, Lord," we pray, "I can't go through this without You." And He holds us.

Insight

Fear can attack you in a waiting period and hold you in a tenacious grip. You must bring every thought captive to Christ.

Waiting for the Spirit

"'Do not leave Jerusalem, but wait for the gift my Father promised, which you have heard me speak about.' . . . All of them were filled with the Holy Spirit" (Acts 1:4; 2:4).

The instruction was clear: Jesus' disciples were to wait for the Holy Spirit to come. After Jesus ascended, the disciples returned to the upper room, continuing in constant prayer. They obeyed Jesus' command and waited.

On the Day of Pentecost, the Spirit came and they were empowered for ministry. Literally these men turned the world upside down. What if they had not waited but had tried to minister without the Spirit? It would have been a total disaster.

When God called Dan and me into prison ministry, He affirmed that call in many ways. For example, in our first trip to the prison in Salem, Oregon, God opened the door through the chaplain so we could visit two men, an unheard of privilege. As we waited to enter the prison, we met a local volunteer who opened her home to us so that we stayed with her on each trip back.

When God's children are walking in the Spirit, God does miracles for us - and we become a miracle.

Insight

When you live and walk in the Spirit, expect the unexpected. God loves to do wonders in and through His children.

DAY 25
Acts 9:1-9

Saul, Blinded and Waiting

"'Now get up and go into the city, and you will be told what you must do.' . . . . For three days he was blind, and did not eat or drink anything" (Acts 9:6, 9).

Saul was headed for Damascus to bring Jesus' followers back to Jerusalem for trial. On the road, he was struck down and blinded. The risen Jesus spoke to him, and Saul's life was turned around.

As Saul waited for the next step, he prayed and fasted. On the third day, the Lord told Ananias to go to Saul. Ananias protested, "Lord, I've heard stories about this man, how much harm he has done to your faithful followers in Jerusalem."

The Lord answered, "Go, Ananias. He is a chosen vessel unto me. I have special work for him to do." And Ananias obeyed. He went to Saul, laying his hands on him so he could see again.

Saul obeyed the Lord and waited in prayer and fasting until he was anointed for ministry and was filled with the Holy Spirit.

We must always stay in tune with the Holy Spirit, not running ahead of Him nor lagging behind. Then we will sense God's power at work in our lives, touching others for the kingdom of God.

Insight

Wait for God's instructions. Don't run ahead of Him, and God will use you to touch many.

Shall Not Be Ashamed

"In you I trust, O my God. Do not let me be put to shame,
nor let my enemies triumph over me. No one whose hope
is in you will ever be put to shame" (Psalm 25:2-3).

As I write this, I am in a waiting period. We lose two children from our day care this month, and the phone remains silent. There are no calls for children.

I knew Jared was leaving to go to kindergarten, but I had no idea Nick would be moved to preschool so young. But God is never caught by surprise, even if I am. He knows how He is going to meet our needs next month with only three children, one of them part time.

We've prayed a full year for a sixth child, and God has not sent one. I've had to bow to His love and wisdom, trusting that He knows my strength and ability.

So we wait on God alone, believing He handpicks the children and parents He wants us to minister to. And we will not be ashamed but will give glory to God as He provides in His time and His way

Waiting on God is never in vain. He comes through for His children.

Insight

Our waiting on God and our faith in His provision will be a witness to all around us, and we won't be ashamed.

2 Thessalonians 3:1-14

Waiting for Jesus' Coming

"The Lord direct your hearts . . . into the patient waiting for Christ. . . . To wait for his Son from heaven, whom he raised from the dead" (1 Thessalonians 3:5; 1 Thessalonians 1:10, KJV).

As believers, we are all waiting for the return of the Lord, and we wonder what is keeping Him as the world seems to be hurtling headfirst into the end times. But God is gracious and longsuffering, giving the human race opportunity to turn to Him while He commissions us to get the Gospel out to all people. So we work, wait, and look up.

A friend asked me, "Do you think the Lord is coming soon?" She would really like her struggles in this life to be over, and I can't blame her. She just lost her job of six years, plus her oldest daughter is moving and taking my friend's only grandchild away.

When we are slammed by one trouble after another, we long for the Lord to come back. We wait patiently and in hope that Jesus' promise to return is real and will happen when we least expect it. In light of this, we can pray, "Lord, I want to stay busy for You until You come for me. Make me a blessing in someone's life today."

Insight

We keep on waiting for Jesus' return, but we wait in momentary expectation and hope.

1 Samuel 13:1-15

One Who Didn't Wait

"'You acted foolishly,' Samuel said. "You have not kept the command the Lord your God gave you; if you had, he would have established your kingdom over Israel for all time'" (1Samuel 13:13).

King Saul and his army were about to engage the Philistines in battle, but first the prophet Samuel was coming to offer a sacrifice and ask God's blessing. The rumors were flying, and Saul's army began to scatter. Still Samuel did not come. So Saul took matters into his own hands and offered the sacrifice. Samuel arrived shortly afterward and said sternly, "What have you done? You should have obeyed God. Because you didn't, God is tearing the kingdom away from you."

Saul's impatience and failure to wait lost him the kingdom. It would go to a shepherd boy named David, who became a man after God's heart.

Saul serves as a warning to us. He shows us the cost of not waiting for God. It results in great loss.

Every time people in Scripture ran ahead of God or took matters into their own hands, it created chaos and loss.

It's better to wait patiently for God to work things out in His own time, to cling to the promises, and hope in Him day by day.

Insight

It is always better to wait and obey God than to run ahead of him and suffer loss.

1 Samuel 13:1-15

Waiting in Hope

"I wait for the Lord, my soul waits, and in his word I put my hope. My soul waits for the Lord more than watchmen wait for the morning. . . . O Israel, put your hope in the Lord" (Psalm 130:5-7).

While 1 have been waiting for the Lord to answer my prayers for His intervention in my need, God has constantly reminded me of His promises.

"Cast all your anxiety on him because he cares for you" (1 Peter 5:7).

"Be still before the Lord and wait patiently for him; do not fret" (Psalm 37:7).

"Trust in the Lord with all your heart and lean not on your own understanding; in all your ways acknowledge him, and he will make your paths straight" (Proverbs 3:5-6).

"Do not worry about tomorrow, for tomorrow will worry about itself. Each day has enough trouble of its own" (Matthew 6:34).

Everywhere I turn in Scripture, God reminds me of His promised care and admonishes me not to worry. So I run over the promises daily. I remember He has never failed me yet and that He is at work behind the scenes. It's a constant battle not to try to figure things out, but to wait in hope.

Insight

God is faithful and He keeps His promises to His children. He is totally worthy of your trust.

Wait Continually

"The Lord God Almighty, the Lord is his name of renown! But you must return to your God; maintain love and justice, and wait for your God always" (Hosea 12:5-6).

Waiting periods-we have them every day. Waiting for the phone to ring. Waiting in line at the supermarket. Waiting for an answer to my letter. Waiting for someone to fulfill an obligation. Waiting for an appointment. Waiting for God to answer our prayers. Waiting for Him to keep His promises.

It seems we continually wait, but the key is to wait on God-to keep our eyes on Him. To cling to His promises, to believe Him and trust Him fully. To wait on Him in the darkness, when we're afraid. To wait for strength to meet our day, for encouragement, in expectation. To wait patiently for our needs, for His blessing. To wait in hope.

Waiting is an essential part of life and not one of us enjoys it. We want things to move. We want the darkness to be over forever. We want Jesus to come. So we pray, "Lord, help me wait, knowing You are using it as part of my training for heaven."

Insight

There will always be waiting periods in our lives. Let's not run ahead of God but wait in hope.

July

DAY 1
Psalm 33

The Thoughts of God's Heart

"The Lord bringeth the counsel of the heathen to nought .
. . . The counsel of the Lord standeth for ever, the thoughts
of his heart to all generations" (Psalm33:10-11, KJV).

He is the unchangeable God - sure, steadfast, totally trustworthy. When all around us comes crashing down, God stands firm. He is our rock, our peace in the midst of turmoil. His thoughts toward us do not change. What He has purposed, He brings to pass in our lives.

God is not so much interested in our comfort as He is in building our character. Don't faint in the day of adversity. Cling to the One who cares for you lovingly, who controls what happens in your life day by day.

In the days ahead this month we are going to seek to discover some of God's thoughts toward us. I trust all our hearts will be encouraged in the daily readings.

Our God is an awesome God and works in ways we cannot even begin to imagine. "Father, as we start this journey, thrill our hearts with the revelation of Your thoughts toward us. Encourage us with bedrock truth. Fill us with Your joy and peace."

Insight

God is our very real and personal God, awesome in praises, doing wonders, and doing them for His children.

Thoughts of Peace

"'I know the plans I have for you', declares the Lord', plans to prosper you and not to harm you, plans to give you hope and a future'" (Jeremiah 29:11).

This promise gives hope, especially when things do not seem to be working out according to our way of thinking.

The future can look pretty grim. What we face can be scary, but God assures us His plans are good. He does not send evil to His children, but uses seeming evil simply to serve His purpose in our lives.

Take Joseph, whose story is given in Genesis, hated by his brothers, sold into slavery, then thrown into prison for something he didn't do. Even when things went from bad to worse, God was with Joseph and was working out His plan to rescue His people. The hatred of his brothers only served God's purpose and would eventually prove their salvation. Today I'm facing a future of caring for a husband with Alzheimer's yet having to supplement the Social Security income at the same time. Right now I do child care. What happens when I have to close the day care? So many questions, but one thing I know-God has a plan and He will make a way through, for me and for you.

Insight

God's plans and purposes are good and He holds your future in His hands.

God's Higher Thoughts

"'My thoughts are not your thoughts, neither are your ways my ways,' declares the Lord. 'As the heavens are higher than the earth, so are . . . my thoughts [higher] than your thoughts'" (Isaiah 55:8-9).

How often I have been thankful for today's key verses. The way I would have handled a situation and the way God worked was directly opposite. God sees the whole picture, while I see only one small corner. He has a much, larger frame of reference, for He sees everything from His eternal perspective. Our greatest concern is that we follow His leading and make wise decisions along the way. Think how it must have been for Jesus' friends, Mary and Martha, when their brother Lazarus was seriously sick. Desperately worried, they sent for Jesus to come, confident that He would heal Lazarus. Instead, Jesus did not come immediately. Lazarus died and was buried before Jesus arrived. The delay was hard for Mary and Martha to understand, but it brought God the greater glory as a healing became a resurrection (John 11:1-44).

When we trust God's higher thoughts, even though we cannot understand why He does not move according to our desires, we make way for Him to bring glory to His name.

Insight

God's ways are not only higher, they are better and bring greater glory to God as He works out His plans in our lives.

A Multitude of Thoughts

"How precious to me are your thoughts, O God! How vast is the sum of them! Were I to count them, they would out-number the grains of sand" (Psalm 139:17-18).

Our God is an exceeding, abundantly, above all we ask or even imagine kind of God. His mercy is higher than the heavens. His compassions are new every morning. His faith moves mountains and withers fig trees. His power is absolute. Who is so great a God as our God?

Does it surprise us that God's thoughts are constantly toward us? That He hears and answers prayer-even the prayer we can't put into words? That He is in control of everything that happens to us? Nothing slips by Him. And it is all for His glory and our good.

Does it surprise us that His creation is so amazing from the starry heavens to the tiniest flower? That no two snowflakes or grains of sand are alike? That no two people on Planet Earth are alike? That God has a detailed life plan for the tiny newborn we hold in our arms? That He has counted the number of hairs on our heads? That He knows our every thought before we think of it? That He knows us and loves us anyway?

Insight

Truly our God is amazing and awesome, always thinking about you and planning for you.

Zephaniah 3:14-20

Rejoicing Over You

"The Lord your God is with you, he is mighty to save. He will take great delight in you, he will quiet you with his love, he will rejoice over you with singing" (Zephaniah 3:17).

When a person comes into God's kingdom, there is great rejoicing in heaven. And God Himself takes great delight in this newborn child. He will quiet the anxieties, fear, and doubts. How often He has to do that for me.

Can we grieve the heart of God? Paul speaks of grieving the Holy Spirit, and He is God. We grieve Him with our pride, our anger, unwillingness to forgive, and our lack of faith.

God begins the work in our lives at the moment of our salvation, and He works to complete it until we see Him face to face. Praise God for the wonderful promise He has given us: "He is able to keep you from slipping and falling away, and to bring you, sinless and perfect, into His glorious presence with mighty shouts of everlasting joy" (Jude 24, TLB).

We fail to trust God and slide into anxiety and worry. Still, God says that He delights in us and rejoices over us with singing. How amazing to think we can bring delight to the heart of God.

Insight

Just think: God is going to take you and get you to your presentation before the throne spotless and with great joy.

DAY 6
Jeremiah 31:1-9

A Major Project

"The Lord appeared to us in the past, saying: 'I have loved you with an everlasting love; I have drawn you with loving-kindness'" (Jeremiah 31:3).

No matter what we do. No matter what we say. No matter how many times we fail Him, God will still love us. We can run to the ends of the earth, but we cannot escape God's love. We can forsake Him, but He will not forsake us. We can be unfaithful, but He will be faithful still.

When we come running back to Him, He will be waiting with arms open wide. He may discipline us, but His love draws us back to Him, forgives us, and restores us to fellowship with Him.

So many men and women in prison have been forsaken by their families. They are left with no one to love and care for them. I write to a number of prisoners, and several inmates have said, "I have only you." That is not true, of course, because they also have the Lord.

When the prodigal son came back after wasting his funds and his life, the father welcomed him home with arms open wide and threw a party.

Have you in any way turned from God? Turn back. He has never stopped loving you.

Insight

We cannot frustrate God's grace. He continues to love us and waits for us to turn back to Him.

DAY 7
Hebrews 13:1-5

I Will Never Leave You

"God has said, 'Never will I leave you; never will I forsake you.' So we say with confidence, 'The Lord is my helper: I will not be afraid. What can man do to me?'" (Hebrews 13:5-6).

Early in our prison ministry, my husband Dan and I were asked to visit a very depressed inmate. Scott was not happy to see us. In fact he was very angry and asked many hard questions which we could not answer. As we left, I thought he would never want to see us again.

The next week I sent Scott a Bible study, a lesson each day. When we arrived to visit him, the anger was gone. He had been reading his Bible seven and eight hours a day. Soon he was moved to another prison, so we were unable to see him again.

We were delighted to receive letter from him in which he told us that he had read the whole New Testament, and parts of it several times. He added, "I can't tell you how great I feel knowing that I'm no longer alone." He could see God's hand at work every day and had received His comfort in time of need.

God's children are never alone, for He has promised to be with us at all times.

Insight

God is faithful to His promise. He is always with you, and His hand is in everything that happens to you.

I Will Guide You

"I will instruct you and teach you in the way you should go; I will counsel you and watch over you. Do not be like the horse or the mule, which have no understanding" (Psalm 32:8-9).

Have you ever made a decision and wondered if was the right one? We have. In 1994 we refinanced our home on a new 30-year mortgage. We dropped the interest rate, but we had a major hassel with HUD. The government had paid most of the interest on our loan. Now they wanted it back. Finally I went to my Senator, and the loan went right through.

With the low interest rates in 2003, we were advised to refinance again, dropping the interest rate. Once again we met roadblock after roadblock. Every time it seemed God had worked things out for us, it was blocked. Now we are borrowing enough to pay off HUD. It is scary, as we are in our retirement years and my husband has Alzheimers.

We need to see God's hand in all of this and have His peace that we are following His guidance. What He promises for us, He promises for you. Whatever your need today, our Lord is committed to instructing you, counseling you, and watching over you. Rely on Him.

Insight

God promises to guide you in large matters and small. As you seek His face and wisdom, respond to His direction.

I Will Always Listen to You

"The eyes of the Lord are on the righteous and his ears are attentive to their cry; the face of the Lord is against those who do evil, to cut off the memory of them from the earth" (Psalm 34:15-16).

Children long for attention-even demand it through their actions. Often the little ones in my day care will cry out, "Earline, look at me!" And I assure them that they have my attention.

Jesus pointed out that we can be tempted to pester God with our prayers. He said, "When you pray, do not keep on babbling like pagans, for they think they will be heard because of their many words. Do not be like them, for your Father knows what you need before you ask him" (Matthew 5:7-8).

Through today's verse God assures us that He is listening to our faintest cry. When our thoughts are confused, our hearts overwhelmed, we don't know what to say or even how to pray, but God hears.

When there are no words to express our heart cries, the Holy Spirit prays for us with groans that cannot be uttered. God hears and begins to answer. What comfort to know we always have the ear of God!

Insight

God is always watching and listening. You have His complete attention at all runes.

Ephesians 1:1-14

I Will Accept You as You Are

"To the praise of the glory of his grace, wherein he hath made us accepted in the beloved, in whom we have redemption . . . the forgiveness of sins, according to the riches of his grace" (Ephesians 1:6-7, KJV).

Many years ago l discovered this wonderful truth: the Beloved is not a place but a person – Jesus Christ, the Son of God. When Jesus died on the cross, He made it possible for God to accept us as we are-warts, wrinkles, and all.

There is no need to attempt to clean up our act before we come to God. He invites us to come just as we are. The familiar old hymn says it so well:

Just as I am without one plea.

But that Thy blood was shed for me;

And that Thou bidst me come to Thee.

O Lamb of God, I come, I come.

We will do just about anything to avoid rejection. That's why God's acceptance of us is so special. Others may reject us, but the One who really matters has accepted us without any effort on our part, not because we are worthy, but because God's Beloved Son bought our redemption through His blood.

Have you ever come to Jesus and been accepted into God's forever family? Come to Him today.

Insight

There can be no greater joy than to be accepted in the Beloved Son of God, once and for all.

Isaiah 43:1-7

You Are Mine

"This is what the Lord says - he who created you, O Jacob, he who formed you, O Israel: 'Fear not, for I have redeemed you; I have summoned you by name; you are mine'" (Isaiah 43:1).

One local television station features what they call "Wednesday's Child." They report on children of all ages who are looking and longing for someone to adopt them - to finally have a home with a mom and dad. They desire to belong, to be considered special by someone.

This is what God has done for us. He made us, then bought us with the precious blood of His Son. He claims us as His own. He says, "You are Mine." And because we are His, we have all the privileges of sonship.

Consider these privileges: He has made us fellow heirs with Jesus. We come under the care of our loving Heavenly Father. We have the gift of the Holy Spirit, strengthening us within, teaching us, comforting us, shedding abroad God's love in our hearts, and bestowing special gifts to use in serving Him. We have access to the throne of grace anytime. We are held by a love that will never let us go. Finally, some day He will take us home to be with Him forever.

Insight

Unworthy as we are, God claims us for His own, placing us under His loving care.

I Will Answer You

"In the day of my trouble I will call to you, for you will answer me" (Psalm 86:1). "Before they call I will answer; while they are still speaking I will hear" (Isaiah 65:24).

Waiting is one or the hardest things to do! We have a need or a concern that we bring to the Lord in prayer. How we long for an immediate answer! But sometimes there is only silence after we have made our request.

God promises He will hear and He also promises He will answer us. We can have utter confidence in Him. That confidence can remain unshaken even when the answer is long in coming.

A number of years ago we lost our business and put our house up for sale. Long months went by and God seemed to be doing nothing. We had to trust throughout the darkness of that long winter. Then suddenly God moved, and all our prayers were answered in one week's time - the sale of our home, the purchase of a home in Boise, and a job for Dan.

God invites us, "Call upon me in the day of trouble; I will deliver you, and you will honor me" (Psalm 50:15). He uses prayer to bring help to us and glory to Himself.

Insight

God's ears are open to His children and the answers to our prayers begin their journey to us the moment they are spoken.

I Will Cleanse You

"If we walk in the light, as he is in the light, we have fellowship with one another, and the blood of Jesus Christ, His Son, cleanseth us from all sin" (1 John 1:7, KJV).

I remember seeing our youngest son Nathan, when he was two or three years old, sitting on the step, clutching his blanket, his little face caked with mud. He was in deep distress, but his unhappy feelings turned to delight once he was cleaned up. Little children need their hands and faces washed, not once but many times a day.

Similarly, as we walk through this old world, our feet get dirty and our garments get spotted. We need daily cleansing, and God provides for that as we walk with Him. Many times a day we need to come to Jesus and ask for His forgiveness and cleansing for our thoughts and words and actions.

We fail God, fall flat on our faces in the mud, but when we confess our sin, He tenderly picks us up again, sets us on our feet, and cleanses us. In trustful confidence we can put our hand in His and walk on together in fellowship.

Praise God for His forgiveness and cleansing. Praise Him for second and third chances to pass life's tests. Praise Him for His grace so freely given.

Insight

God has made the way for us to be cleansed as we walk with Him through this sin-filled world.

Isaiah 40:25-31

I Will Strengthen You

"He gives strength to the weary and increases the power of the weak"(Isaiah 40:29). "I can do everything through him who gives me strength" (Philippians 4:13).

We are on a camping trip as I have been reflecting on this month's theme. My surroundings bring a sense of peace and rest. In quiet moments I have also been reading through 40 years of my journals, and have noticed how many times I wrote, "So weary today." It seems I've always pushed myself to the end of my strength, always setting goals, making plans, and getting very tired. I haven't changed! God promises to strengthen us-to give rest to the weary. When God gives us a task, He gives us the strength to get it done.

Often, though, we need more than physical stamina. We need strength to endure when trials come, and strength to support others when we face difficulties, and they need us to help them trust God's promise.

We may be weak in ourselves, but that weakness drives us to rely on God, to simply trust Him for the strength to endure and to go on even when we think we can't. He promises, "Cast your cares on the Lord and he will sustain you" (Psalm 55:22).

Insight

When we are weak and burdened with cares, God gives special inner strength to our weary bodies and souls.

Psalm 23; 1 Peter 5:1-7

I Will Take Care of You

"The Lord is my shepherd, I shall not be in want. . . I will fear no evil, for you are with me" (Psalm 23:1, 4). "Cast all your anxiety on him because he cares for you" (1 Peter 5:7).

How often God has reminded me of His care and invited me to cast my worries on Him. Once, for example, He sent an angel named Bill. My husband Dan was in the hospital for a knee replacement surgery. Early morning after the surgery, the hospital called me to say that Dan was confused, trying to get out of bed, and asking me to come to him. What to do? My day care children were already there for the day I quickly asked a friend to go to my husband. Then his wife came for the children so I could go to Dan. As long as I held his hand, he stayed calm and in bed. The drugs had sent him deeply into Alzheimer's symptoms.

Then a tall, distinguished gentleman walked into the room. "Hello," he said, "I'm Bill and the sitter for this shift." I didn't know the hospital provided sitters. As we talked, I discovered that Bill was a retired pastor. He was an incredible blessing to me, and prayed with us before I left.

God never runs out of ways to prove He will take care of us. In your need, rely on Him.

Insight

God cares for His children, even sending special people at special times to minister to them.

I Will Restore You

"He makes me lie down in green pastures, he leads me beside quiet waters, he restores my soul. He guides me in the paths of righteousness for his name's sake" (Psalm 23:2-3, KJV).

Have you ever lost something precious to you? Wasted time and opportunity, even years? A friend is deeply concerned for her children in their teen years as she remembers how she spent hers in rebellion. She was greatly comforted when I shared with her God's promise, "I will restore to you the years that the locust hath eaten" (Joel 2:25, KJV).

Many women in prison feel the guilt of their wasted years as their children are growing up without them. But God never wastes anything - even our pain and regret.

God lovingly calls to us, "Turn back to Me. Let Me heal you, restore you, bless you." How patient He is with us, restoring what we have lost, filling our cup of blessing so full that it spills over to all around us.

Give Him the broken pieces of your life. Let Him put you back together, restoring your heart and soul. The most effective prison volunteer is one who has been there, been restored, and comes back to minister to others.

Insight

God lifts up the fallen, restores our soul, redeems our mistakes, then uses us to minister to others.

I Will Give You My Joy

"I have told you this so that my joy may be in you and that your joy may be complete" (John 15:11). "You will fill me with joy in your presence, with eternal pleasures at your right hand" (Psalm 16:11).

Joy can be like a song in your heart, a fountain that bubbles up while over it can be a quiet confidence that God is in control of every detail of your life.

Oswald Chambers said, "Joy is God in your blood." Truly, joy is a God-thing, planted in us by the Holy Spirit. It has everything to do with our relationship with God. There is no greater joy than submitting humbly to Him and then being used by Him to minister to others.

Once I developed a painful elbow. I had golf and tennis elbow, though I play neither game. Finally, I was sent to Darrell for physical therapy. In our first session, he shared he had recently lost his father suddenly from a heart attack. I lost my father the same way. At once I recognized that God had sent me to minister to a young man who was deeply hurting. I shared and prayed with him as we began each session, for Darrell loved the Lord. When I completed my sessions, he gave me a big hug and thanked God for the blessings he had received.

Insight

Joy is a fruit, a product of our relationship with God and a gift of the Holy Spirit that can permeate our lives.

Psalm 107:1-9

I Will Satisfy Your Deep Longings

"Let them give thanks to the Lord for his unfailing love and his wonderful deeds for men, for he satisfies the thirsty and fills the hungry with good things" (Psalm 107:8-9).

Modern media tries to appeal to our here-and now hunger and thirst, but only God can satisfy the deepest longings of our soul. He is the only One who can meet our emotional and spiritual needs, for He has made us. We will be disappointed when we look to another human or any man-made product to meet our needs.

All my life I have wanted to serve God in some special way. The doors to foreign missions closed, then home missions, then local ministry with children. Finally, in our fifties, God called us into prison ministry, and we have been serving Him there ever since. Even with my husband's struggle with Alzheimer's, we still do our prison prayer group and chapel service.

Do you have a secret longing in your heart, something you long to do because you sense that God has called you to do it, has already prepared you to do it, and will equip you for it? Then trust Him to fulfill it in His time and way. If He gave that longing, He will satisfy it.

Insight

God is the only One who can fully satisfy the hunger and thirst in your soul.

2 Corinthians 1:1-11

I Will Comfort You

"Praise be to . . . the God of all comfort, who comforts us in all our troubles, so that we can comfort those in any trouble with the comfort we ourselves have received" (2 Corinthians 1:3-4).

I love to comfort the day care children when they get hurt. Little Morgan always runs to me when she is in pain, crawls up in my lap and sobs against my breast until she feels better.

Several years ago, when I was in much physical pain, I would fall on my knees beside the bed and plead with God for relief. I would picture myself as a child in His lap being comforted, and I would receive strength to go on.

Our Heavenly Father comforts us when we are in pain - not just for ourselves but so we will have words of comfort for others. Much of what God has given me in those pain-filled days I have shared with others who are troubled.

Are you in need of comfort today? Run into your Heavenly Father's arms and let Him comfort you. He is "the Father of compassion and the God of all comfort" (vs. 3). Be still before Him. Listen to His voice. Be open to the work of the Holy Spirit in your life and situation. Then look for someone who needs your word of encouragement.

Insight

God hears our cry, feels our pain, and comforts us in all our troubles so we may comfort others.

Matthew 11:25-30

I Will Give You Rest

"Come to me, all you who are weary and burdened, and I will give you rest. Take my yoke upon you and learn from me, for I am gentle and humble in heart, and you will find rest for your souls" (Matthew 11:28-29).

I am writing today while camped in the mountains. The campground is quiet, while everyone is at the lake. I hear the wind soughing through the pine trees and enjoy watching the birds and squirrels frolic nearby. It is a week of rest, writing, reading, cooking simply, and sleeping until the squirrels chatter above us. It is a time to seek God and review my life as I read 40 years of journals, a time to listen to God speak.

I have left all the problems in the valley below, but I have to return to the valley with its worries and difficulties. When we do only what God asks us to do, the burden is light and the yoke is easy as we walk in step with Him. We get in trouble when we carry yesterday's burdens into today, and carry today's burden while also trying to pick up tomorrow's. It overwhelms us.

Today we are doing well with Dan's Alzheimer's. I try not to think about the tomorrows. It is better to live in day-tight compartments, finding rest as I take Christ's yoke and walk in step with Him.

Insight

God is our great burden bearer. He remembers that we are frail and gives rest when we are weary.

Lamentations 3:22-30

I Will Be Faithful to You

"Because of the Lord's great love we are not consumed, for his compassions never fail. They are new every morning, great is your faithfulness" (Lamentations 3:22-23).

We may not be faithful to God. We may fail to trust Him, yet He remains faithful and trustworthy. He simply cannot fail, for He is God.

A number of years ago our construction business crashed. At that time, we had a bank loan for $4,000. When my husband Dan explained our situation, they agreed to wait for repayment, but we would have to pay the $300 in interest. To raise the needed money, Dan began to sell all of his large construction tools and we made preparation for a yard sale.

Before we could have the sale, however, we received a letter from a lawyer in Oregon. Inside was a check and a note saying, "I cannot tell you why you are receiving this check due to the instructions from my client." The check was for $300. God is so amazing!

When our hearts are humble and we are following His direction in our lives, He is faithful to enable us to live for Him. His love and compassions will never fail.

Insight

God is faithful. When He gives a promise, it is like money in the bank. He will keep that promise to you.

I Will Lift You Up

"The Lord is faithful to all his promises and loving toward all he has made. The Lord upholds all those who fall and lifts up all who are bowed down" (Psalm 145-13-14).

God has provided the way for us to be lifted up in our spirits, no matter what our circumstances are. Yet we allow ourselves to be bowed down because we do not call on Him.

Sin bows us down. We do wrong and try to cover it over. But our hearts are out of fellowship with God. He has provided the way to be lifted up again. He promises, "If we confess our sins, he is faithful and just and will forgive us our sins" (1John 1:9). No matter how many times we fail Him, no matter how many times we have to come to Him and confess those failures, He is ready and waiting to forgive us totally and freely He lifts us up by restoring us to fellowship with Him.

Difficulties also bow us down. We may be bowed down with health problems, constant pain and weakness. We may be bowed down with financial stress or problems with our spouse or children. Employment needs may be an unbearable burden.

Whatever the difficulty that presses you down, give it to God. He will uphold you and lift you up.

Insight

God picks up those who fall down and puts them on their feet again. He lifts up those who are bowed down.

1 Corinthians 10:1-13

I Will Show You a Way Out

"God is faithful; he will not let you be tempted beyond what you can bear. But when you are tempted, he will also provide a way out so that you can stand up under it" (1 Corinthians 10:13).

In our home God is making a way through our battle with Alzheimer's - teaching me these days to bite my tongue and giving me wisdom in controlling the environment. "'You know Lord', I cry 'I'm going to trust You for the wisdom and strength to care for Dan. When his confusion becomes un-bearable, I believe you will make a way of escape for me.'"

I understand the need to simply get away for awhile. At first I was not ready for a support group, but now I'm thankful to go, especially for Dan's sake. He so enjoys sharing with others like himself. I come away feeling blessed that we are where we are in the process. God has made the group become a place of new ministry for both of us.

Sometimes my way of escape is simply a change of attitude - of letting go.

It is easy to think that the temptation we are dealing with is especially unbearable. But whatever the temptation, no mat-ter how it holds us in its grip, we can depend on God to pro-vide a way out.

Insight

God makes a way for us through the most difficult of temp-tations when we cry out to Him.

DAY 24
Isaiah 43:1-7

I Won't Let Trouble Overwhelm You

"When you pass through the waters, I will be with you; and when you pass through the rivers, they will not sweep over you. When you walk through the fire, you will not be burned" (Isaiah 43:2).

Due to medication, we lot Dan mentally after his first knee replacement surgery. I went home, but could sleep only half the night. I wept and pleaded with God to give him back to me as he was before the surgery. I did it again the second night. Then the pain medications were changed, and Dan began to talk again. Each day he became more like himself.

Then unexpectedly the new drugs caused a day of total confusion. I battled with Dan all day. When he finally fell asleep, l went home in despair. I called my son and poured out my heart. After he prayed with me, I was able to go on. Every day after that was better, and soon Dan was himself again.

Today's verse is a promise for those kinds of times-times when we are sure our troubles are going to drown us. When the tears flow and we desperately need encouragement, when we beg and plead and our prayers assail God's throne for the one we love. We can cling to His promises. They are like a lifeboat in heavy seas.

Insight

God takes us through the troubles of this life. His presence keeps us from being overwhelmed.

DAY 25
Psalm 40

I Will Deliver You

"Many, O Lord my God, are the wonders you have done. .
. .Yet I am poor and needy; may the Lord think of me. You
are my help and my deliverer; O my God, do not delay"
(Psalm 40:5, 17).

The Bible is full of accounts in which God delivered His
people. We need these stories to strengthen us to trust Him
when we need His help. Remember how God delivered the
Children of Israel out of slavery in Egypt (Exodus 7-13).

Review how He saved King Jehoshaphat and his army
from the approaching enemy. The king prayed, "We cry out
to You in our great distress. We do not know what to do, but
we will keep our eyes on You." And how would God deliver
them? They were to stand firm and He would fight for them
(2 Chronicles 20).

Then there was Daniel who defied orders not to pray to his
God and was thrown into a den of lions to meet his death. But
God not only saved Daniel's life but restored him to the king's
favor (Daniel 6).

God was with the apostle Paul in a terrible storm at sea.
The ship ran aground, but God delivered. Everyone on board
made shore safely (Acts 27).

What God did for people long ago, He will do for us today,
if we will trust Him.

Insight

*God is faithful. Sometimes God delivers us from trouble;
sometimes He delivers us in trouble, and sometimes He
takes us through trouble.*

DAY 26
Isaiah 49:8-10

I Will Not Forget You

"Can a mother forget the baby at her breast and have no compassion on the child she has borne? Though she may forget, I will not forget you! See, I have engraved you on the palms of my hands" (Isaiah 49:15-16).

In our city we have just had a tragic case of a mother forgetting her ten-week-old baby. As she was driving to day care, she was distracted by a cell phone call. She drove right on to work, leaving her baby in a hot car all day. Medical authorities report that he died in an hour or two. We wonder how a mother could possibly forget her baby.

God assures you that even if a mother could forget her little baby, He won't forget you. He has written your name on the palms of His hands. As His child, you are precious to Him, and He is always thinking about you.

You and I forget. We overlook the needs of people around us. We fail to keep promises we have made, not because we want to avoid an obligation but because we simply forget.

God does not forget us or our deepest heart needs. He never forgets what we have confided to Him in prayer in our desperate circumstances. He remembers that we are but dust - human and frail - and He has compassion on us.

Insight

God could never forget you, for He has written you on His hands and heart. Rest in His love for you.

Psalm 103

I Will Have Compassion

"As a father has compassion on his children, so the Lord has compassion on those who fear him; for he knows how we are formed, he remembers that we are dust" (Psalm 103:13-14).

To have compassion is to feel another's pain with a heart that cares and reaches out to help alleviate that pain. Our God is the God of compassion.

Jesus was tempted in all the ways we are, yet He did not sin. He has been there and knows what we are going through at any one moment. He comes alongside to help. Because He knows exactly the encouragement we need, He will give us that word if we will seek His face.

Recently a problem arose and I needed a word from the Lord. I'm reading my Bible through in a year, so I turned to the assigned Scripture for the day, believing even before I opened my Bible that God would speak to me. The Psalm I read held God's special message for my heart.

I was facing a knotty income tax problem, and my attitude was not good. I read, "I am radiant with joy because of your mercy, for you have listened to my troubles, and have seen the crisis in my soul" (Psalm 31:7, TLB). God led me through that crisis because of His great compassion.

Insight

We have a compassionate and understanding God who sends us a word of encouragement when we need it.

1 Corinthians 15:56-57

I Will Give You Victory

"The sting of death is sin, and the power of sin is the law. But thanks be to God! He gives us the victory through our Lord Jesus Christ" (1 Corinthians 15:56-57).

There really is no need to fail. Christ has already won the victory for us. I knew victory was possible for me when I grieved my father's death, but I was in a deep depression and felt my failure keenly. Why couldn't I grieve victoriously?

We need victory in other aspects of our lives. I am in a waiting period right now, and I wonder if I can come through victoriously. Can I wait without doubting or faltering in my faith? Will I become impatient and fretful or will I confidently rely on God's promises? I am constantly attempting to thank and praise God, though one day my hopes are high and the next day they are dashed.

Remember the story of Mary and Martha when their brother Lazarus died? God brought the greater glory to His name when Jesus delayed coming to heal Lazarus. He performed the miracle of resurrection instead of healing. God works for those who trust Him as they wait.

Victory is ours. Jesus won it once and for all on the cross. We can step into the victory already won.

Insight

Even in the midst of pain and grief, Christ can make us victorious if we put our trust in Him.

I Will Redeem Mistakes

"We know that in all things God works for the good of those who love him, who have been called according to his purpose . . . . If God is for us, who can be against us?" (Romans 8:28, 31).

There is no message I have more joy in giving a man or woman in prison than that God is a Redeemer. He is wonderfully able to take our mistakes and somehow bring good out of them.

Sometimes, though, we have been greatly hurt by the mistakes others have made. God can bring good out of these as well.

No account in Scripture illustrates this truth better than the story of Joseph in Genesis. He was hated by his brothers, sold into slavery, thrown unjustly into prison, only to be forgotten. Yet suddenly he was released to interpret Pharaoh's dreams and to be made a ruler in Egypt.

From this place of power, he saved the lives of the very ones who sold him as a slave. He could say to his brothers, "God sent me here, not you, to save much people alive. God turned your evil act into good" (see Genesis 50:19-21).

Can you trace in your life how God has taken your mistakes and failures and led you into a place of blessing?

Insight

If we love Him, God can take our mistakes and failure of the past and give us a fruitful future.

DAY 30
Psalm 115

I Long to Bless You

"The Lord remembers us and will bless us. He will bless the house of Israel, he will bless the house of Aaron, he will bless those who fear the Lord small and great alike" (Psalm 115:12-13).

God cried, "O Israel, if you had only obeyed me, I would have fed you with honey out of the rock" (see Psalm 81:11-16).

God longs to bless us, but His blessings are for the faithful and obedient, not the wayward and disobedient. So often when people hear our testimony of God's faithfulness to us, they say wistfully, "God blesses you," implying perhaps that He is withholding His goodness from them. Do you want God's blessing? Then live for Him and serve Him with all your heart. God is a lavish giver. He has a generous heart and delights to do wonders for His children. Every day He pours out His mercies and loving-kindness. He fills our cup to overflowing so the blessing spills out to all around us. He satisfies us completely, yet we hunger for more. I understand a little more of Jebez' earnest prayer, "Bless me" (see 1 Chronicles 4:9-10).

Are you hungry for blessing? Open your mouth wide. God will fill it. He longs to bless you.

Insight

God has no favorites. His heart longs to bless all His children. Let's hold up our empty cups for Him to fill.

August

Deuteronomy 26:1-11

God's Mighty Hand

"So the Lord brought us out of Egypt with a mighty hand and an outstretched arm, with great terror and with miraculous signs and wonders" (Deuteronomy 26:8).

Have you ever seen the hand of God in your life? Have you watched Him work in your behalf engineering the circumstances, or have His footsteps been invisible to you?

God delivered Israel from Egypt with mighty signs and wonders, yet His footsteps were invisible in the path through the Red Sea (see Psalm 77:19).

The Psalmist was in distress and he asked God hard questions. Then he looked back and remembered the parting of the Red Sea and God's mighty deliverance of Israel from their slavery.

When we are facing trials of various kinds and become discouraged, it helps to look back and remember God's faithfulness in the past: how He met our needs, how He delivered us, how He comforted us.

The same mighty God who delivered Israel is still at work today in the lives of His children. He still makes a way through the Red Sea places of our lives. He did it for Israel and He'll do it for you. Trust Him. There is no God as great as our God.

Insight

Watch for the hand of God at work in your life. He is always at work behind the scenes engineering your circumstances in love and for your good.

DAY 2
Exodus 15:1-13

Destroyed the Enemy

"Your right hand, O Lord, was majestic in power. Your right hand, O Lord, shattered the enemy in the greatness of your majesty you threw down those who opposed you" (Exodus 15:6-7).

The right hand of the Lord delivers His children and it also destroys the enemy. I'm sure Moses held the rod of the Lord in his right hand. At the command of the Lord, he only had to stretch it out over the sea and the army of Pharaoh was drowned.

Does it seem sometimes that the enemy is winning? Do you feel that you're going to be overwhelmed? But whose power is greater? Who really wins in the end?

When Jesus died on the cross, the enemy appeared to win. But the day that was so black for Jesus' followers was eclipsed by the Resurrection, and the enemy was soundly defeated. Jesus has won for us the victory. Satan can never ultimately win. We need to remember who is on our side and how mighty His hand is.

In our darkest hours when all seems hopeless, our Lord draws close. He invites us to trust Him enough to place our hands in His and wait expectantly for Him to work in our behalf.

Insight

We serve a mighty God who not only delivers us but has soundly defeated our enemy. So stand up and be counted.

Psalm 139:1-18

Guided by His Hand

"If I rise on the wings of the dawn, if I settle on the far side
of the sea, even there your hand will guide me, your right
hand will hold me fast" (Psalm 139:9-10).

No matter how far and how fast we run, we cannot get away
from God. Even the darkness will not hide us, for God is light.

In dark days after the sudden death of my father from a
heart attack, God was there as He guided me to a godly pastor
whose counseling led me out of depression.

In the traumatic days when our business crashed, God
guided us through each step to a new home and a new ministry.

In joyful days when God gave us the desire of our hearts
and my husband Dan became a prison chaplain, God was
there.

In the heartbreaking days when Dan was removed from
his chaplain's position because of Alzheimer's, God was there.

It really doesn't matter where you are or what you're going
through, God is there guiding you with His hand. If you will
only look back, you may be able to trace His guiding hand. If
it is still dark, just count on Him to be there, and thank Him.

Insight

*God guides us by His hand in the darkness and the light.
He never leaves our side, even though we may not sense His
presence.*

He Lifts Up

"The Lord is faithful to all his promises and loving toward all he has made. The Lord upholds all those who fall and lifts up all who are bowed down" (Psalm 145:13-14).

We can never fall so far that we fall out of the arms of God. His arms are always underneath us. As we sink down in depression and despair, God holds us and begins to lift us up.

When you are feeling down, go to the Psalms. Read until you have found the very words that express your heart and until you can begin to praise and thank God. Stay there until God lifts you up in His loving arms.

When I experienced a time of depression, I memorized Psalms 42, 43, and 51. My heart's cry became, "Restore my joy!" I stayed in those three Psalms for a long time.

When we're depressed we tend to withdraw from others. Make yourself reach out, even though you shrink from it. Invite people in for dinner or dessert. Phone a dear friend and share at least once a week. Ask someone to pray with you and for you. Become involved in a small group in your church. Pour out your heart before God. Be really honest with Him. He knows all and loves you completely.

Insight

God is faithful to lift up those who are bowed down in sorrow and discouragement. His arms are always underneath you.

DAY 5
Psalm 145:15-21

A Hand of Provision

"The eyes of all look to you, and you give them their food at the proper time. You open your hand and satisfy the desires of every living thing" (Psalm 145:15-16).

As I write, I'm looking out over a large lake in the mountains of Idaho. I thought about this verse this morning as I watched God's creatures. The birds in the air, the fish in the lake, the deer in the meadow, the squirrel in the pine tree, the carpenter ant on the deck-God feeds them all, and He provides for me, even this brief opportunity to enjoy His creation.

We just made a rush trip to California for my mother's memorial service. Neither my husband nor I can drive that distance any more. How would we get there? Our pastor son asked to lead Mom's service. He flew from Wisconsin to Boise and drove us down. One of my day care mothers has been putting in long hours at her job. For two pay periods she paid me an additional $100, which covered the expense of our trip. In addition, she pushed $25 in my pocket the day before we left saying, "Have lunch."

In spite of my being gone eight working days, all the bills are paid. God is the great provider.

Insight

God provides for His children, meeting our needs in His perfect timing. He can be trusted even in emergencies.

DAY 6
Psalm 31

His Blessed Control

"I trust in you, O Lord; I say, 'You are my God.' My times are in your hands; deliver me from my enemies and from those who pursue me" (Psalm 31:14-15).

Solomon wrote, "There is a time for everything. . . . a time to be born and a time to die" (Ecclesiastes 3:1-2). God times the events of our lives - the birth of a baby, the death of a mother.

When my mother died I observed with amazement how God had dovetailed the lives of family members, preparing us for her home going.

When I received the news, I was preparing for a week's vacation. God perfectly timed her homegoing and the memorial service so I could be there. An aunt had plans to leave for England on July 13. Mom's service was July 12. A cousin who was returning from a vacation was able to stay one more day in order to attend the service. My sister who normally takes her vacation early in July had already changed plans to be gone in September. She was at Mom's side when she needed her.

Do you sometimes feel your life is disrupted by God's timing? We can know His plans are perfect and are for His glory. He is the Blessed Controller of all things, and we can trust Him completely

Insight

God is in control of the big events in your life and of the smallest details. His timing is perfect.

Upheld by His Hand

"So do not fear, for I am with you; do not be dismayed, for
I am your God. I will strengthen you and help you; I will
uphold you with my righteous right hand" (Isaiah 41:10).

There just isn't any need to be gripped by fear because the
hand that upholds us is a righteous hand. To me, that means
God absolutely cannot make a mistake. He knows all things,
works together all things, and controls all things that pertain
to me.

Certainly we have times in our lives when we are dismayed
and overwhelmed. Are we going to cave in through fear or
are we going to trust the arms of our Savior - arms that are
holding us?

When Mom died, my son Nathan flew from Wisconsin to
be with us in Idaho and drive us to California. I couldn't meet
his plane, but when he walked in the door he just took me in
his arms and held me for a long time as my tears flowed. That
gave a little picture of being held and comforted by God. He
holds us tight and does not let us go.

We can feel safe, able to go on facing whatever we have to
face, no matter how painful. Are you safe in the arms of Jesus
- the One who can keep you and care for you?

Insight

*There's a secure place of safety and refuge from the storms of
life - the loving arms of your Savior.*

DAY 8
Psalm 32

His Hand of Conviction

"When I kept silent, my bones wasted away through my groaning all day long. For day and night your hand was heavy upon me; my strength was sapped" (Psalm 32:3-4).

Sometimes we yield to temptation and turn away from God, choosing to go our own way.

We snatch the controls of our lives and head toward shipwreck. Then God's loving hand of conviction brings discomfort and misery as He attempts to turn us back. Long ago David knew that hand - the pressure God brought to bear in his life, revealing his wrong choices and drawing him back.

David responded to that conviction of God, confessing what he had done wrong. Then he experienced God's mercy and forgiveness and he responded with praise.

We pray that God will bring His hand of conviction to bear on those who are straying, asking that they will wake up and come back to God.

We also need to look within in a spirit of humility. We need to confess our own wrong choices, and turn back to God. He waits to hear our cry and will surround us with His loving-kindness and tender mercies.

Insight

God brings people to the end of themselves so that they will begin a life of blessing with Him

Committed into His Hands

"Free me from the trap that is set for me, you are my refuge. Into your hands I commit my spirit; redeem me, O Lord, the God of truth" (Psalm 31:4-5).

When we commit a loved one into the hands of God, we can rest, knowing that one is safe there, whether it be a son or daughter, or a mate, a mom or dad, or a friend.

Blessings come when we learn to let go of the controls and allow God to take over. He will do a much better job.

When we commit our day to Him we can watch as He brings us through - not just the big problems we know we can't handle but also the little things we think we can. Nothing surprises Him.

When we commit our finances into His hands we can rely on Him to guide us in our expenditures and trust Him with the bills.

We can even commit our mistakes to the Lord, the messes we make. In His hands He can make something beautiful out of them.

God is wonderfully able to take care of all matters we commit into His hands. We can safely let go and commit every aspect of our lives into His mighty hands.

Insight

Blessed is the one who can commit themselves into God's hands so He can do whatever He pleases with that one's life.

DAY 10
Psalm 77

I Will Remember

"I will remember the years of the right hand of the most High. I will remember the works of the Lord: surely I will remember thy wonders of old" (Psalm 77:10-11, KJV).

The psalm-writer was deeply distressed and raised some troubling questions. "Is his mercy gone forever? Does His promise fail forever? Has He forgotten to be gracious?" (see vv. 8-9)

Then he says, "I will remember." Remember what? God's deliverance of Israel from Egypt, his miracle of the Red Sea crossing, the destruction of Pharaoh's army. As he remembers, he falls down before his awesome God in worship.

When you become troubled and discouraged, try doing what the psalmist did - remember. Remember how God met your needs in the past. Remember how He brought you through a crisis. Remember how He provided for a trip or a car when you needed one. Remember how He brought a godly friend into your life who helped you in your spiritual growth. Remember how He spoke to you when you needed a special word from Him. Remember that unexpected phone call telling you how much you ministered to the caller. Remember and worship your awesome God.

Insight

It pays to remember how God has worked in the past. I t gives you hope and encouragement for the future.

The Sheep of His Hand

"O come, let us worship and bow down: let us kneel before the Lord our maker. For He is our God; and we are the people of his pasture, and the sheep of His hand" (Psalm 95:6-7, KJV).

He is our personal God, our Good Shepherd, and we are His little flock. He tenderly cares for us and leads us through each day. He personally protects us from all enemies, nurses our wounds and heals our hurts. He restores our soul when we are weary from the demands of life. He leads us to those quiet resting places along the way. He fills our cup full to overflowing so that it spills over to all around us. He blesses us so we can be a blessing to others.

My grandmother wrote after she had been very ill in the hospital, "It would have been so easy for Him to pull the curtain and let me through." She had been in the valley of the shadow, but God had been so close that she was not afraid. Rather, she had been ready to go to Jesus.

Dumb sheep that we are, we have everything we need in our Shepherd. May we keep our eyes on Him and our ears tuned to His voice. May we follow wherever He leads. He has a plan for our lives, so why are we so afraid to follow His leading?

Insight

We belong to the Good Shepherd who meets every need of our lives. We are blessed when we listen and follow Him.

Isaiah 49:15-21

Engraved on His Hands

"Can a mother forget the baby at her breast? Though she may forget, I will not forget you. See, I have engraved you on the palms of my hand" (Isaiah 49:15-16).

In this day of drug addiction, children often become castaways, end up in foster homes and eligible for adoption. They are often forgotten and forsaken by their parents. These children long to belong to someone, to have a mom and dad who will care for them and love them.

Can a mother forget her child? Yes, but there is One who never forgets-God. In fact, He says, "I have engraved you on the palms of my hands."

People often forget us. Recently, for example, my husband had an early morning eye appointment. The person who had promised to sit with my day care children forgot to come, and we missed our appointment. As it worked out, the optometrist was able to fit him in later. I get anxious if my sitter for the day care doesn't arrive on time because I know too well how people may forget!

The prints of the nails in Jesus' palms constantly remind Him of us and of the price He paid for our salvation. We are His, for He bought us with His blood and He will never forget us.

Insight

Our Lord simply cannot forget us for we are written on His palms with a nail.

Safe in His Hands

"My sheep listen to my voice; I know them, and they follow me. I give them eternal life, and they shalt never perish; no one can snatch them out of my hand" (John 10:27-28).

God's hands are awesomely powerful. Whenever the Bible speaks of "the right hand of the most high," it speaks of God's almighty hand, powerful to create - powerful to save, powerful to keep.

In today's verse, God's hand is a place of safety and security. It is a picture of being in Jesus' hand, then with the Father's hands around Jesus' hands, for Jesus and His Father are one. Can there be a safer, more secure place?

Does your heart ache for a rebellious child? Can they run far enough to get away from God? A friend of mine says, "Never stop praying for a rebellious child. One never knows when God will turn them around." She speaks from experience, as she has seen God work in her child's life.

God keeps calling the rebellious back, keeps giving opportunity to turn around, keeps putting believers in their lives to love them to Jesus.

To rebel is to lose, of course, but God keeps seeking the sheep who stray until He brings them back, and we all rejoice in Him.

Insight

You have a place of security and rest, safe in the hands of the Almighty God, your Savior.

1 Peter 5:5-10

Humble Yourselves

"Humble yourselves, therefore, under God's mighty hand, that he may lift you up in due time. Casting all your anxiety on him because he cares for you" (1 Peter 5:6-7).

God does not use proud people. We need to pray that the Lord will humble us, for He uses the humble in heart for His glory: Humility is the mark of a true servant of God.

I've been proud, but God has His ways of humbling me, from the unexpected and devastating "D" I received in Bible school to the day my pastor pointed out how I wounded people with my sharp tongue.

To humble myself is not to think of myself more highly than I ought to think. It is to let another praise me and not my own mouth. It is to be submissive to God, no matter what He asks of me.

My husband Dan has humbly served God in the prison over the last 20 years. Two years ago he received a humanitarian award for his many hours of service. That was timely, as he would soon have to give up his classes and could enter the prison only if I was with him, due to his Alzheimer's.

The humble in heart are truly candidates for God's special blessing.

Insight

God blesses and raises up the humble person. He does not draw close to the proud who rely on themselves for recognition.

Clay in the Potter's Hand

"Yet, O Lord, you are our Father. We are the clay, you are the potter; we are all the work of your hand" (Isaiah 64:8).

God is in the process of making and molding us. He is always shaping our character by the events that take place in our lives. God is much more concerned about our character than our comfort.

Naturally, we will do anything to avoid pain, when it is the very pain we want to avoid that builds Christ's character in us. Character is formed more by the trials we go through than by the times of blessing in our lives. Can people around you see God's hand in your life? Can they see the changes He is gradually bringing about?

One song sung at our wedding was a prayer that as the Potter, God would take us as clay and mold us into the couple He planned us to be. I trust He has been fulfilling that prayer in our lives. I know Dan's Alzheimer's is a great opportunity for God to form His character in me as He molds me to be gentle and patient.

Will you allow God to use the trial you are going through now to mold you into the likeness of His Son?

Insight

God is the Master Potter shaping the clay of our lives into the character of His Son. Our part is to be humble and responsive to Him in the shaping process.

He Holds My Hand

"I, the Lord, have called you in righteousness; I will take hold of your hand. I will keep you and will make you to be a covenant for the people and a light for the Gentiles" (Isaiah 42:6).

David cried out to God, "Don't take Your Holy Spirit from me!" (see Psalm 51:11) We can go through anything so long as we're assured that God is with us and is holding our hand. God says, "Place your hand in Mine. Together we'll tread each step into the future." It's enough to have His presence, knowing He hears the cry of our hearts and cares enough to help.

I dread the next years. Things will not get better, only worse, as there is now no hope for an Alzheimer's patient. I try not to look into the future, but live one day at a time. I can handle today and I try to leave tomorrow in God's hands.

Dan and I are still active in prison ministry, Gideons, and still have the day care children. Thankfully, God has raised up some very special people to pray for us.

Whatever you have to face, know you don't face it alone. One holds your hand and is going through every experience with you. He feels your pain, knows your thoughts, and hears your cry for help.

Insight

The mighty hand of God holds your weak hand. Together you can face whatever the future holds.

DAY 17
Isaiah 41:17-20

Recognizing God's Hand

"So that people may see and know, may consider and understand, that the hand of the Lord has done this, that the Holy One of Israel has created it" (Isaiah 41:20).

Look at recent events in your life. Can you trace hand of God at work? Can others see His hand and give Him praise for what He has done?

Our son Nathan was on vacation in Michigan with his family when my mother died. When he decided to come to lead the service, his plans had to change. His family elected to stay in Michigan another week. That meant Nathan and Evan, the oldest son, needed a ride back home to Wisconsin. Nathan called friends from Wisconsin who were also vacationing in Michigan. They were driving home the very day Nathan and Evan needed a ride, so Nathan could fly to Boise and Evan could go to help with 5-day clubs.

Sometimes we don't recognize God's hand. Sometime His footsteps are invisible, His hand is hidden, or we can't see it through our tears or feel His nearness because of the pain in our hearts.

Look back over your life. Trace God's hand in events and circumstances. Give Him praise. May others see it too and praise Him.

Insight

When people can see God's hand in the events of your life, they are encouraged to give Him praise and to trust Him to work in their lives too.

DAY 18

Isaiah 40:12-26

God's Great Hand

"Who has measured the waters in the hollow of His hand, or with the breadth of His hand marked off the heavens? Who has . . . weighed the mountains on the scales?" (Isaiah 40:12).

Our God is so great and so awesome we cannot begin to comprehend Him. Today, while on vacation, I gaze out on a very large lake and am amazed that "He measured the waters in the hollow of His hand." And this isn't even the ocean!

The sky has been filled with fluffy thunderheads, reminding me that the clouds are the dust of His footsteps.

When I look across the lake and see the mountains, I think that He weighs the mountains. No problem is too big for our great God and no problem is too small. He even knows the number of hairs on our heads.

A Bible school professor challenged us to read Isaiah 40 every Monday morning to get a picture of the greatness of God and be reassured that He is there for us.

When we begin to think great thoughts of God, our troubles diminish to be quite small. We begin to get a proper perspective - His. Then our faith grows as we entrust our troubles into His hands.

Insight

He who counts the stars also counts the moments of your life and knows the thoughts you think even before they come to mind.

DAY 19
Isaiah 40:1-5

Blessing or Judgment

"Comfort, comfort my people, says your God. Speak tenderly to Jerusalem, and proclaim to her that her hard service has been completed, that her sin has been paid for" (Isaiah 40:1-2).

The same hand that bestows blessing also brings judgment. Israel found that out. When they obeyed God, they were blessed. The rains came and the crops were bountiful. God faithfully kept His promises to give them peace and success (Leviticus 26:1-13). However, judgment fell when they turned away from worshiping the true God. They fled before their enemies and drought seared their crops, leaving them hungry.

I watched a young man, so full of faith, begin an aftercare ministry for men coming out of prison. God blessed. Then he turned away from God. First he lost his ministry, then he lost his marriage and his son. Thankfully his ministry continues under other leadership, but because of his disobedience, God can no longer bless him.

Paul warns us that we will surely reap what we sow (Galatians 6:7-8). Sow faith, reap faith. Sow love, reap love. Sow faithful obedience, reap blessing. Sow disobedience, reap judgment. It all comes from the hand of God.

Insight

Both blessing and judgment come from the hand of God. None of us ever really gets away with anything.

1 Chronicles 21:1-13

God's Hand of Mercy

"David said to God, 'I am in deep distress. Let me fall into the hands of the Lord, for his mercy is very great; but do not let me fall into the hands of men'" (1 Chronicles 21:13).

How often I have cried out for God's mercy, asking Him not to treat me as I deserve but to be merciful.

For two years I prayed every day God would pour out His tender mercies on my mother and surround her with loving-kindness and gently take her home. She had Alzheimer's for 16 years and spent the last four, in a nursing home, unable to walk any more and not even recognizing my sister when she visited. Now Mom is rejoicing in the presence of her Savior.

How thankful I am for God's mercy which is higher than the heavens. If it were not for His mercy, we would all fall under His judgment. Christ took that judgment on Himself at the cross so God could visit His mercy on us.

Are you in need of His mercy? He is just waiting for you to cry out to Him, confessing your need.

I remember the night God gave me the words from an old hymn, "The clouds you so much dread are great with mercy and shall break with blessing on your head."

Insight

God is our merciful God, visiting the judgment on His son so that we might escape.

Isaiah 1 50:1-9

God's Saving Hand

"When I came, why was there no one? When I called, why was there no one to answer? Was my arm too short to ransom you? Do I lack the strength to rescue you?" (Isaiah 50:2).

Here in Isaiah, hundreds of years before Christ came, we have a picture of the promised Redeemer and what He would suffer for our sakes.

God would bare His mighty arm to bring us salvation. Jesus would bow in submission to His Father, giving His back to the rods and his face to shame and spitting. His suffering and death would purchase our salvation. His resurrection would make it sure.

Forgiveness is freely offered to all who will come admitting their need, accepting Jesus' sacrifice in their place, and giving themselves to live for Him.

Where are you in your spiritual journey? How far are you from God or how close have you come to giving your all to Him? Perhaps you know Him. Is He asking you to leave your comfort zone to minister to another?

God has power to redeem even the most wasted life. He can take the messes we make and bring some good thing out of them. Will you give Him a chance today?

Insight

God is a Redeemer. He has power to save, to transform a life, and to set a person's feet on the road to glory.

Hidden in His Hand

"He made my mouth like a sharpened sword, in the shadow of his hand he hid me; he made me into a polished arrow and concealed me in his quiver" (Isaiah 49:2).

Who has not needed a refuge to run to in a time of trouble? Where do you turn when the storms of life strike? To a trusted friend, your pastor, a son or daughter, your mate? Or do you turn first of all to the Lord, the only real refuge for us?

The psalmist wrote, "In you my soul takes refuge. I will take refuge in the shadow of your wings until the disaster has passed" (Psalm 57:1).

It's so good to know we have One to run to, One who is always available, One who will never disappoint, who can always be reached on a hot line to heaven.

We are in a cabin on Cascade Lake in the mountains of Idaho for a week. Friends own this cabin and have generously loaned it to us. I'm writing and resting in these beautiful surroundings.

God gives us quiet resting places when we need them. He knows what we are made of. He remembers that we are dust and showers us with loving kindness and tender mercies.

Insight

"God is our refuge and strength, an ever-present help in trouble" (Psalm 46:1). In His strong hand you can rest with an untroubled heart.

Jeremiah Commissioned

"'I am with you and will rescue you declares the Lord. Then the Lord reached out his hand and touched my mouth and said to me, 'Now I have put my words in your mouth'" (Jeremiah 1:8-9).

Jeremiah was young when God called him to be a prophet, and Jeremiah used his youth as an excuse. But God was not accepting excuses that day. Instead, he put His words in Jeremiah's mouth.

Later Jeremiah would find those words a heavy burden. He became the song of the drunkards, despised by many for his prophecies of impending judgment. Finally he decided to keep quiet and avoid further ridicule and rejection. However, he found God's words, were like a fire within his heart and he had to let them out.

He would be put in the stocks in prison and let down in a muddy cistern, and left to die there. Yet God kept His hand on Jeremiah. He protected His prophet and rescued him. He saw he was cared for when Jerusalem fell.

God used Jeremiah, a young man. He spoke to Samuel when he was a young child. No matter who you are, young, old, or in between, God can speak to you and use you. All it takes is a willing, obedient spirit.

Insight

God has given each of us a commission: go, tell all around you about the Lord Jesus and His free offer of salvation.

Daniel 4:34-37

His Sovereign Hand

"He does as He pleases with the powers of heaven and the peoples of the earth. No one can hold back His hand or say to him, 'What have you done?'" (Daniel 4:35).

How often I rest in the knowledge of our Lord's blessed control, His perfect timing of the events in my life.

God sent His Son into the world at the right time in history, into a nation oppressed by Rome. A Roman census would bring Mary and Joseph to Bethlehem for the birth of the baby Jesus. Some 33 years later He would die on a Roman cross, fulfilling prophecy. Roman roads would speed the Gospel throughout the known world.

One day a man walked into our prison prayer group early and introduced himself as our neighbor across the street. He is now in prison for six years. He worked for the health department with the woman who does the inspection for my day care. This was a total surprise as we had never met him or his wife. That evening Dan and I met her. When I asked if we could pray with her, she said, "Yes." After our prayer I gave her a hug and we left. Later I gave them each a copy of Anchor, praying God would plant a seed in their hearts.

Insight

Nothing catches God by surprise. He knows all things and is in control of all things. You can safely trust His sovereign hand.

Psalm 17:1-9

His Loving-Kindness

"Shew thy marvelous loving-kindness, O thou that savest
by thy right hand them which put their trust in thee from
those that rise up against them" (Psalm 17:7, KJV).

The right hand of God is a symbol of His power. He wielded it over Egypt, bringing judgment and destruction. He rescued and delivered His people with a mighty hand. His right hand protects, is our refuge, puts His words in our mouths, and brings us salvation. In today's psalm, the right hand of God brings mercy and loving-kindness.

We only find this word in the Psalms, and it is used only to speak of God. His heart overflows both love and kindness - hence loving-kindness.

God was so good to us as He took us through my mother's memorial service. He had given me time to compose my memories of Mother. Nathan would have to read them for me. Mother had taught two and three-year-olds for many years. One of those children shared at the service. A young mother stood up to say, "I was one of those children she taught and I taught the same songs to my children when they were small."

How very fitting and how it revealed our Lord's loving-kindness.

Insight

Only when we speak of God do we put loving and kindness together. He is both to all of His children.

His Victorious Right Hand

"Sing to the Lord a new song, for he has done marvelous things; his right hand and his holy arm have worked salvation for him. The Lord has made his salvation known" (Psalm 98:1-2).

God bared His arm for us on Calvary and it worked for us a great victory - victory over sin and victory over death and the grave. Death could not hold Jesus in the grave. He broke its bars asunder and came forth alive and well.

There is victory every day all day long. We never need to succumb to the enemy, for he is already a defeated foe. We can live in a victory that has already been won.

"Victory in Jesus" is one of the favorite songs of the men at the prison. It was sung at my dad's memorial service. At my sister's church on Sunday they sang it, plus "When We All Get to Heaven." It seemed God had tailor-made the service for our family. The altar flowers were all zinnias. Mom used to grow them by the basketsful.

Do you need victory today? Believe that Jesus has already won it for you at the cross and in the open tomb. You can say with confidence, "Thanks be to God, which giveth us the victory through our Lord Jesus Christ" (1 Corinthians 15:57, KJV).

Insight

The victory over the enemy is assured. Put on God's armor. Stand strong and true in the lord.

1 Chronicles 29:14-19

All I Have

"O Lord our God, as for all this abundance that we have provided for building you a temple for your Holy Name, it comes from your hand, and all of it belongs to you" (1 Chronicles 29:16).

We only give back to God what He has already given to us. We cannot outgive God.

Our day care income is up this year with four children. This gives us the opportunity to give more to the Lord. Our grandson, Evan, is serving with Child Evangelism Fellowship again this summer doing five-day clubs and witnessing at the fair. We sent him $100. Then at the Gideon convention in June each member was challenged to give $100 for Bibles to be distributed in overseas ministry. Dan and I were delighted to do our part.

Then God started giving back. Sherrie, my single day care mom, has been putting in long hours on her job. She wrote out her check for $100 more than my charge. Then we had applied to a patient assistance program for Dan's arthritis medicine. We will be receiving it free for the next year, a savings of over $800.

Once again we've proven we cannot outgive God. He fills our cup full to overflowing so we can bless others.

Insight

All our resources belong to God. We can only give back to Him what He gave to us in the first place.

DAY 28
Job 2

Good and Adversity

"He said to her, 'You speak as one of the foolish women speaks. Shall we indeed accept good from God, and shall we not accept adversity?' In all this Job did not sin with his lips" (Job 2:10, KJV).

God balances the trials and the blessings in our lives. He took my mother home, but He sent my son to be a comfort and strength in this time of mourning. I can't lean on Dan any more. Rather, he is a care. He is becoming more and more dependent on me, doesn't really want me to leave him alone. But my son has stepped into the gap.

Look for the blessings in your trials, the mercy in the clouds, the calm in the storm. God is always there tempering the trial to make us more like Jesus.

If Dan did not have Alzheimer's, I would never have become part of an Alzheimer's support group. I've met some great people who are all struggling with the same problem. We are rubbing shoulders with a cross section of the world-from an avowed atheist to men and women of faith, and everything in between.

Adversity tenderizes our hearts, broadens our worldview, causes us to touch lives we would otherwise never touch.

Insight

Our trials either become a mirror in which we see ourselves in misery or a window through which God reveals more of Himself.

God's Right Hand

"Though I walk in the midst of trouble, you preserve my life; you stretch out your hand against the anger of my foes, with your right hand you save me" (Psalm 138:7).

The right hand of God is the hand of power. To sit on the right hand of God is to be in the place of power and authority.

David had many enemies. He found himself in need of God's saving power time and again. In the days he was being pursued by King Saul, he found himself on the verge of being caught time and again. Once Saul entered the very cave' where David was hiding. Another time Saul was just around the hill. Still another time David had to flee a city because the people would have turned him over to Saul.

David walked in the midst of trouble and there he experienced God's right hand protecting him, holding back the enemy, and saving his life.

Are you going through a difficult time in your life? Look for the right hand of God holding back the enemy, preserving you in the midst of the trial, and bringing you out safely to the other side.

If God is on our side, we cannot lose. His right hand will bring us through to victory

Insight

God holds all authority. His right hand puts down your enemies. "In all these things we are more than conquerors" (Romans 8:37).

Forgetting God's Hand

"Again and again they put God to the test; they vexed the Holy One of Israel'" They did not remember his power - the day he redeemed them from the oppressor" (Psalm 78:41-42).

When God delivered Israel from Egypt with great signs and wonders, He instituted the Feast of the Passover. It was to be a feast of remembrance of God's great power manifested in their behalf. But, in spite of this, Israel would forget. Later in their history they did not even celebrate the Passover Feast.

God wants us to remember He has been faithful to us in our past. Alan Wright calls them the "God Moments" of our lives, times when God rescued us, met a special need, sent an unexpected blessing, revealed a special word of truth, or took us through a time of adversity. Remembering the "God Moments" gives us hope for the future.

When I face a new need, God helps me find confidence for tomorrow by thinking back to ways He has been faithful in the past. I remember that He has always met my need, never doing the same things twice.

Don't forget God's hand as Israel did. Set your heart to remember and be encouraged.

Insight

Remember the ways God has worked to meet your needs. God's faithfulness in the past gives us hope for tomorrow.

September

DAY 1
Psalm 63

To See His Glory

"I have seen you in the sanctuary and beheld your power and your glory. Because your love is better than life, my lips will glorify you" (Psalm 63:2-3).

David was in the wilderness, probably fleeing from his enemies. He longed to be back home where he could enter the sanctuary and worship God. He longed to see God work in his life in power and glory. He draws near to God in that wilderness and says, "I sing in the shadow of your wings" (v. 7).

How often when we find ourselves in a troubling wilderness, we cry out to God, "Deliver me. Show me Your power and Your glory. Cause me to rejoice."

He answers, "Draw near, dear child. I'm here for you and you will see My power displayed and you will give Me glory."

Sometimes there is a miraculous deliverance and sometimes He simply gives strength to go on. Sometimes things don't change, but God changes us inside, giving new attitudes, and the load is lightened.

My son asked me, "Can you care for Dad joyfully?" Can I? When I face what Alzheimer's is doing to him every day? It is a soul-searching question.

Insight

We long to see God display His power in our lives and He longs to do so, that we may give Him the glory and praise.

John 1:10-16

We Saw His Glory

"The Word became flesh and made his dwelling among us. We have seen his glory, the glory of the One and Only, who came from the Father, full of grace and truth" (John 1:14).

Jesus came from heaven to earth to reveal the Father to us. As we looked in His face, we saw the face of the Father. As we looked at His heart, we saw the heart of God for His children.

We saw His glory when He touched a leper and said, "Be clean." We saw His glory when He touched a blind man and he could see. We saw His glory when He touched a lame man and he could walk. We saw His glory when He rebuked a demon and a child was set free and He helped a father believe. We saw His glory when He tenderly took young children in His arms and held them close to His heart. We saw His glory when He rebuked the religious leaders for their pride and sham of religion. We saw His glory when He forgave them from the cross.

So you want to know God the Father? Get to know Jesus, for He has revealed Him in all His glory. As we observe Jesus' life here on earth as He ministered to others, we see the heart of the Father God for us.

Insight

Our response to seeing the glory of God is a longing to glorify Him by our love for Him and our obedience to His commands.

DAY 3
Psalm 34

Exalt His Name Tog ether

"My soul will boast in the Lord; let the afflicted hear and rejoice. Glorify the Lord with me; let us exalt his name together" (Psalm 34:2-3).

I love to hear how God is working in a person's life. I rejoice to see God putting the pieces of the puzzle together in my life or theirs.

Recently I had a new little girl in my day care. It was working out perfectly, but after only one week she went back to her original sitter. Her practice teaching was put off until fall, so she wanted Jilly back. I could not understand what God was doing. Her coming had been such an answer to prayer, and now she was gone.

Then I had an interview for two little boys. These parents had no problem with my husband's Alzheimer's and chose to leave their two sons with us. If I still had Jilly, I wouldn't have had room for two more children. I began to see what God was doing and the pieces of the puzzle fell into place.

So we rejoice with those who rejoice and we weep with those who weep. We share the trials as well as the triumphs-the joys as well as the sorrows - for God takes us through them all. Together we can exalt His name and give Him glory.

Insight

Praise, no matter what our circumstance, frees God to work. Prayer with praise brings God's grace to us and glory to Himself.

Presented Before His Glory

"To him who is able to keep you from falling and to present you before his glorious presence without fault and with great joy - to the only God our Savior be glory" (Jude 24-25).

When our oldest son was in junior high band their uniform required them all to wear white pants. Imagine, a junior high boy in white pants! I don't believe we ever did get him to a band function spotless.

Yet, amazingly, Jesus Christ is going to present us one day before the presence of His Glory and He is going to see that we are spotless - without fault. What a day that will be for us! And what a day that will be for Him, for His heart will be filled with great joy at our presentation. We are His blood bought children, precious to Him and the delight of His heart.

Once in a rare while, God gives me a day care child who is a real sweetheart. That child brings me much joy and delight. As I hold the little one close, I imagine God holding me close and singing over me: "You are so precious to Me. I love you so much. You bring Me great joy." These words I would sing over my precious toddler. How much this child has taught me about God's love for me.

Insight

Revel in God's great love for you. It is His work to get you ready for your presentation. You don't have to clean yourself up. Simply yield to His work in your life.

DAY 5
Ephesians 3:14-21

The Riches of His Glory

"That he would grant you, according to the riches of his glory, to be strengthened with might by his Spirit in the inner man" (Ephesians 3:16, KJV).

God gives good gifts to His children and one of His greatest gifts is His Holy Spirit who dwells within us and makes the things of Christ real to us. He strengthens us down deep inside, quiets us with His love so we can remain calm and serene no matter what a day brings forth.

He works through the mighty resurrection power of God. He roots and grounds us in the great love of God.

He enables us to grasp the great love of God and experience it in new ways in our lives. He literally fills us up with all the fullness of God.

By His Holy Spirit we can be filled with God's "love, joy, peace, patience, kindness, goodness, faithfulness, gentleness, and self-control" (Galatians 5:22-23).

How does all this come about? By faith. By believing the promises. By depending on the work of the Spirit within, not on ourselves. For if we depend on ourselves, we fail. Only His Spirit enables us to live victoriously all to the glory of God.

Insight

Heaven came down and then glory filled my heart with all that I need to live this day for Jesus.

2 Corinthians 4:1-12

Treasures in Jars of Clay

"God, who said, 'Let light shine out of darkness,' made his light shine in our hearts to give us the light of the knowledge of the glory of God in the face of Christ" (2 Corinthians 4:6).

In Jesus' day people had little clay lamps which filled with oil were used to light their way in the darkness.

We are like those little clay lamps, filled up with the oil of the Holy Spirit. The light of Jesus shines forth from us to the world around us. We may be common clay pots but we contain a treasure - the living Son of God. As others see Christ in us, they are drawn to God and He is glorified.

As we gaze on the face of Jesus our faces begin   to reflect His radiance, His glory. Like Paul, we can rejoice to be that common clay pot in the hand of God used every day to bring blessing to others. No fine china for us, used only on special occasions.

It probably means getting dirty, being washed often, and being poured out in some uncomfortable places where we'd rather not be.

God remembers that we are but common clay. He is aware of our weakness, our humanness. But He fills us up with Himself and when others see the light shining from within us, they know it is Him.

Insight

The glory light of God is best displayed in common clay vessels, full of weakness, but revealing the light shining from within us.

2 Corinthians 4:8-18

Light and Momentary Troubles

"We do not lose heart . . . . For our light and momentary troubles are achieving for us an eternal glory that far outweighs them all" (2 Corinthians 4:16-17).

Paul speaks of being hard pressed, perplexed, persecuted, and struck down. He suffered much for Christ. How did he endure all he went through? By keeping his eyes fixed on Jesus. He looked, not at what was happening around him but on the eternal. His circumstances were only temporary but the unseen was forever. From his heavenly perspective, Paul saw his troubles as light and momentary and bringing him eternal glory.

He also endured because his inner man was being renewed day by day by the Holy Spirit. You see, one of the Spirit's jobs is to strengthen us in our inner person. When God quiets us with His love down deep inside, the storms of life do not shake us. We find strength to endure and go on.

Are you being shaken today? Get alone with God. Let Him quiet you with His love deep inside. Let Him speak peace to your fears and worries. As you bask in the warmth of His love, He will replace your weakness with His strength and you will begin to see your troubles from an eternal perspective.

Insight

No trouble on this earth can erase the glory that God has planned for us through those very troubles.

Let Your Light Shine

"Let your light so shine before men that they may see your good works, and glorify your Father; which is in heaven" (Matthew 5:16, KJV).

What does it mean to let our light shine? Jesus said, "People don't light a lamp and hide it under a bowl. Instead, they put it on a stand and it sheds light to all who are in the house" (see 5:15).

Do we ever try to hide our light? Refuse to let it shine? Cloud it by our disobedience?

Just shine for Jesus. Do what He asks you to do. Shed light in the dark corners where He places you. Do whatever task He places before you. Then what will happen? All around will see Christ in you and will glorify God.

Do you ever hide your light because you are afraid of what people will think and say? Is it hard to shine in your place of work? Your home? Remember the oil lamps we use when we're roughing it? We have to clean the chimney often. God is always in the process of cleaning our chimney so we will shine brightly for Him. God uses us to shine light on people we never dreamed we would touch. Be a shining light for Him.

Insight

God has made you a light in a dark and discouraging place. Ask Him to help you shine out from your stand to all around you.

1 Corinthians 5:12-20

Bought with a Price

"Do you not know that your body is the temple of the Holy Spirit . . . and you are not your own? For you were bought with a price; therefore glorify God in your body" (1 Corinthians 6:19-20, KJV).

Stop and think! God bought you and paid for you with the precious blood of His Son. You now belong to Him body and soul. Join me as I reflect on this awesome truth.

My body has become a temple, a dwelling place of God's Holy Spirit. What kind of house cleaning is He doing?

How do I treat this body that is now His? Exercise it, feed it, clean it?

What about my spirit? How do I feed the spiritual part of me? Exercise it? Clean it?

What kinds of words come out of my mouth? What kind of thoughts do I have?

Is the law of kindness in my tongue? Does the love that the Holy Spirit sheds abroad in my heart spill out to all around me?

Do I reach out with Christ's love to those who do not know Him-nearby and around the world?

I cry out, "Purify me, Lord. I long to live for You with all my heart. May I bring honor to Your name by the way I live."

Insight

Your body and soul belong to God alone. Keep yourself pure so that God may be glorified in you.

2 Corinthians 9

For Your Giving

"Each man should give what he has decided in his heart to give, not reluctantly or under compulsion, for God loves a cheerful giver" (2 Corinthians 9:7-8).

My brother, sister, and I have just sold the family property in California. Each of us received a large sum of money. Now we can give thousands to bless others instead of hundreds. My brother just gave $10,000 to my youngest son, Nathan, a struggling pastor with children in their teens. What an incredible blessing this gift has been to them, and what glory it brings to God.

All three of us will be giving money to God's work here and there. I wonder if our parents can look down from heaven and be pleased with the way their children are handling their inheritance. Do they join us in praising God for His overflowing goodness and give glory to God for the way His kingdom is being blessed around the world?

Whether we give out of our poverty or out of riches, God is pleased, and it brings glory to Him.

Has God challenged you to give recently? Did you obey Him? Your generosity will result in much thanksgiving to God. People will be blessed, and God will be glorified.

Insight

God promises that when we give, it shall be given to us, good measure, pressed down and shaken together. Our cup will overflow.

John 14:1-14

Asking in Jesus' Name

"I will do whatever you ask in my name, so that the Son may bring glory to the Father. You may ask me for anything in my name, and I will do it" (John 14:13-14).

Our prayers in Jesus' name bring glory to God. Jesus encourages us to pray. When the answers come, our hearts are filled with joy and we give praise and thanks to God.

God has delight in answering the prayers of His children. He is generous beyond our imagining, able to do abundantly above anything we ask or think.

A number of years ago we anticipated a move from Weiser, Idaho to Boise. We prayed for three things: the sale of our Weiser home, a job for Dan in Boise, and a home for us there.

In the spring, our home sold. Answer number one. We drove to Boise and bought the first house we looked at. Answer number two. But Dan still did not have a job. The mortgage company gave us 30 days to provide proof of employment. Dan went to Boise, stayed with friends, and hit the streets. A week later he was hired at a door factory in Nampa. Answer number three. God had met our needs but not in the order I thought He should. His way brought the greater glory.

Insight

God moves and works through the prayers of His children, filling our hearts with joy and bringing Him glory.

Bearing Much Fruit

"If you remain in me and my words remain in you, ask whatever you wish, and it will be given you. This is to my Father glory, that you bear much fruit" (John 15:7-8).

In a vineyard, Jesus is the vine, trunk, root, and sap, and as children of God we're part of Him.

The life of the Son of God flows through us producing fruit. Can we clog the channel through sin and disobedience?

How do we stay closely connected to the vine? Through obedience. How do we remain or abide in God's love? By obeying His commands.

God has a plan for our lives and it includes a crop of fruit. So as the Master Gardener, He prunes even fruitful branches so they will bear more fruit. He is totally glorified when we bear much fruit.

But the pruning hurts. The Father allows painful trials in our lives and we cry out, "Why?"

We need to keep our eyes on what the Father is doing - making us more like His Son. He is conforming us into the image of Jesus - making us more compassionate, more patient, more loving, more joyful, more yielded to the Father.

Let's not resist His pruning. Submit to the Father's will. Bear much fruit and glorify Him.

Insight

Remember that the branch can not bear fruit of itself. Apart from being vitally connected to Jesus, we cannot produce life-giving, Christ-exalting fruit.

DAY 13
Romans 5:1-8

Glory in Tribulation

"We glory in tribulations also: knowing that tribulation worketh patience; and patience, experience; and experience hope" (Romans 5:3-4, KJV).

God is glorified as He builds His character in us. The more we become like Jesus, the more God is glorified. Because we know God is at work through whatever He allows to happen in our lives, we can rejoice even in the trials.

When my husband Dan was diagnosed with Alzheimer's, I realized God must have a lot of work to do in the garden of my life. I saw, first of all, He was working on the fruit of gentleness, then patience, and kindness. Caring for Dan will build Christ's character in me in ways nothing else could. God has special blessings all along this path I am traveling.

I don't want to fail this test but Dan does things that drive me crazy. There are times I lose it and even yell at him. Sometimes I don't know whether to laugh or cry as I see his confusion, whether to help or let him muddle through on his own.

But this I know, God is building His character in me, and every day I have opportunity to become more like Jesus.

Insight

It is not in the easy places of life that character is built, but when the going gets tough and we need to depend on Jesus.

1 Peter 4:1-11

God Given Ability

"If anyone ministers, let him do it with the ability which God supplies, that in all things God may be glolified through Jesus Christ" (1 Peter 4:11, KJV).

Is God asking you to step out of your comfort zone and do something for Him? It can be scary and decidedly uncomfortable - but oh the joy when you obey!

Do you feel someone else is better qualified for the ministry, but God is calling you? Go and do it with the ability God has given you. He loves to work through our weaknesses.

When I was first asked to go to a woman in prison, I said, "No." Another volunteer went and I missed God's blessing. I felt very inadequate. What would I say? How could I help? Yet as God gave me other opportunities, I went and found that the Holy Spirit gave me the words I needed.

Today some of my most precious times are with the women at the Community Work Center as we study God's Word together.

If God is calling you to minister to someone, go. Obedience brings great joy, and you have the best helper in the Holy Spirit.

Insight

God delights in working through our weakness, giving us the words and ability to serve Him that He may be glorified.

John 11:1-44

Sickness for God's Glory

"The sisters sent word to Jesus, 'Lord, the one you love is sick.' . . . Jesus said, 'This sickness will not end in death. No, it is for God's glory so that God's Son may be glorified through it'" (John 11:3-4).

Mary and Martha's brother Lazarus was sick, so they sent an urgent message to Jesus. They knew He had healed others, so they were certain He would come immediately and heal their brother. But days went by, and no Jesus. Lazarus died and was buried. By the time Jesus arrived, Lazarus had been in the grave four days.

Both Martha and Mary accused Jesus, "If only You had come my brother wouldn't have died!"

Jesus was deeply touched by their grief even as He was led to Lazarus' tomb. He commanded them to open the tomb and called Lazarus to come forth alive. What rejoicing and what glory to God as he was resurrected!

Is all sickness for the glory of God? Certainly some is. Can we go through cancer treatment to the glory of God? Two of my friends have done so.

Is my husband's Alzheimer's for the glory of God? Certainly He can be glorified in how we go through these days. Do others see attitudes that lift up Jesus? I certainly hope so.

Insight

Lazarus' illness was for the glory of God. So may ours be as we check our attitudes and align them with His will for us.

The Day of Trouble

"Call upon me in the day of trouble; I will deliver thee and thou shalt glorify me" (Psalm 50:15, KJV).

The day of our greatest trouble came in Dan's contracting business. Our pastor advised Dan to go to a lawyer. The lawyer said that if it went to court we would lose. Dan and I both turned to the Lord and cried out to Him in the words of this great promise in Psalm 50:15. Dan had made several mistakes and we were facing an impossible situation of our own making - or so we thought.

As Dan returned to work on the remodel, our client dismissed him, and we were free. We only had thousands of dollars to pay the bank and lumberyards. We would sell our home to clear these debts.

This day of dire trouble and God's deliverance became a major turning point in our lives. God was uprooting us and moving us to Boise where we would have a more fruitful prison ministry.

Who could foresee that God would take a time of trouble and turn it into a time of blessing in our lives and to many others through our years of prison ministry?

Insight

God brings great glory to Himself as He takes our times of trouble and brings much good out of them to others and us.

Our Wonder Working God

"Who among the gods is like you, O Lord? Who is like you-majestic in holiness, awesome in glory, working wonders?" (Exodus 15:11)

How often I have prayed, "Lord, do a wonder for me as You did for Israel long ago."

We were facing losing two children from our day care when school started. I was longing for another infant to care for. But who would trust us with their newborn when I have a husband with Alzheimer's?

Then a friend called to ask if I had an opening for an infant. Of course I said, "Yes." It seemed a young unwed mother would be moving from California to Idaho to be near her family. She needed day care for her four-month-old baby. A phone call later committed me to care for this wee one. Before Chelsea even moved from California, she landed a job in Boise - not 10 minutes from my day care. Soon she had an apartment close by also.

God had put it all together so quickly for her and for me. We had the baby two weeks before school started. Now we have a special ministry to this young mother and her baby. Our wonder working God had perfectly met our needs.

Insight

God delights to do wonders for His children, and we delight to give Him all the credit for what He does.

DAY 18
John 17:1-19

Jesus Glorified His Father

"I have brought you glory on earth by completing the work you gave me to do. And now Father, glorify me in your presence with the glory I had with you before the world began" (John 17:4-5).

Every step He took from the day of His birth to day of His death, Jesus glorified His Father. He did always those things that pleased the Father. He was the beloved Son.

As He prayed this prayer in John 17, He was saying, "My work is done and I am ready to lay down My life now for all humankind. I've taught these 12 men for three years and prepared them for their worldwide task."

"In obedience to You, I've healed the sick, cleansed the leper, forgiven the prostitute, raised the dead to life again, made the blind to see, the lame to walk, the deaf to hear. I've taught by story and example about the kingdom of God and You, My Heavenly Father. Now it is time for the final great act - My death and resurrection. Then I will be home with You."

When the day comes for me to meet Jesus, I hope I can tell Him, "I've done all You asked me to do."

Will Jesus be able to say to you and me, "Well done, good and faithful servant"?

Insight

May our lives, like Jesus' life, bring great glory to God on this earth. May we do all He asks of us.

God's Tradeoff

"To give unto them beauty for ashes, the oil of joy for mourning, the garment of praise for the spirit of heaviness . . . that he might be glorified" (Isaiah 61:3, KJV).

Jesus came and did all that Isaiah had prophesied. He healed the brokenhearted, preached the good news to the poor, released the prisoners, comforted those that mourned.

When you have nothing to give Him but the ashes of your mistakes, He can bring beauty out of them. He is always ready to exchange our mourning for His joy, to put praise in our hearts and mouths in the place of our despair. When He does, how we will honor Him and magnify Him!

God was with me in the dark days of depression after the sudden death of my father. He took what I considered my greatest failure and used it to minister to many, for the issue of Anchor on suffering that came out of those days brought the most reader response ever to any I had written.

Isn't that just like God? Redeeming our mistakes and bringing good out of them? Taking our failures and making them a blessing to others? Give God the ashes of your life that He may replace them with a crown of beauty.

Insight

God's great exchange - giving us something beautiful and good for the ugly things in our lives.

Romans 3:21-26

Falling Short of God's Glory

"For all have sinned and fall short of the glory of God, and are justified freely by his grace through the redemption that came by Christ Jesus" (Romans 3:23-24).

No matter how hard we try, we cannot measure up to God's goodness. We fall far short of what we need to enter heaven's glory.

But there is One who has done it all for us Jesus, the Son of God. He died on the cross, taking on Himself all our sin and shame. He, who was sinless and had never done any wrong, paid for all our wrongs. When we accept Him and all He has done for us, then His righteousness is put on our account. We are justified - made right; our debt paid in full. We are made free and whole, on our way to heaven.

You know you've fallen short of God's glory. You've made too many wrong choices. Now will you make one right choice? Accept Jesus as your Savior today.

He promises to accept you just as you are, warts, wrinkles, and all. He will justify you "freely by his grace." He will wipe the slate clean, set your feet on the narrow path of eternal life, and put a song in your heart.

Insight

Jesus tells us that narrow is the way that leads to life. Only a few will find it. Be one of the few.

DAY 21
Ephesians 1:3-13

To the Praise of His Glory

"In him we were also chosen, having been predestinated according to the . . . purpose of his will in order that we . . . might be for the praise of his glory" (Ephesians 1:11-12).

How does God view us? First, He thought of us before the foundation of the world and chose us to be His very own.

Then He planned to adopt us into His family before we were ever born.

He accepted us "in the Beloved." This is not a place but a person, God's own dear Son. He accepted us just as we are.

Why did He do all this for us who are so undeserving? That we might be to the praise of His glory.

He sealed us with His Holy Spirit, the earnest of our inheritance. We are His forever, and the Son will present us faultless before the Father's throne one day with great joy (see Jude 24). What a day that will be!

God's plans and purposes embrace our lives here on earth and all of eternity. Those plans are good and perfect. They all fit into a pattern in the unique tapestry of our lives, the dark threads as well as the gold threads.

Insight

God's plans and thoughts are so much higher than ours are. Our only need is to trust our Heavenly Father's love.

1 Corinthians 1:20-31

God Chose the Weak

"He chose the lowly things of this world and the despised things - and the things that are not - to nullify the things that are, so that no one may boast before him" (1 Corinthians 1:28-29).

God chooses to work through our weaknesses. Do you feel like a nobody, and that God couldn't possibly use you? Rejoice! You are the very one God wants to use.

You say, "I can't sing, can't speak, can't lead." Believe God has a place in His vineyard that only you can fill, a task only you can do, a life only you can touch. Humbly offer yourself to God and let Him use you. He only asks for a willing heart that will respond to His leading.

When God called me to prison ministry, I told Him that He had the wrong person. I had never been where they are. But Dan and I stepped willingly through the doors God opened, and we were filled with joy. Dan went on to have a wide and effective ministry, even becoming a prison chaplain for a year until Alzheimer's struck him. We still go in together and lead a prayer group each Sunday. Dan can no longer sign his name or talk very well, but his compassionate spirit still shines through.

Insight

Remember God chooses to work through our weakness so that all the glory will go to Him.

DAY 23
2 Corinthians 3:7-18

Changed into His Image

"We, who with unveiled faces all reflect the Lord's glory, are being transformed into His likeness with ever-increasing glory, which comes from the Lord, who is the Spirit" (2 Corinthians 3:18).

As the moon reflects the glory of the sun, our faces reflect the glory of the Son of God. When people look at you, do they see Jesus in your eyes, your smile? Do they hear His kindness in your voice, sense His joy in your spirit?

We will be changed into His likeness as we gaze on His face and keep focused on our Savior.

How are we going to keep focused on Him day after day? By seeking His face in His Word. Ask the Holy Spirit to make the truth a reality in your life. Spend some time quietly listening for His voice to apply the Word to your life.

We can easily lose our focus. Our lives become crowded with busyness and our time with God is shut out. We slip and fall and don't get back in God's grace. Financial problems begin to choke us. Illness lays us low. It's hard to focus when we are in pain. We grow so tired we can hardly go on another day.

Jesus left the crowd to be alone with His Father. Is He calling you to draw away also?

Insight

As we keep focused on Jesus, we are being transformed into His image moment by moment, day by day.

2 Corinthians 12:1-10

Boasting in Weakness

"He said to me, 'My grace is sufficient for you, for my power is made perfect in weakness.' Therefore I will boast all the more gladly about my weakness" (2 Corinthians 12:9).

Some time ago my brother was ill, and today's verse was what I prayed for him. I would phone him every Sunday and pray with him. I watched as God used those days of my brother's weakness to touch one life after another.

He is a professor and dean of students at a Bible college. Hundreds began to pray for him. He continued teaching, though he was not sure he could get through the day, and God touched lives.

My brother says he was not sure that he ever reached the point Paul reached where he could boast in his weakness, but God continued to touch lives through him.

God told Paul, "My grace is sufficient for you for my power is made perfect in weakness." Are you, am I -willing to learn the reality of this truth? To actually boast in difficulties, hardships, weaknesses? When we realize how weak we are, how much we need God's grace and strength, then we become strong in the strength of the Lord, and God is glorified.

Insight

God not only works through weaknesses, but when we are at our weakest, God shows His strength.

Philippians 2:5-11

Humbled and Exalted

"At the name of Jesus every knee should bow, in heaven and in earth, and under the earth, and every tongue confess that Jesus Christ is Lord, to the glory of God the Father" (Philippians 2:10-11).

Jesus is God, and He has a glory that we are yet to see. But He laid aside that glory to come to earth as a helpless babe and be made in the likeness of men. He became a servant to all-to the poorest of the poor, the lame, the blind, the leper, the tax collector, the prostitute. He reached out and touched us in our need.

At the Last Supper He took the place of the lowest servant, kneeling down and washing His disciples' feet. Then He said to us, "Do as I have done." If I am to have the mind of Christ, there is no one too lowly for me to serve.

Jesus was humble and obedient even to death on a cross. Then came His resurrection and exaltation. One day every knee will bow before Him to the glory of God. He stepped down from His glory as the Son of God and returned to His glory.

Humility comes before honor. This is true for us as well. God tells us to humble ourselves and He will lift us up (1 Peter 5:5).

Insight

When we have the mind of Christ, we serve humbly and willingly all God puts in our path.

Suffering Before Glory

"Now if we are children, then we are heirs - heirs of God and co-heirs with Christ, if indeed we share in his suffering in order that we may also share in his glory" (Romans 8:17).

God elevates us from servant to friend to child of God. So we call God our Father by the Spirit who indwells us. We can run into our "Abba's" arms at any time. His ears are open to our cries and His heart is touched by our pain.

We become heirs of God, inheriting all that God has planned in heaven for us. We cannot begin to conceive what God has prepared for those who love Him.

But first we are going to go through some suffering here on earth. "Although He was a Son, he learned obedience from what he suffered" (Hebrews 5:8). If Jesus learned obedience through suffering, why do we think we will escape? But Paul adds, "Our present sufferings are not worth comparing with the glory that will be revealed in us" (Romans 8:18).

It will be worth it all when we stand before His throne one day. So we can hold our heads up and thank Him for the pain, quit complaining and feeling sorry for ourselves.

Insight

Our sufferings on this earth are building up for us an eternal glory that far outweighs them all.

Suffering for God's Glory

"Neither this man nor his parents sinned," said Jesus, 'but this happened so that the work of God might be displayed in his life'" (John 9:3).

One of the ideas in this world is that suffering is a result of sin in our lives.

When the disciples saw the blind man, they asked Jesus, "Who did this sin? This man or his parents?" "Neither," Jesus answered. "This blindness is for the glory of God."

When we were young marrieds, Dan was kicked by a cow and had his knee torn up. Some believers who observed his accident said, "He must be out of fellowship with the Lord. God allowed this to happen to bring him back." This is not always a true observation, though it did cause Dan to walk more closely with the Lord.

In the case of the blind man, he was blind so Jesus could make him see and bring glory to God.

Job's friends thought his troubles were because of sin in his life, but they were wrong.

I can care for Dan in a manner that glorifies God or I can feel sorry for myself. Much better that others give glory to God for the way we are walking through these days.

Insight

Some suffering is a result of sin, but other suffering is simply for the glory of God.

Philippians 1:3-11

Living to the Glory of God

"This is my prayer: that your love may abound more and more in knowledge and depth of insight , so that you may be able to discern what is best and may be pure and blameless" (Philippians 1:9-10).

Paul prayed such wonderful prayers for other believers. They make good prayers for us to pray also.

Paul surely had the mind of Christ when he wrote other believers, "I pray for you with joy. I'm confident God will complete the work He is doing in your life. I have you in my heart and I long for you. I pray that your love would abound more and more, that you may be pure and filled with the fruits of righteousness."

As I wrote to prisoners with whom I correspond, I shared that was how I thought of them and prayed for them.

Then I turned my thoughts toward God. He said to me, "I have you in My heart and I pray for you with joy." We know Jesus prays for us and the Holy Spirit prays for us. How do you think they are praying? Maybe much like today's prayer in Philippians and oh so much more. I wonder, what kind of persons will we be if God's prayers for us are answered?

Insight

It is awesome to think the Trinity is praying for us and those prayers will be answered.

Glory at His Birth

"An angel of the Lord appeared to them and the glory of the Lord shone around them. . . . But the angel said to them, '. . . I bring you good news of great joy'" (Luke 2:9-10).

When God's Son came to earth, His birth announcement was surrounded with glory.

The shepherds on the hillside were murmuring and nodding around their fire when a brilliant light burst around them. Heaven's glory filled their sight and heaven's chorus filled their ears. They were terrified.

But the angel spoke, "Don't be afraid. A wondrous thing has happened this night. A Savior has been born. You will find the baby wrapped in swaddling clothes and lying in a manger."

Then the angels sang praises to God and left the stunned shepherds trying to find their voices. "Let's go see this baby," they said.

How will I react when I actually see the shining glory of my Lord? Will I be struck dumb, or will words of praise pour from my mouth?

We see God's glory every day in creation, but for now it is veiled. Some day we'll see it in all its shining beauty. We will fall before Him with love, and praise, and worship.

Insight

A vision of the glory of God transforms the viewer. One is never the same again.

Luke 23:44-49

Glory in His Death

"Jesus called out . . . , 'Father, into your hands I commit my spirit.' The centurion, seeing what had happened, praised God and said, 'Surely this was a righteous man'" (Luke 23:46-47).

Jesus brought heaven's glory to earth in His birth and brought glory to His Father in the agony of His death. Though His death was unspeakably ugly, He died with dignity.

Many stood there that day watching Him die and heard the words from His lips, "Father, forgive them for they know not what they do." They heard Him welcome a thief into His kingdom, make provision for His mother, cry out in agony, "My God, My God, why have You forsaken Me?" and at the end, "It is finished."

All this so impressed a centurion standing nearby that he gave praise to God saying, "Surely this was a righteous man!"

Jesus' work of redemption was done. His Father was glorified.

In heaven the praise song will ring out through out eternity in glorious celebration, "Worthy is the Lamb, who was slain, to receive power and wealth and wisdom and strength and honor and glory and praise" (Revelation 5:12).

Insight

Whether we live or whether we die, may it be our determination to glorify God with our lives.

October

Remember God's Miracles

"I will remember the deeds of the Lord; yes, I will remember your miracles of long, ago. I will meditate on all your works and consider all your mighty deeds" (Psalm 77:11-12).

When the going gets tough and things are difficult, we need to remember. Remember how God rescued us in the past. Remember His faithfulness to meet our needs when it looked impossible. Remember how He has kept His promises.

When we remember past miracles we are encouraged to trust Him for today's problems. We need to apply the character of God to our problem. Too often our minds pray from the problem to God. We are consumed with our pain when we need to fill our minds with God's loving-kindness and mercies.

When I knew I was losing my husband Dan to Alzheimer's I cried out to God, weeping and praying through the early morning hours when I could not sleep. I was consumed with the pain. Then I chose to stop focusing on my loss and to begin focusing on the incredible mercy of God. That was a turning point for me. Oh, the pain was still there, but I found so much to be thankful for as I rested in the arms of my Savior.

Insight

It pays to remember who God is and how He has helped us in the past. Then we are confident that He will take us through our tomorrows.

God Remembers Us

"As a father has compassion on his children, so the Lord has compassion on those who fear him; for he knows how we are formed, he remembers that we are dust" (Psalm 103:13-14).

When our children are hurting, we hurt with them. We cry out to God in their behalf, asking for His grace and mercy to be poured out on them.

When we are hurting, God's heart is touched and He hurts with us. As we call on Him, He moves to rescue us from our trouble.

He never forgets that He formed us out of clay. He is completely aware of our humanity and our inherent weakness. He feels our discouragement and moves to lift us up. Lovingly He takes our mistakes and failures and redeems them, even bringing good out of messes we have made.

Do not be discouraged when you fail God by stumbling over the rocks in your path or getting off the path completely. He will keep putting road blocks in your way to turn you back to Himself. Remember that you cannot sink lower than His protective arms, for they are always under you. He is the lifter up of those who are down. Remembering our human weakness, He is patient and gentle with us.

Insight

When we forget God remembers. When we fall down, God is ready to pick us up and set us on the right path again.

God Forgets Our Sins

"Remember these things, O Jacob . . . . I have made you . . . . I will not forget you. I have swept away your offenses like a cloud, your sins like the morning mist" (Isaiah 44:21-22).

God remembers His children but He forgets our sins, sweeps them away, throws them in the deepest sea and puts up a "No fishing" sign. Sins, once forgiven, are under the blood forever and will never come back to haunt us. We are able to move forward in a new freedom to love and serve Him with the rest of our lives.

This is a wonderful truth for any of us, but especially for the man or woman who has made a mistake that sent them to prison. Their experience of incarceration often turns them to God. They are redeemed and leave prison to serve God with all their hearts.

God is always ready to forgive - His arms are open wide to the prodigal. He is ready to forgive and forget, to reinstate you into the family of God. He can still use you, no matter how great a sin you have committed. He is the God of new beginnings. The promise He made to Israel long ago extends to us: "I will forgive their wickedness and will remember their sins no more" (Hebrews 8:12).

Insight

God welcomes us with open arms when we turn back to Him. He forgives and forgets our sin and waywardness.

When We Can't Sleep

"On my bed I remember you; I think of you through the watches of the night. Because you are my help, I sing in the shadow of your wings" (Psalm 63:6-7).

What do you do when you can't sleep? I weep and cry out to God because when I am wakeful it is usually because I am facing a crisis.

This was true in December 2005 when I was losing my husband Dan. For two nights I wept and prayed through the hours until dawn. Then on Christmas morning God led me to Psalm 63. I determined to sing in the shadow of God's wings even as my heart was grieving.

On Christmas night our youngest son Nathan flew out from Wisconsin. He borrowed a guitar and we sang songs of praise around Dan's bed.

Four days later, on December 29, Dan graduated to glory. We were surrounded with godly nurses, aides, and a wonderful hospice team. I stayed under those wings of God, close to His heartbeat of love for me, singing through my tears.

No matter why sleep eludes us we have a choice: to center on our heartache or to focus on the Lord and His love and understanding of our needs. We will find Him faithful to uphold us.

Insight

When you can't sleep, do you turn your thoughts to God and His character? Do you pour out your heart and give thanks for His incredible mercy?

Hebrews 13:1-6

Remember to Entertain Strangers

"Keep on loving each other as brothers. Do not forget to entertain strangers, for by so doing some people have entertained angels without knowing it" (Hebrews 13:1-2).

When Daniel, our firstborn, was a toddler and I was expecting Jonathan, we were running a ranch for troubled boys in Placerville, California. Strangers often stopped by to visit the ranch and observe the work going on there.

One day an older couple stopped and toured the ranch. It seemed an ordinary encounter. Then a few weeks later a box arrived filled with baby things for our soon-arriving baby. Included was a check to buy a new dresser, which we really needed. A women's group had put these things together for us. Truly we had entertained angels unaware.

Hospitality has been a large part of our lives. We have been blessed as we often entertained visiting missionaries and other servants of God.

Sometimes, though, we have opportunity to welcome "ordinary" people, like the couple who visited the ranch. God has a special outcome when we reach out to include them. He says, "Accept one another, then, just as Christ accepted you, in order to bring praise to God" (Romans 15:7).

Insight

God blesses you when you open your home to others. You might even entertain angels unaware.

Remember to Share

"And do not forget to do good and to share with others,
for with such sacrifices God is pleased" (Hebrews 13:16).

I love to share with others. A special joy comes when we send a meal to a family with a newborn baby or after surgery, or to take fresh baked cookies to a doctor's office.

Recently I gave a gift from my inheritance to a home for women coming out of prison. I have a heart for this ministry as I work with women on the inside and know it is hard for them as they get out. A month later my sister sent a check. I also received a letter from a family in Pennsylvania containing a check from their inheritance. The amazing thing is that their envelope was postmarked five months before I received it. Delivery was held up, but it was God's perfect timing for me. I needed the money when it arrived more than when it was mailed.

Sharing brings pleasure to both the receiver and the giver, but that's not all. Today's verse comes from a passage about worship-no longer sacrificing animals, but pouring out praises to God and sharing with others, worship that gives God pleasure.

Insight

God is pleased when we share. What a wonderful incentive to reach out to others in practical expressions of our worship!

James 1:19-27

The Life God Blesses

"The man who looks intently into the perfect law that gives freedom, and continues to do this, not forgetting what he has heard, but doing it-he will be blessed in what he does" (James 1:25).

My prodigal came home. John's divorce was final, his job was ending, and he needed to move. So he came home to live with us, bringing his 20-year-old son with him. He quit drinking three weeks before coming, and doesn't miss it. He started going to church and growth group with us and now his life is back on track with God.

Four days after moving in with us, he was hired in a metal fabricating plant in a job he loves and working with a great crew.

He started giving a portion to God out of his paycheck even though he was deeply in debt.

A month later my husband got sick, spent five days in the hospital, then was moved to a nursing home. Five weeks later he was gone to glory.

There is no doubt in John's mind that God brought him home to take care of me and He is blessing John for his obedience.

God promises to bless us when we do not forget what we have heard in His Word but put it in practice in our daily living.

Insight

God sees it all - every desire to remember His Word and obey it, and He promises to bless us when we actually do it.

Philippians 3:12-21

Forgetting What Is Behind

"Forgetting what is behind and straining toward what is ahead, I press on toward the goal to win the prize for which God has called me heavenward in Christ Jesus" (Philippians 3:13-14).

Some things we need to remember and other things we need to forget.

For example, remember God's commands and obey Him. Remember to praise and thank Him every day. Remember to reach out to help others. Remember to listen to God and do what pleases Him.

But we need to forget past mistakes and failures. We can learn from them but put them behind us as we move on. Past mistakes need not cripple our future. We can let God redeem them, bring good out of them, and shape us into the image of Christ.

As we stood at my husband's graveside, my brother challenged us to move on into the future, saying, "There's still work for us to do."

At first I could not go back to the prison. I just didn't have the heart to go without Dan, as it was a ministry we had together. Two months later I returned to continue the prayer group we had started five years ago. The door was wide open, and the men were glad to have me back.

Insight

There is a time to put the past behind us and by faith move toward our future with God.

God Remembers the Humble

"Declare among the people his doings. When he maketh inquisition for blood, he remembereth them: he forgetteth not the cry of the humble" (Psalm 9:11-12).

When we realize how poor and needy we are and call on God, He hears and remembers us. We are helped when we also remember:

Remember how He heard the cry of the Hebrew slaves in Egypt and moved to rescue them.

Remember when the Israelites cried out under the oppression of the Midianites. He raised up a deliverer in Gideon.

Remember too in Jehoshaphat's reign when the coalition of armies came against Judah. God heard their cries and told them what to do. Their praises brought victory as God destroyed their enemies.

Remember that God heard the prayer of Daniel in a den of lions and shut the lions' mouths.

Remember that God heard Paul and Silas singing at midnight and He opened the prison doors.

God does not forget the prayers of His humble servants. He hears, rescues, and delivers them.

Remembering leads us to believe God's promise to hear us when we call out to Him in humility and honesty, pouring out our hearts to Him.

Insight

"God lives in a high and holy place, but also with him who is contrite and lowly in spirit, to revive the spirit of the lowly and to revive the heart of the contrite" (Isaiah 57:15).

DAY 10

Isaiah 49:14-21

God Never Forgets

"Can a mother forget the baby at her breast? . . . Though she may forget, I will not forget you! See, I have engraved you on the palms of my hands" (Isaiah 49:15-16).

We may forget a birthday, an appointment, or fail to remember a face, but God can never forget you and me.

Have you seen someone write a date or phone number on their hand so they won't forget something important? Well, God is saying, "I have written you on the palms of my hands. Your name and image are always before Me. I won't forget you. My thoughts are ever toward you."

"Then why is God silent?" you ask. "Why have all these things happened to me? Where is His protection?"

God gives us promises, not explanations. Don't lose your faith when the storms of life come. Cling to His promises. In desperate times count on His everlasting love for you. Begin to thank God for who He is and what He did in Bible times. Remember that He cannot change. He is still rescuing His children in time of trouble. He invites you, "Call upon me in the day of trouble: I will deliver you, and you will honor me" (Psalm 50:15).

Insight

God has written our names in blood on His own Son's hands. He simply cannot forget us after paying such a price.

2 Timothy 1:3-14

My Maker Is My Husband

"You will forget the shame of your youth and remember no more the reproach of your widowhood. For your Maker is your husband - the Lord Almighty is his name" (Isaiah 54:4-5).

Walking in the shoes of widowhood is uncomfortable at first. Eventually, I trust I will get used to it.

I feel vulnerable without Dan by my side.

For now my Maker is my special protection day by day.

I am amazed how God sent my son home to live with me just two and a half months before He took Dan home. Family property in California sold in September and I received my inheritance. When I had to place Dan at Life Care in December, the funds were available to pay for his care. God so perfectly timed the events of the past year that I can only praise Him for His loving care for my needs.

No matter where you are in your life, you can count on God to remember your inner needs. He is the special protector of the widow and fatherless, but He will never forget any of His children. He understands intimately our loneliness and heart needs. He moves in compassion to bring heart healing. Our part is to come to Him honestly admitting our dependence on Him.

Insight

Truly God is the special protector of the widow and fatherless. But He also provides for us whatever our need when we depend on Him.

John 14:15-31

When We Need Reminders

"The Counselor, the Holy Spirit, whom the Father will send in my name, will teach you all things and will remind you of everything I have said to you" (John 14:26).

Everything we read or hear falls down into our subconscious. That's why it is so important to store God's Word there. It builds an effective buffer zone between our conscious and subconscious minds and gives the Holy Spirit something to work with when we are in trouble. He can bring back to our conscious mind just the word of encouragement we need at the moment.

God gave us the Holy Spirit to remind us of truth we need to live by, to counsel and comfort us, to open our eyes to new truth from His Word. He is Teacher, Comforter, Counselor, Friend, and Helper to us.

We often need reminders from the Holy Spirit-in times of family disagreements, when we are being treated unfairly at work, or are under pressure to make a decision and need guidance. Our needs go on and on. At such times the Holy Spirit will be faithful to remind us of Scripture we have treasured or will lead us to discover new truths in the Word to meet our need.

Insight

When Jesus left this earth, He sent the Holy Spirit in His place to be every thing we need to live for Him.

2 Timothy 1:3-14

Remembering to Pray

"I thank God, whom I serve . . . as night and day I constantly remember you in my prayers. Recalling your tears, I long to see you, so that I may be filled with joy" (2 Timothy 1:3-4).

Paul was closely attached to Timothy, his son in the faith. He prayed for him day and night. He remembered how they had parted in tears and he longed to embrace him again in joy.

I hate good-byes and always cry. I love arrivals because they bring joy. With my family scattered across the country, those arrivals are too few.

I pray for my loved ones every day, but when someone I love is in crisis, I know what it is to pray day and night. My heart is so burdened that I intercede for that one constantly.

I'm thankful for all the prayer that went up for our family as we went through Dan's homegoing. We were remembered before the throne constantly, and God sustained us, pouring out His incredible mercy on us and surrounding us with His loving-kindness.

Let's remember to pray for others. It's a great privilege to enter God's presence and intercede for them. Our prayers may be the very thing that God will use to see them through their crisis.

Insight

Prayers of intercession bring God's power and blessing to the lives of His children.

Remember Jesus' Promise

"In everything I did, I showed you that by this kind of hard work we must help the weak, remembering the words the Lord Jesus himself said: 'It is more blessed to give than to receive'" (Acts 20:35).

God has a giving heart. Out of His great love and goodness He gives generously to His children.

He pours out His blessings day after day and fills our cup of joy to overflowing. As His children, He encourages us to be giving, to have a heart of compassion for those in need.

"Give and it shall be given you. A good measure, pressed down, shaken together and running over, will be poured into your lap. For with the measure you use, it will be measured to you" (Luke 6:38).

Follow this promise and God will bless you. As you give in faith, you will discover God has a bigger shovel. We simply cannot outgive Him. He always remembers His promise and is amazingly creative in the ways He gives back to us.

I've tested this promise over and over and can report amazing experiences of God's blessing to both the receiver and the giver. As we draw close to God, He opens our hearts to see needs. So don't forget to give even out of your need. No one is too poor to give something.

Insight

God has a special place in His heart for the poor and needy, broken and wounded. So should we, His children.

Put Yourself in Their Place

"Remember those in prison as if you were their fellow prisoners, and those who are mistreated as if you yourselves were suffering" (Hebrews 13:3).

Dan and I were prison volunteers here in Boise for the last 20 years. Prison volunteers are known for their bleeding hearts, as we care for the men and women we minister to. At the very beginning we were taught to be "trust-suspicious," not to believe everything we are told because many will take advantage of us. The danger increases now that I'm a widow, yet I am confident God will protect me.

Are we to risk caring for those in prison? Yes. Are we to care for the mistreated? Yes. Are we to care for the widow and fatherless. Yes.

I took Anita into my home straight from the work center. Two weeks later she told me that she had to appear in court in California. She left never to return. A year later I learned she had lied to me and broken her probation. I had done what I felt God wanted me to do. Now it was in His hands.

When we obey God, He takes responsibility for the consequences of our obedience. Our part is to respond to His desire that we reflect His love to others who have needs.

Insight

Reaching out in love and compassion is never wrong in God's eyes. He rewards us when we take the risk and trust Him for the results.

Deuteronomy 6:1-12

The Test of Prosperity

"When the Lord your God brings you into the land . . .
then when you eat and are satisfied, be careful that you do
not forget the Lord who brought you out of Egypt" (Deuteronomy 6:10-12).

When we go through trials and difficulties, we stay close to
the Lord because we need Him so desperately.

But when things are going well, we tend to get careless in
our prosperity. We tend to put God on the back burner and
slack off on prayer and study of the Word.

Moses warned Israel, "When you come into the land and
settle down in that new home, when your herds multiply and
you have a bumper crop, don't forget who gave it all to you."

The test of prosperity is much harder than the test of adversity. When we are desperate, we seek God, knowing we have
nowhere else to go. But when things are going well, we tend to
forget Him, assuming we can manage everything on our own.

When I received my inheritance, my greatest fear was that I
would do something foolish and not be wise with this money.
God has guided me through each decision and even my sons
said, "You did good, Mom," when I made my car purchase.

Insight

*The harder test is prosperity, for we tend to forget God. Adversity forces us to seek God and acknowledge our complete
dependence on Him.*

Divine Testing

"Remember how the Lord your God led you . . . to humble you and to test you in order to know what was in your heart, whether or not you would keep his commands" (Deuteronomy 8:2).

Dan and I had the privilege of celebrating 50 years of marriage. All the family came home, and we had a wonderful weekend together. Six months later, Dan would be gone. But those happy memories of that weekend would carry us through Dan's homegoing. The actual events of that weekend celebration would prepare us for Dan's memorial service.

It is good to remember how God has worked in our lives in the past. How He has met our needs in one crisis after another. How He has answered prayer, taught us, encouraged us, carried us through illness and loss of a business.

Why do the tests come? To test our faith, to see if it's based on solid rock or sifting sand, to burn away the dross and bring us forth as pure gold. To see if we will trust God when the going gets rough.

Remembering is good! Don't fall apart when tests come. Rely on God's unchanging love. Cling to His promises. Recall the many times He has been faithful to you, and depend on Him for the future.

Insight

Remembering how God has worked in your life in the past gives you encouragement for today and tomorrow.

Numbers 15:37-41

Why the Tassels?

"You will have these tassels to look at and so you will remember all the commands of the Lord, that you may obey them" (Numbers 15:39).

God gave Israel many ways to be reminded of His commands so that they would obey them.

One way was to use blue thread in the tassels on their clothes. Every time they looked at their robe they would be reminded to obey God.

They also put Scriptures in little boxes and put them on the doorframes of their houses. God instructed Moses to put His truth in a song and teach it to Israel. Words in music tend to stay with us and are easily brought back to our minds.

We can do the same thing today. We can put Scripture reminders on our walls, in our wallets and on our computer screens. We can listen to the truth in song as we drive or do routine tasks. Surrounding ourselves with reminders like these can be very powerful.

One of the ways I'm moving on from Dan's death is by filling my house with praise music from morning till night. Words of one song have especially worked their way into my heart - "God has no problems, only plans."

Insight

Let's constantly surround ourselves with reminders of who God is, what He does, and what He wants us to do.

Genesis 9:1-17

A Reminder in the Sky

"Whenever I bring clouds over the earth, and the rainbow appears in the clouds, I will remember my covenant between me and you and all living creatures of every kind" (Genesis 9:14-15).

Whenever I see a rainbow, I think of God and His promise. But God didn't put the rainbow in the sky only for us to enjoy but to remind Himself of His covenant. Does God need a reminder? Hardly!

Yet somewhere in the world there is a rainbow every day. God's promises are the solid rock on which our faith stands.

How do we get through those stormy periods of darkness when we can't feel His presence? We rest on His everlasting arms that are underneath us. We can never fall out of them. We can echo the psalmist's cry, "Why are you downcast, O my soul? Why so disturbed within me? Put your hope in God, for I will yet praise him, my savior and my God" (Psalm 42:11).

We can make the commitment to place our hands in the hand of Jesus and together tread each step into the future. He will hold us up when we stumble in the darkness and give us hope as we anticipate the rainbow that will soon appear. He will always be faithful to His promise.

Insight

When the storm passes, God will place a rainbow of promise in your life. You can count on it.

Genesis 40; 41:1-9

A Forgotten Promise

"The chief cupbearer; however, did not remember Joseph; he forgot him. . . . Then the chief cupbearer said to Pharaoh, 'Today I am reminded of my shortcomings'" (Genesis 40:23; 41:9).

If anyone ever felt forgotten, it must have been Joseph. He was torn from his family as a young man, sold into slavery, accused of a crime he did not commit, and thrown into prison.

While in prison he interpreted the dreams of Pharaoh's butler and baker. He asked the butler, when he was restored to favor, to speak to Pharaoh on his behalf, but the butler promptly forgot him. Two more years would go by. Then Pharaoh had a dream, and the butler remembered Joseph. The interpretation of that dream would catapult Joseph into leadership in Egypt.

When someone asks us to pray for them, do we glibly respond, "Yes," and then promptly forget our promise? Or do we faithfully pray for that need and rejoice with them in God's answers?

Too easily we make promises and forget them. Like the butler, we get busy and go on with life, forgetting those we need to remember. God has a rich ministry for us as we learn to remember the promises we have made.

Insight

God never forgot Joseph and He will never forget you. His purposes and plans for you are right on time.

Joshua 4:1-7

Stones of Remembrance

"When your children ask you, 'What do these stones mean?' tell them. . . . These stones are to be a memorial to the people of Israel forever" (Joshua 4:6-7).

The Israelites faced a daunting challenge. Ready enter the Promised Land, they had fears of what lay before them. First they needed to cross the Jordan River. As they approached, God held back the water and made a dry way for them all to cross.

Joshua instructed twelve men to each pick up a stone from the dry riverbed. They piled these stones on the other bank. Every time an Israelite saw that pile of stones, he remembered how God had stopped the waters of the Jordan. God provided stones of remembrance so parents could tell their children of His presence in their lives.

Do you have stones of remembrance? Instead of real stones, we may keep a journal, or marks on a calendar, or notes in our Bible. These reminders mark a time of special rescue or deliverance, such as a day when God met a special need, He gave a word of encouragement or revealed a truth to your heart just when needed. Go back and remember. Thank God for His hand in your life and pass these testimonies on to your children.

Insight

When we remember God's faithfulness in the past it greatly encourages us to look to Him to day to meet our needs.

1 Samuel 1:1-19

A Vow to be Remembered

"If you will only look upon your servant's misery and remember me, and not forget your servant but give her a son, then I will give him to the Lord for all the days of his life" (1 Samuel 1:11).

Hannah was the beloved wife, but she was barren. She longed to hold a child she could not conceive.

On their annual trip to Shiloh to worship and sacrifice to the Lord, her husband gave each in his family portions of meat, but to Hannah he gave a double amount because of his tender love for her.

The other wife taunted Hannah constantly because she was childless. Finally Hannah could stand it no longer. She went to the door of the tabernacle and poured out her grief and pain before the Lord. She promised that if He would give her a son, she would give him back to the Lord to serve Him all his life.

God heard Hannah's plea. When that son was born and was weaned, Hannah kept her promise and gave him to God.

Have you ever poured out your heart to God, as Hannah did? "Remember me? Lord, You see my situation and my need. I'm getting desperate down here." God has not forgotten you and His answer could be just around the corner.

Insight

God hears the desperate cries of your heart. He remembers you and is working for your good even in the waiting periods.

Remembering at Death's Door

"When my life was ebbing away, I remembered you, Lord, and my prayer rose to you into your holy temple" (Jonah 2:7).

God had given Jonah marching orders. "Go to Nineveh and preach for me there." The wicked city of Nineveh? That was the last place Jonah wanted to visit, so he took a ship in the opposite direction.

When God sent a violent storm and their lives were in peril, Jonah admitted to the sailors that he was the cause of their trouble. "Throw me into the sea," he said, "and the storm will be over."

God saved Jonah from drowning by preparing alternate transportation in the belly of a great fish. Inside that great fish, Jonah remembered to pray, and God heard him. Soon the fish spit him out on dry land. God was giving Jonah a second chance. The once-reluctant prophet obeyed, went to Nineveh, and was effective in leading that great city to repentance.

Do we wait to pray to God until we are in desperate circumstances? Or do we turn to Him at the first sign of trouble? Is prayer a last resort or a first step when storms come? Let's learn from our mistakes. God waits to turn our trouble into blessing.

Insight

God speaks to us when He allows storms in our lives. When we turn to Him in our trouble, He rescues us.

DAY 24
Matthew 26:69-75

Words to Be Remembered

"Immediately a rooster crowed. Then Peter remembered the word Jesus had spoken: 'Before the rooster crows, you will disown me three times.' And he went out and wept bitterly" (Matthew 26:74-75).

Jesus has warned Peter that his prideful boast was going to become his biggest failure. And when it came down to standing up for Christ or denying Him, Peter failed miserably. After the Resurrection, Jesus would totally restore Peter and commission him to feed His sheep.

Scripture is full of warnings. We need to remember them or like Peter, we too will fall. To fail is not fatal. God will give one test after another until we pass. He is the God of second chances - even third and fourth ones.

God also gives special words of encouragement. For example, when my husband Dan was diagnosed with Alzheimer's, He spoke to me in the words of an old hymn, "The clouds you so much dread will break with blessing on your head." I clung to that through our six-year battle with the disease.

Has God impressed on you a warning from His Word or a word of encouragement? Remember His words often. They will keep you and guide you through all the days.

Insight

Remember that God has a special mercy for each hour, a warning to keep us from harm or a word of comfort or encouragement for every trial.

DAY 25
Luke 23:35-43

Jesus Remembers

"Then he said, Jesus, remember me when you come into your kingdom.' Jesus answered, 'I tell you the truth, today you will be with me in paradise.'" (Luke 23:42-43).

A dying thief hung beside Jesus on a cross. I doubt he had ever heard Jesus teach on the Resurrection, yet he believed Jesus was someone special. That took faith. In his desperation he requested, "Remember me." Jesus rewarded his faith with a promise He kept that very day.

God remembered a thief dying on a cross. And He remembers you and me, no matter where we are or how difficult our circumstances. He remembers His promises to us and keeps them.

You may be in a prison. You may be in a difficult marriage. Perhaps you've been out of work for months. An unresolved family conflict may be eating your heart out. You may be desperately trying to get justice after being cheated financially. Perhaps you have recently lost a loved one to death and you see no end to your grief.

God knows who needs encouragement or a word of comfort. He speaks to our heart just the word we need to hear, reminds us of just the promise we need to cling to. He will never forget us.

Insight

God does not forget His children or His promises to them. He knows their pain and hears their cries. He has the power to help them in time of need.

Luke 24:13-35

Remembering Jesus' Words

"The Son of Man must be delivered into the hands of sinful men, be crucified and on the third day be raised again.' Then they remembered his words" (Luke 24:7-8).

Jesus prepared His disciples for His death. He told them what was going to happen, but they did not grasp the significance of the events to come.

After His resurrection, He walked with two disciples from Jerusalem to Emmaus. As they traveled together, He explained the recent events in Jerusalem from Old Testament teaching.

When they arrived at their destination they asked Jesus to stay with them. As He gave thanks for the bread, they suddenly recognized Him. After He disappeared from their sight, the light dawned and they remembered clearly what He had taught them. It all began to make sense.

Have you ever gone through a crisis and simply could not understand what God was doing in your life? You felt as if you had blinders on. Then once on the other side of the event you could look back and see some of what God accomplished through it.

God does not always give us good hindsight, but sometimes we see God's hand in it all in a remarkable way.

Insight

We live by promises, not explanations. Remember the promises - cling to them - when you cannot understand what God is doing in your life.

"In Remembrance of Me"

"He took bread, gave thanks and broke it, and gave it to them, saying, 'This is my body given for you; do this in remembrance of me'" (Luke 22:19).

God gave Israel a remembrance feast, the Passover. They were to remember their deliverance out of Egyptian slavery. The little lamb that was sacrificed became a picture of a future deliverance from the slavery of sin.

Hundreds of years later Jesus gave us a remembrance feast-the Lord's Supper. We are to remember how Jesus gave His blood and body to rescue us from the slavery of sin. Jesus said, "Every time you eat the bread and drink the wine, remember what I have done for you."

We can almost hear Him say, "Remember how much I love you, enough to lay down my life for you. Remember how merciful I am, not treating you as you deserve. Remember how much grace I give you, not requiring payment of your great debt. Remember how receiving Me as your Savior and Lord gives you eternal life. Remember the work I have begun in your life. I will finish it. Remember that some day I will present you before God's throne with great joy, a trophy of My grace."

Insight

God gave us ways to remember all He has done for us. Remember and give thanks.

Forget the Past

"Forget the former things; do not dwell on the past. See, I am doing a new thing! Now it springs up; do you not perceive it? I am making a way in the desert and streams in the wasteland" (Isaiah 43:18-19).

God often tells us to remember. Remember how He has been faithful in the past. Remember past miracles, victories and rescues, words of encouragement.

And there are things we need to forget. Forget past mistakes that we have asked God to forgive. Learn from them and move on, letting God redeem them and bring good out of them.

God is getting ready to do a new thing in your life. Have you just been through divorce? There is life after divorce. Have you lost your mate of many years? There are new; exciting experiences for you as you go on alone. Have you lost a job of many years? God still has a plan for your future and will open new doors. Have you lost a close friendship because of a misunderstanding or a cruel betrayal? Trust God to bring about reconciliation.

When life does not go as you planned, look for God's plan. He is in the process of doing new things in new ways. Get your eyes off the past and focus on the good future that lies ahead.

Insight

What gets your attention gets you. Let it be God's love and His faithfulness, not your failures.

DAY 29
Exodus 2:23-3:10

God Remembered

"God heard their groaning and he remembered his covenant with Abraham, with Isaac and with Jacob. So God looked on the Israelites and was concerned about them" (Exodus 2:24-25).

The Children of Israel were groaning and crying to God in their slavery in Egypt, and their cries came up to God before His throne. As He saw their misery and heard their cry, He began to move to rescue them from slavery.

He remembered promises He had made to Abraham, Isaac, and Jacob that He would make of them a great nation and give them a land of promise.

Do you feel that God has forgotten you? That He is not listening to your desperate pleas? That He is doing nothing to change your circumstances?

Dan and I went through a winter of crying out to God when He appeared to be doing nothing for us. Then suddenly our prayers were answered all at once. God had been working silently behind the scenes all the time.

He remembers His promises to His children and He is faithful to keep them. Cling to what God has said in His Word. He will come through for you. He is always at work, silently preparing for the miracle you need.

Insight

Even if the answers are slow in coming, you can be sure God will keep His promises to you. He is at work behind the scenes.

A Book of Remembrance

"Those who feared the Lord talked with each other; and the Lord listened and heard. A scroll of remembrance was written in his presence" (Malachi 3:16).

Did you know there are books in heaven? Did you know your name is written in the book of life if you are God's child?

Malachi speaks of a book of remembrance being written. Many Israelites in his day had chosen not to follow God, but some still loved and faithfully worshiped Him. They feared God and encouraged one another. God listened to their conversations and wrote down their names. He knows those who put Him first, and they are precious to Him. Not one of them will be left out of His book of remembrance.

God remembers His own, and He will complete the work He has begun in us. He rejoices over us, singing a love song in our ears. He will get all of His own safely to Heaven. We may not be considered of worth by the world around us, but Jesus promises that not one believer will be lost or forgotten. In fact, some day Jesus will present each of us before His Father's throne with great joy, trophies of His grace. What a day that will be!

Insight

You are so special to God that He writes your name in His book of remembrance. He will not forget you.

DAY 31
Psalm 119:49-56

God's Promise, My Hope

"Remember your word to your servant, for you have given me hope. My comfort in my suffering is this: Your promise preserves my life" (Psalm 119:49-50).

How many times have you come to God with one of His promises and held Him to it? I have over and over.

When our business crashed, Dan and I cried out to God, and He delivered us. When Dan was diagnosed with Alzheimer's, He gave me a promise that even this would be a blessing in my life.

One day I sat on the stone bench by the little stream tumbling down the hill at the cemetery where Dan's body is resting. I prayed, "Lord, I have this grave in my life. Use it for Your glory."

The very next day at the work center, a woman came in early to our Bible study. She was totally distraught. Her mother was dying and she was not allowed to be there with the rest of her family. I listened, remembering times when God had met my need as I called on Him in times of complete desperation, then prayed with her.

God is amazing in the way He uses the pain in our lives. Remembering His promises, He comforts us so we may comfort others.

Insight

God's promises are our hope and comfort in the trials of life. Hold Him to them. "Lord, remember what You have said to me."

November

DAY 1
Isaiah 55:8-11

Has Revealed Himself

"The secret things belong to the Lord our God, but the things revealed belong to us and to our children forever . . ." (Deuteronomy 29:29).

Have you ever heard a child explain who God is? You've probably marveled how the youngster seems to know more than some adults do about the Lord. That childlike faith and understanding is commendable. The Bible has revealed to us all we need to know about our Creator.

Still there are questions we will never have answers to this side of heaven. There are things we simply cannot comprehend with our limited minds. There are mysteries that the Bible speaks of but does not explain. Because our thoughts are not like God's and our ways are not like His, we may grow frustrated about uncertainties. We may feel like giving up when the Bible doesn't seem to speak directly to a problem we are experiencing. But everything He has revealed to us in Scripture is all we need to know for the most important and basic problem we have: our sin problem. He sent His Son to live a perfect life in our place and pay the penalty for the sin that we all carry. If you know that, you know VERY much, indeed!

Insight

We can never know everything about God, but we can know all that we need.

DAY 2
Romans 8:35-39

God Loves Me Forever

"The Lord appeared to us in the past, saying: 'I have loved you with an everlasting love; I have drawn you with loving-kindness'" (Jeremiah 31:3).

There is one unalterable truth-God loves me. Stand firm on this foundation because life is full of uncertainties.

Your best friend gets cancer, and there are no more cozy chats with a cup of tea. A son or daughter is killed in Iraq, and sorrow engulfs your soul. A black cloud of depression enters your life, and you cannot function as usual. You get an infection and end up in the emergency room of the hospital. The hot water heater goes out and costs too much to replace. You are down to the last dollars in your bank account. Sickness sidelines you, and you don't work for weeks. The bills pile up. There never seems to be a shortage of troubles.

But Paul says that neither life nor death can separate us from God's love. Nothing that happens today and nothing that will happen tomorrow can affect God's love for you.

Look for the silver lining in the clouds in your life. God doesn't waste anything-not even our sorrow or pain or distress.

Insight

There is one rock solid truth in this world on which you can stand: God loves you.

1 Corinthians 1:21-31

He Works Through My Weakness

"But God chose the foolish things of the world to shame the wise; God chose the weak things of the world to shame the strong" (1 Corinthians 1:27).

My husband had Alzheimer's six and a half years but never let it stop him from serving in the prison. He was removed from his chaplain position, but he continued to serve as a volunteer as many hours as he could, going out to the prison seven days a week. In time he couldn't speak very well, but the men stepped up to help him.

When he could no longer drive, I drove us out for our Sunday prayer group. When he could no longer sign his name, I signed us in and out. The men loved him and wanted him there. We were at the prison just six weeks before he died, closing the chapter on his work here on earth.

Don't let weakness stop you. God uses the weak in special ways. When we are weak, we depend on God all the more, and others see Christ in us. We are vessels of clay showing forth the glory of God. Weakness keeps us humble and dependent on God. On our own we have so little strength, but through Him we can do all things (see Philippians 4:13).

Insight

God chooses to work through the weak so that the glory goes to Him.

DAY 4
1 Timothy 1:12-17

Redeems My Mistakes

"I thank Christ Jesus our Lord, who has given me strength, that he considered me faithful, appointing me to his service" (1 Timothy 1:12).

Wasted years - we all have them. Mistakes – we all make them. But God is a specialist in redeeming our mistakes and bringing good out of them.

I mentor Mary, a former drug addict. It is such a joy to see her life change and see God restore much of what has been lost. I'm sure she regrets the wasted years, but God gives great hope for the future. Her past is part of what is shaping her for the Lord today.

I have considered my greatest failure sinking into depression after the sudden death of my father. But God redeemed my despair in a special way. I was half-finished writing a piece on suffering when my dad died. I put it aside, feeling unable to write another word. Four months later I picked it up and finished it. That particular devotional writing meant a great deal to me and to others.

Don't despair and become discouraged when you fall short. Let God give you beauty for the ashes of your failure. He can turn our lowest into glory in the highest for Him.

Insight

God is above all a Redeemer, taking broken lives and making them whole again.

He Tests My Faith

"Consider it pure joy, my brothers, whenever you face trials of many kinds, because you know that the testing of your faith develops perseverance" (James 1:2, 3).

Last summer I began having unrelenting right hip pain I was planning on touring Israel with my brother in eight months, so I needed to find an answer to my pain. I went to the doctor and discovered I'm full of arthritis - not a pleasant thought! Next I was off to the pain clinic to be injected with three different injections, none of which worked. Finally, the doctor decided it was a muscle problem and sent me to a chiropractor.

The treatments were helpful in the beginning, but then I had a major setback. Time was running out before my trip was to start. However, by the time I left for Israel, I was pain-free.

All through this difficult time, I was reflecting on the verse in James about suffering. How do I count the pain as joy? What does it mean to "let patience have its perfect work" in me?

I believe in every trial we go through, God is building patience and endurance in us. We just want to get through the trial as quickly as possible, but we must let patience have its perfect work.

Insight

God is working in the trials in our lives to produce the fruit of the spirit in us, especially patience.

DAY 6
Romans 8:32-39

He Calls Me a Conqueror

"Who shall separate us from the love of Christ? . . . we are more than conquerors through him who loved us" (Romans 8:35, 37).

I don't know what kind of trouble you are going through today, whether it is health problems or financial tests or sudden calamity. You may be asking God, "Have you deserted me? If you are in control, why have you let this happen to me?" You may be very angry at God for allowing these things to touch you. You are overwhelmed and feel that if one more thing happens, you will fall apart.

Well, fall apart in God's arms and let Him begin to lift you up and enable you to become more than a conqueror. Stop trying to fix things on your own. You have the Creator of the Universe to do that for you!

Because of Christ's life and death for me, I can begin to forgive those who hurt me so deeply. I can begin to let go of my anger and thank God for who He is. I can pray with thanksgiving and have the peace that passeth understanding. I can let this trial deepen my relationship with God and produce in me the fruit of the Spirit.

Insight

We become more than conquerors in the trials and calamities of life by submitting to God, not by fighting Him.

DAY 7
Hebrews 4:14-16

He Feels My Pain

"For we do not have a high priest who is unable to sympathize with our weakness, but we have one who has been tempted in every way, just as we are - yet was without sin" (Hebrews 4:15).

Are you just plain poor and needy today? Needing relief from pain? Needing strength to go on? Needing rest desperately after several sleepless nights? In your need have you cried out to God, "Have mercy on me and bring relief?"

There is One who along with you feels your pain, your fatigue, your weariness, and your discouragement. He knows how weak you are and how tempted to despair. He lives in your body with you and feels every feeling with you. He understands and is waiting to help.

Max Lucado writes that when healing hasn't come, God may be answering prayers we are not even asking.

Look for the blessings in the trials. Look for God's mercies. "He heals the brokenhearted and binds up their wounds" (Psalm 147:3). He has mercy and grace for you this moment. Praise God He sent His Son not only to bear our sin for us, but also to endure every manner of suffering there is and to do so in a perfect life. That's the Savior I want!

Insight

Hold fast to God in the storms of life. Jesus has been where you are. He understands and can help you through the storm.

DAY 8
Psalm 103

He Is Forever Merciful

"Bless the Lord, O my soul, and forget not all his benefits . . .
Who redeemeth thy life from destruction; who crowneth
thee with lovingkindness and tender mercies" (Psalm
103:2, 4 KJV).

How often have you cried out for God's mercy? How often
have you received it? How often have you missed it? There is a
song with a phrase, "God gives a special mercy for each hour."
What comforting words those are! His mercies are new every
morning. God never runs out of mercy. We cannot diminish
His supply.

I roomed with Mary, a college student, on my trip to Israel.
Her mother is dying of cancer, and there are nine children
in the family, the youngest of whom is 10 years old. Mary
dropped out of school to help at home, but God gave her the
opportunity to take this trip to Israel. Our hearts were immediately knit together as I shared with her how to look for the
mercies of God. "They will be there, but you can miss them
if you are not watchful," I told her. "Let the joys of this trip to
Israel carry you through the days ahead."

God remembers that we are dust. Often in ways we least
expect, He lightens the load, eases the pain, and encourages
the heart.

Insight

*God does not treat us as we deserve. He knows our weakness
and pours out His mercy on us every moment.*

He Hears My Cry

"The eyes of the Lord are on the righteous and his ears are attentive to their cry; the righteous cry . . . and the Lord hears them; he delivers them from all their troubles" (Psalm 34:15, 17).

Every so often I throw myself down on my knees and cry out to God, "Help me, I can't do this. You're going to have to move men in my behalf, give me strength to go on, shut off my mind so I can sleep, solve this problem."

He hears. He even hears my groanings, my silent cry 1 can't put into words. He gives us the Holy Spirit to help us with our daily problems in our praying. So often we simply don't know how to pray about a matter. Then the Holy Spirit begins to pray for us without words, and those prayers are answered.

We do not escape troubles, but the Lord helps us in each and every one. He puts the right people in our lives at the right time to help us. The other day when I was so discouraged, four different people called, and three of them prayed for me over the phone. God not only hears, but He goes even one step further. He delivers us out of all our troubles. So let's praise Him no matter what happens.

Insight

The Lord hears our cries, sees the desperate situations in our lives, feels our heart needs and delivers us from all our troubles.

He Is With Me in Trouble

"'He will call upon me, and I will answer him; I will be with him in trouble, I will deliver him and honor him'" (Psalm 91:15).

God is not merely on the outside looking in on the events and details of our lives; He is living these things with us.

He lives in your body with you. He feels the brain tumor pressing on your skull, the arthritis forcing its pain, the lupus weakening you, the Alzheimer's confusing your thoughts. And somehow He is there when you can't think right or have no strength. He is there for you to grasp when dizziness or fear strike. He is there in the darkness of depression.

Jesus is with me in this trouble. He'll sell the house, settle the debts, feel the pain of my divorce, pick up the pieces of the business crash and enable me to heal and start over.

He will be with me beside the bed of a dying loved one, comfort me in my sorrow, speak the very word I need to hear. He is with me when I am afraid, worried or anxious, when I face having to say goodbye to one I love, when I send a child off to college. His name is Emmanuel - God with Us.

Insight

The Lord is close to those whose hearts are breaking. He is in each and every trouble with us and He can be trusted to help.

DAY 11
Psalm 119:1-8

He Forgives My Sin

"Have mercy on me, O God, according to your unfailing love; according to your great compassion blot out my transgressions. Wash away all my iniquity and cleanse me from my sin" (Psalm 51:1, 2).

Lord, I've made such a mess of my life. I was determined to go my own way and it has been a disaster. In my distress, I started to drink and do drugs. I've lost my marriage, my children, my home and I've ended up in the county jail. Lord, I'm at the bottom. Can you forgive me for the mess I have made of my life?"

"I do forgive you, my child. Give your heart and life to me, and I will rescue you from the pit of despair. I will restore the years the locust hath eaten. For I know the plans I have for you, plans for good and not for evil, to give you a future and a hope" (see Jeremiah 29:11).

Not only does God forgive our sins, but He casts them into the depths of the sea. "As far as the east is from the west, so far has he removed our transgressions from us" (Psalm 103:12). Have you ever come to God and given your heart and life to Him? Do it today. He is waiting to receive you and forgive you and make you part of His forever family.

Insight

Run into His arms today and find mercy and loving-kindness.

He Will Strengthen Me

"So do not fear, for I am with you; do not be dismayed, for I am your God. I will strengthen you and help you; I will uphold you with my righteous right hand" (Isaiah 41:10).

Who of us doesn't need strength in this life? Many are the days in the day care that I have in my home when I just pray I can make it to nap time and rest.

Life gets so busy for most of us. Our jobs and hectic schedules keep us on the go long before sun up and beyond sun down. We are in daily need of strength.

There are things which test us and try us, and we find that in our own strength we are unable to go on. God promises to give us that strength and to help us.

Is God challenging you with a difficult job or task? He will strengthen you for it.

Do you have ongoing health problems? His promise is for you, too.

Are you a caregiver for an elderly family member? Special strength is yours. No matter what God calls us to do, He gives strength for the task.

I worried about keeping up with the college kids on a tour to Israel, but God saw me through the long journey and gave me strength for each day.

Insight

God never gives us a task but that He gives us the strength to get it done.

He Knows My Name

"But now, this is what the Lord says - he who created you, O Jacob, he who formed you, O Israel: 'Fear not, for I have redeemed you; I have called you by name; you are mine'" (Isaiah 43:1).

Jesus never saw crowds; He saw individuals and He ministered to the needs of each one. One day in a crowd a single desperate woman reached out and touched His garment and was healed. Jesus knew it.

God has known you from the top of your head to the tip of your toes. He numbered all the moments of your life even before you were born. He knows when you sit down and when you rise up. He knows the thoughts in your mind before you think them. He knows every word on your tongue. He knows your abilities and talents, for He placed them in you.

He knows the load of care you carry today and invites you to lay it at His feet. He is familiar with the stresses and strains of your life and will make a way through it for you.

He is your personal God. He called you by your name. He gave you a task He has fitted you for. He has engraved your name on the palms of His hands. You belong to Him, for He is your personal God.

Insight

He who sees the smallest sparrow fall, who numbers the hairs of your head, calls you by name to the task He has prepared for you.

Matthew 6:25-34

He Knows My Need

"So do not worry, saying, 'What shall we eat?' or 'What shall we drink?' or 'What shall we wear?' . . . your heavenly Father knows that you need them" (Matthew 6:31, 32).

How often have you found that the things you worried about never happened? You planned for the future, yet it did not at all turn out the way you expected. As we faced the future with Alzheimer's, I thought the time would come when I would be forced to close the day care in my home and care for my husband full-time. As Dan's disease progressed, I wondered how I would have enough income to make ends meet.

Instead Dan got sick and was hospitalized, needing nursing home care afterwards. Five weeks later he was gone, and I never even closed my home day care center at all. My son and grandson had come to live with me so that I had all the help I would need. Income was indeed adequate to meet my needs.

God's ways astound us, though really they ought not to. After all, He holds the universe in His hand. His ways are so much better than mine. "Therefore do not worry about tomorrow, for tomorrow will worry about itself. Each day has enough trouble of its own" (Matthew 6:34).

Insight

Leave the tomorrows with God. Live one day at a time. God will take care of today and tomorrow, too.

DAY 15
1 Corinthians 10:1-13

He Makes a Way of Escape

"No temptation has seized you except what is common to man. And God is faithful; he will not let you be tempted beyond what you can bear. . ." (1 Corinthians 10:13a).

When the pain doesn't end, when the days go by and you don't get better, when healing takes so much longer than you anticipated and you become impatient, remember, many others have walked this way before you. Your suffering is not unique. There are those who understand what you are going through. More importantly, there is One who understands!

Dan and I eventually joined an Alzheimer's support group. As the caregivers shared their struggles and stories, we cried together and laughed together. It was good to be with others going through the same difficulties.

Bear patiently whatever God brings into your life, be it pain or struggle, and look for His way of escape. Sometimes He provides escape by the support of others around you; other times by settling you on your knees alone with Him. God will give you the strength to face that which you are sure you cannot bear. Look for His mercies and be thankful. He will faithfully see you through.

Insight

God is never caught unaware by the surprises of life. They are all in His plan.

DAY 16
Hebrews 10:16-25

He Keeps His Promises

"Let us hold unswervingly to the hope we profess, for he who promised is faithful. And let us consider how we may spur one another on toward love and good deeds" (Hebrews 10:23, 24).

Look back over your life and count the times God has been faithful to keep a promise or meet your needs. Can you even count that high? Has He ever failed you? Can you trust Him?

God has a great track record in my life. I cannot count one failure. He may not have met my needs in the way I thought He would, but the way He did brought Him the greater glory.

My son has lived with me for the last year and a half, but he has just taken a job in Portland, Oregon. It was a big adjustment when he came, and now it will be a big adjustment to have him leave. Still I know it is God's plan for now. It will leave me alone for dinner and in the evening three nights a week. Since losing my husband, Dan, I have not often had to face the loneliness. Now I will be alone a lot more. But I know God will be with me because He promises to never leave me or forsake me. We all can rest assured that He cares for us and can sing along with young ones that we "are standing on the promises of God!"

Insight

In what promise are you trusting right now? God will be faithful to meet your needs in the way that is best.

Lamentations 3:18-23

He Is Full of Compassion

"Because of the Lord's great love we are not consumed, for his compassions never fail. They are new every morning; great is your faithfulness" (Lamentations 3:22, 23).

Jesus had a heart of compassion. He wept over Jerusalem. He wept at the grave of Lazarus. A leper said, "Lord, have compassion on me and heal me," and Jesus said, "I will. Be thou clean."

The heart of God yearns over his children. He feels our pain and encourages us to hang on saying, "You will get through this also."

He understands the agony of divorce, the rending of the one flesh, the anger that consumes you. He will gently lead you to Himself, heal the wounds, and enable you to love and trust again.

He bore the agony of the cross so we could know the healing of our souls.

There is no emotion you go through but that He can identify with it. He has been where you are. When His disciples ran away and when His father forsook Him on the cross, He knew loneliness. When all the sins of the world were laid upon Him, He knew pressure. He knew what He was facing and begged the Father for another way. Still He said, "Not my will but thine be done."

Insight

Christ totally identified with us becoming a man, living here on earth land suffering and dying for us.

DAY 18
Isaiah 30:18-33

He Guides My Steps

"Whether you turn to the right or to the left, your ears will hear a voice behind you, saying, 'This is the way; walk in it'" (Isaiah 30:21).

This promise came to Israel in a time of adversity. God comes to us in our times of trial with clear and specific direction. He says, "This is what I have for you now. This is the next step."

Often when we are troubled and feel desperate, we start trying all the doors ourselves. We want to fix things. We look for opportunities, and then we listen for His voice saying, 'This is where I want you for now." I need to listen to Him first and then act.

I wasn't going to write an Anchor this year, but God impressed upon me the value of considering all that I know of Him. It turned out to be the foundation for this writing. He even provided the time in my schedule to complete the work!

In 2 Chronicles 20:12 Israel said to the Lord, "We do not know what to do, but our eyes are upon you." God gave them their battle plan, and they won a great victory.

Do you need guidance? Listen for His voice.

Hear Him out before you try solving things. He will guide your steps.

Insight

God's guidance in times of trouble is very clear, so start listening for His voice.

Deuteronomy 33:26-29

He Holds Me in His Arms

"The eternal God is your refuge, and underneath are the everlasting arms. He will drive out your enemy before you, saying, 'Destroy him'" (Deuteronomy 33:27)!

This is a comforting verse. I can never fall out of God's arms. If His arms are underneath me, then He must be carrying me. I'm secure, and I'm close to His heart.

When I was a young child, my family would come home late from visiting relatives, and we three children would have fallen asleep in the car. I was big enough to wake up and walk into the house on my own, but I would pretend to be asleep so that my father would carry me in. It felt so good to be in my father's arms.

You may be experiencing great weakness right now. Remember that underneath are the arms of your heavenly Father carrying you through ill health, depression, cancer, heart attack or worry.

What a comforter our God is, uplifting us in our hardships and trials and strengthening us to go through them. Why does He do this? So that when others go through similar trials, we can pass on to them the same help and comfort God has given us, and so that He might be glorified.

Insight

The more we undergo sufferings and trials, the more God showers us with comfort and encouragement.

DAY 20
Psalm 57

He Protects Me

"Have mercy on me, O God, have mercy on me, for in you my soul takes refuge. I will take refuge in the shadow of your wings until the disaster has passed" (Psalm 57:1).

The verse that was the greatest comfort to me when I lost Dan was Psalm 63:7: "Because you are my help, I sing in the shadow of your wings." God brought my attention to Psalm 63 on Christmas morning, and I continued to ponder that Psalm the following week when Dan went home to glory. I could imagine myself tucked underneath God's wing, warm and protected, feeling the beating of His heart for me.

As I entered the first days of my widowhood, I determined to sing in the shadow of His wings. Wonderfully, I found much to praise Him for.

Dan had a short nursing home stay with kind people caring for him. Two of my sons were at my side. God's timing was perfect, giving my brother the opportunity to lead Dan's memorial service on his Christmas break from the Bible college where he teaches. Our hospice team was superb. They were there to comfort and guide us. In all of these ways God sheltered me under His wings until these calamities had passed.

Insight

There is wonderful comforting peace in the shelter of God's wings, near to His heart.

He Holds My Hand

"I was senseless and ignorant; I was a brute beast before you. Yet I am always with you; you hold me by my right hand" (Psalm 73:22, 23).

We hold the hand of the dying. We hold the hand of the toddler learning to walk. We hold the hand of the one we love as we stroll through the park, as we say our vows at our wedding. We take the hand of a friend as we pray for him or her.

My physical therapist closed the doors, sat down opposite me, took my hand in hers and prayed for me. I felt stress mounting that day as I dealt with an inner ear problem, not being able to watch my two little girls, not having normal income. My son had just lost his job. Worry consumed me, but that act and prayer were so comforting. Sometimes God uses others to be the hands for Him.

Are you going through a particularly tough time? Do you need comfort and encouragement? I pray God sends someone to hold your hand and pray for you. On that distressing day three unexpected phone calls came, each one ending with a friend praying for me. Listen for God's voice saying, "Put your hand in mine and together we will tread each step into the future."

Insight

I know who holds tomorrow, and I know who holds my hand - the living, eternal God.

Psalm 139:13-18

God Planned and Created Me

"I praise you because I am fearfully and wonderfully made; your works are wonderful, I know that full well. My frame was not hidden from you when I was made in the secret place" (Psalm 139:14, 15a).

Do you know that you are one of a kind? That when God made you, He broke the mold? You are unique, gifted for the special plan and purpose God has your life. He has people only you can touch through your personality.

He wove you with skill in your mother's womb, giving you the inborn talents, abilities, intelligence, face and form that please Him. He loves you just as you are. You are his work of art, an original masterpiece!

Love and accept yourself just as you are: one of God's precious human beings. There is much pressure in our world to convince us that we need more material goods, money or status to be accepted. Really, all we need is more of Jesus Christ in our lives. Fulfill the purpose for which He made you to love Him, fellowship with Him and glorify Him.

He planned every day of your life even before you were born. Every day was written in His Book. Look up and say, "Thank you for the experiences you are putting me through right now, for they are forming Your character in me."

Insight

God planned you and designed you in your mother's womb. You are one of a kind, God's unique creation.

God Knows My Ways

"When he is at work in the north, I do not see him; when he turns to the south, I catch no glimpse of him. But . . . when he has tested me, I will come forth as gold" (Job 23:9, 10).

Either we are going into a trial, are in one, or coming out of one. God is never caught by surprise by the things that happen to us, even though we are. Trials and troubles are part of living on this sin-cursed earth. We will not escape them. But God has divine purpose in each and every one. He is refining us as gold is refined. That means He turns up the heat until He sees His face reflected in the molten ore.

He balances the blessings and trials in our lives. He surrounds us with His incredible mercies. So often we miss His mercies, because we are not looking for them. In the midst of immense heartache and suffering, Job trusted in God and in His ways, believing even while all was being taken from him that God would cause him to emerge in the end as something "like gold."

Do you want to be like Jesus? To come through the test like gold? Welcome the trial. Count it all joy. Cry out to the Holy Spirit to do in you what you know you can't do on your own.

Insight

When the trials of life buffet you, know God's hand is on you and His purpose is being fulfilled - building your character.

He Lifts Me Up

"The Lord is faithful to all his promises and loving toward all he has made. The Lord upholds all those who fall and lifts up all who are bowed down" (Psalm 145:13b, 14).

Here is a promise for the depressed: He lifts up those who are down. Do you remember whose arms are underneath you? He always lifts up. When it is dark and you can't see, reach out your hand. He will take hold of you and lift you up.

David wrote, "Why art thou cast down, O my soul? And why art thou disquieted within me? Hope in God: for I shall yet praise him for the help of his countenance" (Psalm 42:5, KJV). David rested in the surety of his God even while trouble surrounded him.

In my own dark time I memorized Psalms 42 and 51. I never quit reading my Bible and praying, but my spiritual life seemed as dry as dust. I began counseling with a godly pastor. I made myself walk a mile a day. I forced myself to call people to talk to each week. We still welcomed guests into our home, though Dan had to carry the conversations. I was an encourager but much in need of encouragement. Eventually, the black clouds were gone and God made me an encourager once again.

Insight

We all sink low at times, but we have a God who lifts us up again in His time.

DAY 25
Matthew 11:25-30

He Gives Rest for the Weary

"'Come to me, all you who are weary and burdened, and I will give you rest. Take my yoke upon you and learn from me . . .'" (Matthew 11:28, 29).

God understands when we become burdened by the circumstances of life. The stresses of one week alone were weighing me down: physical ailment, strains with finances and job security, sleeplessness. Perhaps these things sound familiar to you or have at one time in your life. I wrote down everything I was anxious about and handed it to God. I asked for help with the interrupted sleep patterns. Even after one full night of restful sleep, the world looks like a different place! His gentle invitation is to come to Him and find that sweet rest we need. The apostle Paul, whose own life was brimming with trials, reminds us in Philippians 4:6 to "not be anxious about anything, but in every thing, by prayer and petition, with thanksgiving, present your requests to God." The burdens of life are not too insignificant to present before our loving God who made us and cares for us. He will keep in perfect peace those whose minds are fixed on Him (see Isaiah 26:3).

Praise God for the rest He gives!

Insight

Jesus invites us to come and find rest in Him alone.

Psalm 23

He Restores My Soul

"He makes me lie down in green pastures, he leads me beside quiet waters, he restores my soul. He guides me in paths of righteousness for his name's sake" (Psalm 23:2, 3).

I had orders from my physical therapist to get as much rest as possible on the weekend so my inner ear could heal. Yet I got up on Saturday morning, intent on doing the shopping and facing the tasks for the day. Overcome with dizziness, I found I simply had to give up and spend the entire day in bed.

I recalled David's words from Psalm 23: "He makes me lie down in green pastures." God was literally making me rest through the dizziness. The pastures are lush and green where He would have us rest. Our soul is nourished there. Jesus spoke of the peace He would leave with us: peace not as the world gives (see John 14:27). It is a peace that restores because that peace is Jesus Christ himself.

Most of us do not like to be out of our normal routine. In those times when God must literally make us stop and rest, you may chafe at it as much as I did. But today, I'm truly refreshed and ready to go back to work, grateful for the work He has done for me!

Insight

The resting places of life become places where God restores us deep down inside - our soul.

God Works While I Sleep

"He will not let your foot slip - he who watches over you will not slumber; indeed, he who watches over Israel will neither slumber nor sleep" (Psalm 121:3, 4).

While I sleep, He is protecting me, healing me, restoring me, and setting in order every detail of my life. Why do I seem to forget that God is in control of all things? Why am I surprised by bumps in the road of life?

At the beginning of Psalm 4, David calls out to the Lord in his distress. He was familiar with troubles and anguish far more serious than my "bumps in the road." I never have had to run for my life as David did. Though he was a man after God's own heart, he knew great suffering. But he rested firm on what he knew of the Lord so that by the end of Psalm 4, he could say confidently to himself (and to us thousands of years later!) that he would lie down and sleep in peace, knowing the Lord alone would keep him.

So why do I fret over life's circumstances, even to the point of losing sleep? I falter because I am a sinner in a sin-tainted world, in need of a strong, perfect Savior. Praise God my Savior works while I sleep!

Insight

God is always at work in every part of my life. In fact, He never sleeps.

He Carries My Burdens

"Cast your cares on the Lord and he will sustain you; he will never let the righteous fall" (Psalm 55:22). "Cast all your anxiety on him because he cares for you" (1 Peter 5:7).

Once there was a man walking down the road carrying a heavy load. Along came a farmer in a wagon. He stopped and invited the man to ride. The farmer chanced to look back and see the man still carrying his burden. "Friend, why don't you lay your burden down?"

We are so much like that stranger on the road. We have a Savior who carries us, but we insist on hauling our load ourselves. As a result, we grow very weary and overwhelmed.

Somehow we have to learn to cast our load of care on the Lord, who is most capable of carrying it, of solving the problems, healing the hurts, and providing the needs.

God moved my prodigal son home to help me shortly before Dan died. He has been such a blessing to me, and now God is moving him to Portland, Oregon. I'm happy for him but am finding it difficult to let go. It is time for me to do in my heart what my head knows is true: cast my burden on the Lord and rest in His care.

Insight

We will have no rest and peace until we can fully cast all our cares on the One who cares for us.

DAY 29
Luke 1:34-38

God Can Do the Impossible

"'For nothing is impossible with God.'" "'I am the Lord's servant,' Mary answered. 'May it be to me as you have said.' Then the angel left her" (Luke 1:37-38).

Do you really believe God can do what man cannot? That He is working on your behalf at all times? That He will heal you if He chooses to? Or that He will give you the strength to live with debilitating illness?

I never thought I could handle having a spouse with Alzheimer's, yet I did and cared for Dan until the last six weeks of his life. Yes, there were times of frustration when he couldn't communicate what he wanted to say. But we always managed. I watched God answer all our prayers. I prayed Dan would not become fearful and angry. He stayed gentle and sweet, easy to care for. I prayed the care would not be too much for me. It wasn't until I was forced to put him in a nursing home. A friend prayed that God would spare me the worst of Alzheimer's. God was indeed very merciful and did just that.

I don't know what you are facing, but I know our God and He is there for you in the difficult places of life.

Insight

God makes a way through the Red Sea places of our lives, doing what we think is impossible.

2 Corinthians 12:7-10

God's Grace Is Sufficient for Me

" . . . I will boast all the more gladly about my weakness, so
that Christ's power may rest on me" (2 Corinthians 12:9).

God's power shows up best in weak people. He loves to
work through our weakness. It is there that I feel God's nearness.

God is able to heal, but He may choose not to. Paul had
some kind of infirmity; he begged God three different times
to heal him. God did not heal Paul. Rather He gave him a
promise saying, "My grace is sufficient for you, for my power
is made perfect in weakness."

So Paul actually said he was glad to boast about how weak
he was. The weaker we are, the more we depend on Him. Do
we ever feel grateful for our weaknesses? Would we confess
with Paul that we are glad to be a living demonstration of
God's power?

We can do the same because we can rely on the all-sufficient grace of God, grace that has never once failed. Let's give
thanks for our weakness, trusting God to display His glory in
us, rejoicing in our trials. By the power of the Holy Spirit, we
will be able to count as joy the troubles the Lord has ordained
to use in our lives.

Insight

*No matter what we have to face, we have the all-sufficient
grace of God freely given and made real by the Holy Spirit.*

Romans 8:28-34

He Works for My Good

"And we know that in all things God works for the good of those who love him, who have been called according to his purpose" (Romans 8:28).

Not only does God love us implicitly, as seen in this month's meditations, but He uses our struggles to make us more like Christ. In Jeremiah 18:6 He says, "O house of Israel, can I not do with you as this potter does? Like clay in the hands of the potter, so are you in my hand . . ." A lump of clay is tough until the craftsman kneads it and pulls it, shaping it gradually into the form he envisions.

Troubles abounded for God's Old Testament chosen people, the Israelites, but God, like the potter, knew His purposes and design for them. He was there through the battles, the slavery, the famine. His promise to make them His people and save them never wavered, not even when they felt forsaken. The Potter was shaping them as it seemed best to Him (Jeremiah 18:4).

There is no shortage of anxiety for us either. The writing of these devotionals came out of weakness in my life. Still God's guidance has been clear, and I've grown along with you as we meditated on and rejoiced in all that we know about God.

Insight

Praise God that "Jesus loves me, this I know!"

December

Isaiah 6:1-8; 2 Corinthians 8:9

Down from His Glory

"No one has ever gone into heaven except the One who came from heaven - the Son of Man" (John 3:13).

Every year I look forward to singing favorite Christmas carols. Today the beautiful song words addressed to Jesus come to mind, "Thou Didst Leave Thy Throne," and I stop to reflect on their meaning.

God in heaven looked down and saw our terrible need, and in His plan, before the earth was formed, Jesus would leave heaven and come to earth. The Son of God would become the God-man, like us yet truly God. He would be clothed in human flesh, experience the cycle of human life from birth to death, but as God, would be raised from the dead.

No longer need mere mortals tremble with fear in the presence of Almighty God. In Jesus He became approachable, touchable. God came near in the person of Jesus. One could eat with Him, walk with Him, talk with Him. He came to reveal the Father, share our sufferings, bear our wrongs. He gave up heaven's riches to embrace earth's poverty. He submitted Himself to His Father's will, knowing it would cost Him everything - even His life.

Why? So that we might be given the gift of eternal life by believing in Jesus as our Lord and Saviour. Yes, Jesus became poor so that we might become rich. He became sin for us so we could be free from its penalty.

O the Wonder

God came near in the person of Jesus so that I can personally know Him. That's the message of Christmas.

DAY 2

Luke 1:26-38

The Virgin Mother

"The virgin will be with child and will give birth to a son, and will call Him Immanuel" (Isaiah 7:14).

Hundreds of years before the birth of Jesus, Isaiah prophesied that a virgin would be with child, and that child would be the Son of God.

In order for this child not to be tainted with Adam's sin, His birth must be supernatural. God would be the Father, and a virgin the human mother.

When the time had come, the Angel Gabriel appeared to a young woman named Mary, who lived in the little village of Nazareth. He announced that she had been chosen by God to bear His Son.

Astonished, Mary asked the angel, "How will this be . . . since I am a virgin?" (Luke 1:34)

When the angel explained that this would be brought about by the power of the Holy Spirit, Mary's response was beautiful in its simplicity. She reverently bowed her head and said, "I am the Lord's servant. . . . May it be to me as you have said" (v. 38).

This devout and obedient young woman became the instrument in God's hands for the entrance of His Son into the world. Did she realize the price she would have to pay? Probably not.

Are we willing to submit to God's plan for our lives? While we can't see ahead to what obedience may cost us, we can trust God's wisdom and love in choosing that plan for us.

O the Wonder

A miracle birth for a miracle Child. God the Father, Mary the mother.

DAY 3
Luke 2: 1-7

The Son of Mary

"She gave birth to her firstborn, a son" (Luke 2:7).

When we held our firstborn in our arms we were deeply proud, yet totally inexperienced. We loved our son, but we would make our share of mistakes as we raised him.

It's hard to imagine that God would make Himself so vulnerable that He would come as a tiny baby into this sinful world. A baby is helpless, completely dependent on adult caregivers for all his needs. Yet the Son of God allowed Himself to be cuddled, fed, and changed, like any other infant.

Babies are little miracles. To the delight of their parents they grow, develop, and learn. Jesus' earthly parents must have thrilled to His first smile, the first tooth, the first step, and the first word.

God entrusted His Son to be raised by a pair of earthly parents. Because Mary and Joseph were human, they would make their share of mistakes, but even these would only help this child develop into the perfect man God intended Him to be.

Yes, God made Himself vulnerable, touchable, and reachable for our benefit. Jesus experienced all we will ever experience from infancy to adulthood. He fully identified with us in His birth and in His life on Planet Earth. We can count on Him to understand our frailties, our frustrations, and our pain.

O the Wonder

God came to earth as a helpless baby, so tiny and vulnerable, that He might save me from my sin.

DAY 4
Philippians 2:5-10

"She wrapped Him in cloths and placed Him in a manger, because there was no room for them in the inn" (Luke 2:7).

Emily Elliott acknowledges Jesus' coming with these words in her Christmas song, "But in lowly birth didst Thou come to earth, and in great humility."

Mary was a simple peasant girl married to a working class tradesman named Joseph. She did not visualize God's Son being born in a palace. That would have been beyond her dreams. I'm sure, though, Mary would have chosen to have her baby in her snug little home and to have placed Him in the little bed they had prepared for Him.

Instead, she and Joseph found themselves on the road to Bethlehem shortly before the baby was due. They must register for the census along with many others. On arrival, they discovered that Bethlehem's crowded inn could not even spare them a room, so they were forced to take refuge that night in the stable. There Mary gave birth to the Baby Jesus, wrapping Him in soft cloths she had prepared and placing Him in the hay of a cattle manger. What a humble birth for the very Son of God!

Truly Jesus identified with the poor in His birth and later on in His life. He came to serve, and He did so in humility. He served as "one of them," not as an outsider reaching down to do good to people who were beneath Him.

O the Wonder

"He was rich, yet for your sakes He became poor, so that you through His poverty might become rich" (2 Corinthians 8:9).

DAY 5
John 3:16-18

"For God so loved the world that He gave His one and only Son" (John 3:16).

As Christmas approaches we think about giving gifts to those we love. I make out a Christmas list, and next to each name write something that person needs. My giving isn't prompted by need alone. I also give because I love.

God looked down and saw our poor and needy state, but He gave not because of our need but because of His love for us. And how much did He love us? Enough to give His one and only Son as the sacrifice for our sins. His Father's heart would break to watch His Son die, yet He would rejoice because it would be the means of bringing many children into His family.

That tiny Baby in the manger was a gift of the Father's love. Jesus was a gift to the world of humans, given freely for each person. All we have to do to make that gift ours is to receive Jesus Christ into our hearts and lives. Then we'll go on to live for Him and serve Him, not because of the need around us, but because He has given us His love to be expressed unselfishly.

Truly God showed us the way when His love gave us His Son. Yes, it was love that was born that night so long ago. Now as we prepare to celebrate Christmas, let's open our hearts in a new way to receive His love. Then, out of our fresh understanding of His love, let's go out to express it unselfishly.

O the Wonder

I marvel with humility that God would love me so much that He would give His Son for me

The Son, God's Gift

"Thanks be to God for His indescribable Gift!" (2 Corinthians 9:15)

Today as I prepare my thoughts for Christmas, song words whisper their way into my heart, "This Gift of God we'll cherish well."

We all love to give and receive gifts, and the peak of gift-giving is Christmastime. My daughter-in-law loves to shop and finds a great deal of joy in buying gifts for those she loves. My best friend feels a gift should be handmade, and that it is more appreciated because of the love that goes into the labor. But a gift is still a gift, whether we purchase it or make it.

We work for many things in this life. An education does not come without effort. Our employment earns us wages, benefits, and vacations. But a gift cannot be earned nor worked for-only received. Those gifts under the Christmas tree with your name on them are yours. But to make them truly yours, you must take them and open them.

At Christmas we remember that God gave us the gift of His Son. He wrapped His Gift in soft cloths and placed Him in a manger. When Jesus grew to man hood, God allowed Him to be placed on a tree, an old rugged cross. The gift has your name on it, written by God with love: "Whosoever will."

The gift is yours. Have you reached out to receive it? Have you accepted the gift of God's Son?

O the Wonder

God freely gave His Son for me, a gift with no strings attached. All I have to do is receive Him.

Hebrews 1:1-3; Philippians 2:6-8

"True Man Yet Very God"

"Although He was a Son, He learned obedience from what He suffered and . . . became the source of eternal salvation" (Hebrews 5:8-9).

A Christmas song reminds us that God's Gift came to be "true Man yet very God." This is the wonder of what God accomplished in the Incarnation. God became man, yet did not lay aside His deity.

Jesus became like His creation in every way but one. He was sinless because He was God. He took on our humanity but not our sin nature.

Because He was man, Jesus was born as an infant. Throughout His time on earth He experienced every thing we could possibly experience in this life, and then He died. Because He was God, He came back to life from the dead.

He became like us in every way except for our sin. Because He did, He understands all our pain and suffering, our temptations and weaknesses. And because He is God He can help us, pouring out His grace and mercy in our times of need, giving us His strength to endure pain and withstand temptation.

We are to ask Christ to give us His mind, His way of thinking and responding so that we become willing, as He was, to lower ourselves for the sake of others. If the very Son of God was willing to humble Himself and become a man, how much more should we be willing to humble ourselves and become servants to people around us.

O the Wonder

Today I ponder the mystery that God became truly Man in every respect, yet He was no less God.

"She Bore to Men a Saviour"

"Today in the town of David a Saviour has been born to you; He is Christ the Lord" (Luke 2:11).

The promise, spoken through God's prophets, had been made for hundreds of years. Ever since Adam and Eve had disobeyed God and plunged the human race into ruin, God had promised to send a Saviour-Messiah. By faith Israelites through the ages had looked for the fulfillment of the promise. As they had sacrificed each little lamb, their hearts had longed for the Saviour's coming.

When the angel announced to Mary that she was chosen to bear this very special Baby, she sang, "My soul praises the Lord and my spirit rejoices in God my Saviour" (Luke 1:46-47).

Young as Mary was, she immediately recognized that the promise was at last being fulfilled and this Child would rescue her and the rest of the human race from their sin.

The name Saviour denotes "to save, rescue, deliver or protect, to heal and make whole."

How we each need a Saviour -

one to rescue us from our sinful, wayward lifestyle;

one to rescue us from the shackles of sinful habits;

one to preserve us and keep us unto eternal life;

one to heal our deep wounds and make us whole.

Do you need rescuing and healing today? Come to Jesus the Saviour.

O the Wonder

God sent Jesus to be my Saviour, to rescue and preserve me, to heal and make me whole.

Matthew 2:1-12

Born a Child, Yet a King

"Magi from the east came to Jerusalem and asked, 'Where is the one who has been born King of the Jews?'" (Matthew 2:1-2)

Again God's promise: This child to come would be born into the tribe of Judah and be destined to rule the nations. He would come from David's family and rule on David's throne. His kingdom would be one of peace, justice, and righteousness. Unlike the kingdoms of this world, His would last forever. How Israel longed for this King to be born! They had no realization, however, that He would first become a Saviour.

When the wise men came to Jerusalem searching for the newborn King, they arrived at Herod's palace. But the new King was not to be found in the royal residence. Instead, the wise men were directed to the little town of Bethlehem, and the miracle star that had guided them throughout their journey finally rested over a humble cottage. There the wise men found the Child with Mary, a humble peasant maid.

God opened the eyes of these visitors from the east. He revealed to them that this was indeed the King whom they were seeking. Immediately they bowed the knee and worshiped Him, presenting gifts fit for a king.

That Child born so long ago is also our King, and as such deserves our worship. And He welcomes it! No matter what pressures we face today, no matter what demands are being made on us, let us take time to kneel before the Lord our Saviour and King.

O the Wonder

The Ruler of the universe has come down to rule and reign in my heart.

Matthew 1:18-25

Our Lord Emmanuel

"The virgin will be with child and will give birth to a son, and they will call Him Immanuel - which means, 'God with us'" (Matthew 1:23).

As my partner and I were sharing with the women at the prison recently, two little sparrows flew into the room through the open window. Badly frightened by their unexpected surroundings, they became frenzied when they could not find their way out again. They flew up into the corner of the room, then to the edge of the open window, but never out the opening. I watched with sympathy, but was not able to help them. I was rooted to the floor while they were out of reach up at the ceiling. No amount of my shouting directions or pointing the way out could have helped them. If only I could have taken wings and spoken sparrow language I could have led them safely out again.

In a way, that is what God did for us when He sent His Son to earth. Jesus took on human form, spoke our language, understood our deep heart needs, and showed us the way to freedom. He became Immanuel, God with us.

Jesus fully identified with us, tasting every human experience and emotion. He knew joy and sorrow, laughter and tears, close relationships and betrayal, the touch of devotion and the scourge of the whip. Yes, Jesus became one with us so that we earth beings could be one with Him and taste the joys of heaven.

O the Wonder

Jesus loves and understands me perfectly this very moment because He became Immanuel - God with us.

Prince of Peace

"And He will be called Wonderful Counselor, Mighty God, Everlasting Father, Prince of Peace" (Isaiah 9:6).

We sing, "Hail the heaven-born Prince of Peace," but what does the name imply to us today?

Years ago when our youngest son was a tiny baby my husband became emotionally ill. We drove to the Narramore Foundation in Los Angeles and spent three weeks in intensive counseling.

We were back home only one week when Dan had a total relapse. I called our local doctor early one morning and asked for help. Angrily he washed his hands of us, saying that what we were doing would not work and that my husband needed hospitalization and shock treatments.

How could I tell Dan what the doctor had just told me? I felt alone and afraid! I remember standing at the stove stirring the oatmeal, unable to face my husband. Satan seemed to whisper, "See, you can't trust God anymore."

I looked up and said in my heart, "Lord, if I can't trust You, there's nothing left."

Immediately the enemy left, and a deep peace enveloped my soul. After three more weeks of Christian counseling Dan was well on his way to healing, and the old symptoms have never returned.

Do you need peace today? Open your heart to the peace Jesus has promised you (John 14:27).

O the Wonder

Jesus is the Prince of Peace for the world and for my troubled heart.

Revelation 21: 1-7

Alpha and Omega

"'I am the Alpha and the Omega,' says the Lord God, 'who is, and who was, and who is to come, the Almighty'" (Revelation 1:8).

Jesus was there in the beginning creating with the Father, and He will be there when this world is folded up and a new heaven and earth come into being. And at a point in time, as we know it, He came to earth as a tiny baby. He grew up, served, died, and rose again from the dead.

Alpha and Omega are the first and last letters of the Greek alphabet. In our verse for today Jesus is telling us, "I am the beginning and the end and everything in between." He was there when I was born and He will be there when I breathe my last breath, and He is with me all the days in between those two events. There is nothing that can happen to me outside of His control.

As David writes so well in Psalm 139,
"You were there
While I was being formed in utter seclusion!
You saw me before I was born
and scheduled each day of my life
before I began to breathe.
Every day was recorded in Your Book"
(vv. 15-16, TLB)

Today, right now at your point of need Jesus is there. He knows your innermost secrets and understands your deepest pain, and because He also knows the end, He sees the good He has in store for you.

O the Wonder

Jesus is there for me in the beginning and at the end, and every day in between.

Born to Die

"Look, the Lomb of God, who takes away the sin of the world!" (John 1:29)

When painting the scene of Jesus' birth artists often add an aura of glory over the stable. In reality, though, over the manger hung the shadow of a cross. This Holy Child, innocent of all earth's wrongs, was destined for a cruel inhuman death. He would become God's once-for-all sacrifice for the sins of the world. The greatest thing He would ever do for people would not be the healing of the sick, the blind, the leper, the feeding of the hungry, nor the stilling of the storm, but in giving His life for each one of us.

As Joseph trembled with fear and wonder, the angel told him, "Do not be afraid to take Mary home as your wife, because what is conceived in her is from the Holy Spirit. She will give birth to a son, and you are to give Him the name Jesus, because He will save His people from their sins" (Matthew 1:20-21).

Jesus would bear it all, all of our sorrow and suffering. He would bear all the punishment that I so richly deserved. He would save me from sins' consequences by translating death into eternal life.

He wants to be your Saviour today. Have you realized that you have sinned, that your feet are on the wrong path? Have you ever personally asked Jesus to save you and forgive you? Let Him set your feet on the right path and lighten your way into His presence.

O the Wonder

*Jesus came to earth to become God's perfect sacrifice for sin.
He same to save me personally.*

Isaiah 53:7-12

How Silently He Suffered

"He was led like a lamb to the slaughter, and as a sheep before her shearers is silent, so He did not open His mouth" (Isaiah 53:7).

After Jesus was arrested in the Garden of Gethsemane He was first taken before the high priest and Jewish council. There they determined to find Him guilty of a crime that demanded the death penalty. Many bore false witness against Him, but Jesus remained silent.

Finally the high priest charged Jesus under oath, "Tell us if You are the Christ, the Son of God." Jesus answered, "Yes, it is as you say" (Matthew 26:63-64). He was only telling the truth, but for this He would be condemned to die.

Jesus bore silently the humiliation and pain of the spitting, mockery, and beating. As He was taken before Pilate and then Herod He still refused to defend Himself, but suffered the mockery and ridicule of the soldiers silently.

Back before Pilate the accusations continued. Still Jesus made no reply. Pilate was amazed as Jesus let matters take their course. He never defended Himself but spoke only the truth, and for that He was crucified. His trial was a farce. He died unjustly, an innocent Man dying for the sins of the human race. He fulfilled God's plan knowing that suffering was a part of that plan.

Could we resist the urge to defend our innocence when wrongly accused? Could we suffer silently as Jesus did?

O the Wonder

Jesus, who did no wrong, suffered silently for the wrongs I have committed.

John 19:28-37

Brokenhearted

"The Spirit of the Sovereign Lord is on me. . . . He has sent me to bind up the brokenhearted" (Isaiah 61:1).

Does it seem strange to sing at Christmas, "His heart upon the cross was broken"? But Jesus' suffering is part of the Christmas message.

There's no pain like emotional pain-the discovery of an unfaithful spouse, the rending of a divorce, the betrayal of a wayward child, the sting of unjust criticism, the loss of a loved one. All these things crush us and lead us to despair and brokenness.

But there would be One who would be broken for us. His heart would bear not only His own sorrow but also the pain and suffering of all people of all time.

Because Jesus suffered so much, saw so much, understood so much, He can mend our broken hearts. When we're sure we have been shattered beyond repair, He can pick up the pieces and put them back together, bringing healing and restoration.

A few years ago my father died suddenly of a heart attack. Immediately I was plunged deeply into grief, then into black depression. I lost my zest for life so that every day I had to force myself to go through the motions of living. Eventually I sought out a godly pastor, and through his biblical counseling and God's help I was able to put the depression behind me.

Today I'm a person of hope once again. Jesus has bound up my broken heart. Let Him give you hope too.

O the Wonder

Jesus' heart was broken for me so that He can heal my broken heart and give me hope.

DAY 16
John 19:38-42

Dead and Buried

"Because it was the Jewish day of Preparation and since the tomb was nearby, they laid Jesus there" (John 19:42).

We all know the first verse of the Christmas carol, "We Three Kings." Perhaps many of us are not so familiar with this phrase from the fourth verse:

Sorrowing, sighing, bleeding, dying,

Sealed in the stone cold tomb.

The gift of myrrh from the wise men may well have pictured the death of the Saviour, for it was used for embalming.

Years later the disciples watched their Leader die a terrible death by crucifixion. They were hurt, confused, and leaderless. The Shepherd had been smitten and the sheep were scattered. They trudged down that hill in despair and hopelessness. Going into an upper room, they locked the door, hiding for fear of the Jews lest they be killed also.

Jesus was dead. His body was taken down from the cross and sealed in a stone tomb. It was a dark, hope less time for the disciples. But God's plan was being fulfilled, though they did not understand. Jesus must become a suffering Saviour. He must bleed and die as the sacrifice for the sins of the world.

The beauty of Christmas is not in sweet carols, tiny lights, or gently falling snow. Rather, the beauty is that God was willing to send His Son to earth, knowing fully what lay ahead for Jesus.

O the Wonder

That Jesus would suffer, bleed, and die, the innocent for the guilty.

Luke 24:1-12

Risen from the Grave

"Why do you look for the living among the dead? He is
not here; He has risen!" (Luke 24:5-6)

Gloom had settled over Jesus' followers. Their Friend and
Leader was dead and buried. The women prepared additional
spices to anoint His body, then waited out the long day of the
Sabbath to perform their one last act of love and respect.

Very early the next morning they went to the tomb. As they
hurried on their errand of tender caring they wondered who
would roll away the stone that covered the entrance to the
tomb. But when they arrived, they were astonished to find the
tomb was open and the body of Jesus was gone.

Suddenly two men in shining apparel stood by them.
Frightened, the women immediately bowed down. But the
angels reassured them by asking, "Why do you look for the
living among the dead? He is not here; He has risen!" (vv. 5-6)

As we read the Gospel accounts we note how slow the disciples were to believe the wonderful truth of Jesus' resurrection, that He had actually come to life again. But once they
grasped what had happened, their hearts were filled with indescribable joy.

How could death possibly have kept the Son of God prisoner? Jesus is life itself. Because He has gained the victory
over death, we have nothing to fear, because we too shall live
eternally if we have put our trust in Him.

O the Wonder

Jesus rose from the dead, giving us hope and life eternal.

1 Corinthians 15:20-28

Victory Over the Enemy

"The sting of death is sin, and the power of sin is the law. But thanks be to God! He gives us the victory through our Lord Jesus Christ" (1 Corinthians 15:56-57).

There's no doubt about it: death is an enemy that delivers a sting to each of us. But Jesus came to break the power of Satan, through whom death came to the human race.

When Satan entered God's perfect creation and tempted Adam and Eve to disobey, it looked as if he had won. God's perfect creation was spoiled. But God pronounced judgment on Satan, saying there would come a day when he would be utterly defeated.

Still Satan would try to destroy the kingly line through which Christ would come-from evil Queen Athaliah slaying the king's sons to wicked King Herod killing all the boy babies in Bethlehem two years old and under. But God saved baby Joash (2 Kings 11) and He warned Joseph to flee with Mary and the Baby Jesus to Egypt (Matthew 2:13-15).

When Jesus' enemies condemned Him to death by crucifixion, Satan must have thought he had finally won. But it was to be his greatest defeat. Satan had the power of death, but Jesus would put this last enemy down forever.

At His resurrection Jesus gained the victory over death, taking the sting out of death for us and giving us resurrection hope.

O the Wonder

Jesus became victor over death, and He gives that victory to us when we put our trust in Him.

John 1:1-18

Light for Our Darkness

"People living in darkness have seen a great light; on those living in the land of the shadow of death a light has dawned" (Matthew 4:16).

Another Christmas song speaks of another result of Jesus' coming: "The night of darkness ending."

Before Jesus was born the nation of Israel lived in a time of darkness. For 400 years there had been no visitation from God. But suddenly the angelic appearances broke the silence. The time of darkness was past. The night was coming.

John called Jesus "the true light that gives light to every man" (John 1:9). Jesus spoke of Himself as "the Light of the World" and promised, "Whoever follows Me will never walk in darkness, but will have the light of life" (8:12).

Then why do periods of darkness come in our lives? I remember a time when a dark cloud of depression pressed me down. As I prayed for help, the Holy Spirit shone a ray of light into my life and showed me that I was harboring anger with my husband for a poor financial decision made months before. When I responded to the Spirit's revelation and forgave Dan, the cloud was gone.

We may not understand why we have times of darkness, when God seems far away and unresponsive to our needs. But we can trust God in the dark silent places of our lives. Jesus is still the Light of the World, and He will come to us in His time.

O the Wonder

Jesus is the light of my world and will shed His light in the dark areas of my life.

Romans 5:6-11

God and Sinners Reconciled

"God was reconciling the world to Himself in Christ, not counting men's sins against them" (2 Corinthians 5:19).

Through Adam the human race was plunged into sin, and we grew up as the enemies of God. In the fullness of time God sent His Son to become the sacrifice for sin and to bear our penalty. He made the way for us to change our attitude of enmity to God, accept what Christ as done for us, and be reconciled to God. Once we have been reconciled to God we long to have right relationships with others.

Once a dear friend and her husband were deeply hurt by an incident that took place in our church. They left our church, and my friend did not speak to me again. I could not understand why she had cut me off, since I had not been involved in what happened other than being present. My hurt deepened as I waited week after week for her to make the first move to restore our friendship.

After several months I decided to go and talk to her face to face. We spent an afternoon together as she shared how she had blamed me for not speaking up and defending her husband.

As we talked that afternoon away our differences were reconciled. She who had become my enemy was once again my friend. My simple action had brought about a change in her attitude. My relationship with God enabled me to seek reconciliation with her.

O the Wonder

When I was an enemy of God He sent Jesus to pay my penalty so I could become His friend.

Matthew 11:28-30

My Burden Bearer

"Cast your cares on the Lord and He will sustain you; He will never let the righteous fall" (Psalm 55:22).

Jesus came to be our burden bearer. The Authorized Version gives us "Cast thy burden upon the Lord" (KJV).

One day Jesus would stand amid the crowds and offer this invitation, "Come to Me, all you who are weary and burdened, and I will give you rest" (Matthew 11:28).

An old story is told of a man walking along a road carrying a heavy load on his shoulder. In time a farmer overtook him and invited him to climb in the wagon and ride. After a while the farmer looked back to see the man standing in the back of the wagon, still carrying his load. "Sir, why don't you put your burden down?" the farmer asked.

"I never thought of it," the man replied with a weary sigh.

Are we not often like that man in the story? We accept what Jesus has done in offering to carry our burden, but we never lay it down and enjoy the relief that Jesus offers us.

"Cast all your anxiety on Him because He cares for you" (1 Peter 5:7). Are you carrying a heavy load of worry today? Does physical weakness or pain weigh you down? Or concern about a loved one? Cast your care on Jesus, believing in His loving care for you.

O the Wonder

Jesus came to bear my burden and free me from an anxious load of care.

DAY 22

Isaiah 61:1-3

Healing

"He hath sent Me to heal the brokenhearted, to preach deliverance to the captives, and recovering of sight to the blind, to set at liberty them that are bruised" (Luke 4:18, KJV).

All around us are hurting people, people going through hard experiences and in need of healing, both physical and emotional. But I have never seen as much pain in people's lives as I have seen among the women in prison. As they open up and share around the table often there are tears.

My heart aches as I have listened to many sad stories. Some will say, "I came to know the Lord a long time ago, but I quit going to church and I slipped away from Him." Now in prison, these women renew their commitment, get into God's Word again, pray, and determine to get out and make it. How we pray that they will take the steps necessary to stay close to the Lord. We grieve whenever we see them break their parole and end up back in prison.

Jesus came to save us from the penalty of our sins. He also came to bring healing and wholeness to our broken lives. There's no pain so great as emotional pain, but this is God's specialty. We have His promise, "He heals the brokenhearted and binds up their wounds" (Psalm 147:3).

When Jesus took our punishment He brought us peace, and by the wounds He suffered we find healing (Isaiah 53:5).

O the Wonder

Jesus came to heal all the broken places of my life. How I praise Him!

DAY 23
Romans 8:28-30

To Make Us Like Jesus

"Being confident of this, that He who began a good work in you will carry it on to completion until the day of Christ Jesus" (Philippians 1:6).

A line in the favorite carol, "Away in a Manger" is a prayer that God will "fit us for heaven to live with Thee there." Something wonderful happens in our lives from the moment we come to know Jesus as Saviour, and it continues until we see Him face to face. As we walk with the Lord we are becoming more like Him every day.

What was Jesus like when He lived on earth? He was compassionate, wise, humble, faithful, patient, long suffering-for a beginning. If we become aware of the fruit of the Spirit being manifest in our lives, we know we are becoming like Jesus (Galatians 5:22-23).

When we look around at other believers and when we look within we realize God has a lot of work to do to make us "fit for heaven."

God can use everything that comes into our lives to conform us to the image of His Son. It's easy to see this in major events, perhaps, but He can also take the minor, everyday experiences to shape our characters.

I'm not naturally a compassionate person, but since I'm in a ministry where compassion is needed, I'm trusting the Holy Spirit to give me more of Christ's compassion. Do you see an area in your life in which you need to grow? Look to God to bring about the needed growth.

O the Wonder

God is at work within me to make me like Jesus and to fit me for heaven.

Freedom from Fear

"By His death He might destroy him who holds the power of death . . . and free those who all their lives were held in slavery by their fear of death" (Hebrews 2:14-15).

Jesus came to release us from the sins and fears that grip us. Have you ever looked deep within yourself and asked, "What am I afraid of?" Most of us tend to bury our fears until something happens to bring them to the surface. If you find anxiety crowding out the peace in your heart, look for the fear.

Many years ago my husband developed walking pneumonia, then developed a severe reaction to the medication he was given. He was unable to understand what was happening in his body and mind. The medication caused him to become very fearful. He was filled with dread that he was losing his mind and lived in fear of death.

Nothing seemed to reach him. I would quote favorite verses from the Bible, but he found no strength or comfort in them. His physical and emotional problems overshadowed everything else, and he had no power to combat the fear. We sought Christian counseling and began the long upward climb to wholeness once again.

As my husband's body began to heal and right itself the fear gradually faded. But throughout the difficult experience God wonderfully carried him through the days when he could not trust and patiently waited until his faith became vibrant once again.

O the Wonder

Jesus came to deliver me from my fears and make me whole.

Jesus Brings Hope

"Through Him you believe in God, who raised Him from the dead and glorified Him, and so your faith and hope are in God" (1 Peter 1:21).

In the carol, "O Little Town of Bethlehem," we sing, "The hopes and fears of all the years are met in Thee tonight." For hundreds of years Israel had been hoping for a Messiah, a deliverer, a Saviour. One day God sent His Son as a tiny baby, and that hope was fulfilled. God kept His promises to Israel, and He will keep His promises to us.

Hope is built into our lives by the trials we go through. As God allows the storm to sweep over us, He draws us close to His side and reveals Himself to us. His promises shine especially brightly when we walk in darkness.

When Dan, my husband, was ill and we were waiting for our first counseling session, I rocked my tiny baby in the middle of the night and pleaded with God for my husband. I prayed for hours while the enemy battered my soul.

Then, when the darkness seemed greatest, God brought a verse to my mind, "When the enemy shall come in like a flood, the Spirit of the Lord shall lift up a standard against him" (Isaiah 59:19, KJV).

Suddenly I was infused with hope that the Lord would push back the darkness and carry us through. My hope was not a hollow wish, but was based on God's Word, and He kept His promise.

O the Wonder

Jesus came to give us an eternal hope, and that hope anchors our souls.

John 15:9-17

Joy of Every Longing Heart

"I have told you this so that My joy may be in you and that your joy may be complete" (John 15:11).

When Jesus came to earth He not only brought hope but He also brought joy. Think of the great rejoicing at His birth by the angels, the shepherds, Mary and Joseph, Simeon, Anna, the wise men, and many others who recognized who He was.

Do you remember when you held your firstborn in your arms? After months of anticipation and planning, the baby was there. Your heart overflowed with gratitude and wonder at this little miracle of life.

Jesus' birth brought wonder and joy. Then 30 years later He began His earthly ministry. Think of the joy He brought to a man born blind when he could see again; the incurable leper when he was made clean and whole; the paralyzed man when he could walk again; the demon possessed man when he was freed to express his love of righteousness.

We think of Jesus as a man of sorrows from the words of Isaiah 53, but what joy must have filled His heart to help each hurting person He touched!

For us there is the joy of knowing Jesus, serving Him, and seeing others come to know Him. We experience this joy when we turn from being absorbed with ourselves and look to Him. As His joy seeps into our hearts we experience a deep longing to share that joy with others, and as we do so, our joy is multiplied.

O the Wonder

Jesus came to bring joy to my sad and aching heart.

DAY 27
Psalm 145:1-7

Sing His Praises

"Glory to God in the highest, and on earth peace to men on whom His favor rests" (Luke 2:14).

Many of our Christmas carols include praise to God. The uplifting theme of praise is in contrast to the lowly shepherds who crouched in terror as the skies around them lit up with angels. In trembling amazement they listened to the message the angel brought.

Suddenly the night sky was filled with a burst of praise to God. Then once again the men were wrapped in darkness, and all was quiet.

"Let's go see this thing that has happened," the shepherds said to one another (see v. 15). After they had hurried to Bethlehem and found the Baby in the manger just as the angel had said, they returned to their flocks praising God.

We too need to praise God for who He is and for what He has done. How do I praise God? One way is by using the words of the praise psalms and praying them back to God.

We praise God simply because He is worthy of our praise. Rather than being a magic formula to get things from God, praise is recognizing who God is and what He has done.

Take a moment to think of a difficult situation that you or someone dear to you is facing. Ask God to help you begin to praise Him as you pray about that difficulty today.

O the Wonder

God is so great and He has done so much for me. When I stop to reflect on it, I praise Him!

Room for Jesus

"She gave birth to her first born, a son. She wrapped Him in cloths and placed Him in a manger, because there was no room for them in the inn" (Luke 2:7).

Bethlehem was crowded the night when Mary and Joseph arrived. The census ordered by the emperor in Rome had caused an unusually large number of people to fill the little town. By the time Joseph had knocked at the door of the inn, every room had been filled to overflowing.

We can picture Joseph begging the innkeeper for even one small corner, but there was simply no room. Then the inn-keeper suggested that there might be a corner of the stable where they could rest for the night. And so it was that Jesus entered the world He had created, but the only bed for Him was a cattle manger in a humble stable.

Each year my heart almost melts as I sing in the refrain of one of the Christmas songs, "There is room in my heart for Thee."

Yet I recognize that it is much the same today. The world has no room for Jesus. He is shoved aside unrecognized and finally rejected. But to those who will open their hearts to Him and make room for Him, He brings life eternal. When Jesus comes knocking at the door to your heart will you say to Him, "There is no room"? Or will you open your heart and welcome Him in? Yes, Jesus, there is room in my heart for You.

O the Wonder

There was no room in the inn so long ago, but there's room in my heart for Jesus today.

Mystified Angels

"Of which salvation the prophets have enquired and searched diligently, who prophesied of the grace that should come unto you . . . . which things the angels desire to look into" (1 Peter 1:10, 12, KJV).

In our December 1980 issue of Anchor, Constance P. Bemus wrote of a mystery of Christmas:

Imagine how hospital personnel would feel if their most famous surgeon put on janitor's clothing and went about cleaning the boiler room, or how airplane passengers would react if their pilot came down the aisle serving coffee and tea.

So you can begin to imagine how the angels wondered that first Christmas Day when they saw their majestic King born in a stable on the low, lost, contaminated planet of earth.

How they must have marveled at the mystery of Jesus, who for a time was made lower than the angels (Hebrews 2:9).

We can't know how much God's angels understood of His marvelous plan to have His Son suffer for man's salvation, and then have subsequent glory. But the Apostle Peter tells us that these are matters that angels desire to look into. By "look into," Peter must have meant comprehend, since angels saw Jesus' birth. They were there and announced and praised, but they announced and praised a mystery they understood as little as we do.

O the Wonder

What a mystery that Jesus the infinite Son of God came to earth as a tiny baby - for me.

DAY 30
Matthew 2:9-12

Come, Let Us Adore Him

"On coming to the house, they saw the Child with His mother Mary, and they bowed down and worshiped Him" (Matthew 2:11).

That night was special. The Baby who was born was special, for He was the very Son of God become man. At the moment of Jesus' birth all the angels stopped to worship Him.

When the wise men found this Child, their first response was one of worship. How much more should we bow our knees and worship Him too.

O the Wonder

Jesus is here. Let's publish the News by bowing down and worshiping Him alone.

DAY 31
Luke 2-15-20

Publish the News

"When they had seen Him, they spread the word concerning what had been told them about this Child" (Luke 2:17).

We sing, "Go Tell it on the Mountain." The shepherds were filled with wonder at all they had seen and heard, but they did not keep the good news to themselves. They told everyone they met about this Special Child. Jesus has come. Let's spread the Good News to all the world.

O the Wonder

I'm a bearer of the Good News that Jesus has come to save us from our sins.

CPSIA information can be obtained
at www.ICGtesting.com
Printed in the USA
FSHW021404050120
65292FS

9 781733 550369